KU-570-472

# In Care and After
## A Positive Perspective

Edited by
**Elaine Chase, Antonia Simon
and Sonia Jackson**

Routledge
Taylor & Francis Group

LONDON AND NEW YORK

First published 2006
by Routledge
2 Park Square, Milton Park, Abingdon, Oxon OX14 4RN

Simultaneously published in the USA and Canada
by Routledge
270 Madison Avenue, New York, NY 10016

*Routledge is an imprint of the Taylor & Francis Group*

© 2006 Elaine Chase, Antonia Simon and Sonia Jackson

Typeset in Goudy by
Keystroke, Jacaranda Lodge, Wolverhampton

All rights reserved. No part of this book may be reprinted or
reproduced or utilised in any form or by any electronic,
mechanical, or other means, now known or hereafter
invented, including photocopying and recording, or in any
information storage or retrieval system, without permission in
writing from the publishers.

*British Library Cataloguing in Publication Data*
A catalogue record for this book is available from the British Library

*Library of Congress Cataloging in Publication Data*
In care and after : a positive perspective / edited by Elaine Chase, Antonia Simon, and
Sonia Jackson.
      p. cm.
   "Studies . . . carried out at the Thomas Coram Research Unit at the Institute of
Education, University of London"–Ack.
   Includes bibliographical references and index.
   ISBN 0-415-35253-3 (hardback) – ISBN 0-415-35254-1 (pbk.) 1. Foster
children–Great Britain. 2. Foster home care–Great Britain. 3. Youth–Institutional
care–Great Britain. 4. Youth with social disabilities–Great Britain. I. Chase, Elaine,
1962– II. Simon, Antonia. III. Jackson, Sonia. IV. University of London. Thomas
Coram Research Unit.
   HV887.G7I63 2005
   362.73'0941–dc22                                                           2005013780

ISBN10: 0–415–35253–3    ISBN13: 9–78–0–415–35253–6 (hbk)
ISBN10: 0–415–35254–1    ISBN13: 9–78–0–415–35254–3 (pbk)

# Contents

# Contributors

All editors and contributors to this book were, at the time of writing, researchers at the Thomas Coram Research Unit at the Institute of Education, University of London.

## Editors

**Elaine Chase** has worked as a practitioner and researcher in the field of health promotion, both in the UK and internationally, for the past 15 years. The main focus of her research is the health and well being of children and young people, especially those who are marginalized and/or disadvantaged.

**Antonia Simon** is a statistician with responsibility for advising on research methods, providing statistical support and expertise to a range of studies and conducting extensive data analysis in the fields of health and social care affecting children and families.

**Sonia Jackson OBE** is a Professorial Fellow of the Institute of Education and was previously Professor of Applied Social Studies at the University of Wales Swansea. She has directed many studies on early-years services and children in care, most recently a five-year study of care leavers in higher education.

## Contributors

**Sarah Ajayi** has been a researcher since 2002 on the By Degrees project, a study of the experiences of care leavers in higher education. Her other research interests include the experiences of minority ethnic care leavers in education and applied psychology for non-Western cultures.

**Sofka Barreau** has worked as a researcher at the Institute of Education since 2000. Her main research interests are the private fostering of West African children and teenagers, the childcare and social care workforces, and child development.

**Claire Cameron** has worked as a researcher since 1992. Her main research interests are the childcare and the social care workforces, care work over the life course and international comparative studies, including pedagogy and residential care.

**Abigail Knight** has been a researcher at the Institute of Education since 1995. Her particular interests include the health and wellbeing of looked-after children and young people, disabled children and their families, and children's rights.

**Christine Oliver** joined the research unit six years ago. Her research interests include advocacy for children, young people and adults; historical developments in the care of looked-after children; inequalities in health care; mental health care and sexuality and the family.

**Charlie Owen** is a Senior Research Officer with responsibility for contributing to research methods and data analysis, especially secondary analysis of large datasets. He also teaches research methods within the Institute of Education

**Edwina Peart** has a wide range of research experience, particularly in education and development. She has worked both in Britain and in a number of African countries on projects funded by a range of agencies including DFID and UNESCO. She was a research officer on the Private Fostering study.

**Pat Petrie** is a professor in education within the research unit where she directs research on social policy relating to children's out-of-school lives. Recent work includes a study of social pedagogy, with special reference to looked-after children in Europe.

**Margaret Quigley** has worked since 2002 on the By Degrees project, a study looking at the experiences of care leavers in higher education.

**Valerie Wigfall** has been a researcher at the Institute of Education since 1997. Most recently she has worked on studies of residential care, fostering in Europe and services for vulnerable young people, particularly care leavers.

# Foreword

For workers of my generation, who qualified fifty years ago, this book raises the intriguing question of when and why we stopped using the strengths of our clients and became fixated on their weaknesses and problems. In the possibly over-confident probation service of the 1950s we had clear expectations of what our young charges and their families could achieve. Getting boys to school to study, supporting the mothers who were usually the emotional heart of the home and helping fathers into work were basic objectives. Impediments to achievement were more often environmental than personal or familial – in particular a pervasive class system that imposed successive, often impermeable, ceilings to progress. Cohorts of children had their life chances virtually decided at the age of 11. The best we could often do for our probationers was to help them hit the ceiling. For some children, ironically, being in care helped propel them through it.

I cut my teeth on child care as one of the first Directors of Social Services. Immensely fortunate in inheriting a highly professional children's service in Kensington and Chelsea, I had a group of colleagues who taught me what child care was about and a set of members motivated to do the best they could for 'their' children. This blend of professional certainties and patrician *noblesse oblige* looks immensely old-fashioned from the perspective of 2005. We certainly believed that we knew best, and children's rights were no more than a whisper. But the system did deal with the whole child, and successfully withstood the compartmentalising tendencies of specialist services.

The reaction against professionalism in social work and against all forms of authority in society caused this system to unravel. Evidence of incompetence in child protection and of abuse in residential care completed the loss of political and public confidence. Child protection in the last quarter of the twentieth century became dominated by a procedurally driven approach. Initially justified, perhaps, its ultimate bankruptcy was demonstrated by the inexplicable failures of social and health services, and of the police to protect Victoria Climbié.

The 1997 government deserves credit – in spite of its blind spots – for its efforts to improve the lives of children. The attack on child poverty is central. The structural reorganisation of children's services, however, while it has attractive aspects, will not necessarily deliver what is hoped for. A temporary drop in performance frequently follows the turbulence of organisational change. Implementation is therefore crucial. So is the focus on disadvantaged and marginalised children, whose need for consistent champions will be as great under the new dispensation as under the old: there is an immutable law that political and public concern always returns to the interests of the majority in the mainstream. The workforce remains the key to successful services: workers in residential care educated to post-qualifying levels, and all the agencies concerned with child welfare and protection staffed by confident and mature professionals capable of reliable and responsible decision-making.

The world has moved on, however, since we thought that professionals always knew best. I applaud the emphasis in this book on the potential of these young people and the prime importance of involving them in all the decisions that affect them. Twenty-five years ago I looked forward to a time when children in care might have a real say in deciding their future – a vision far from fully realised even now. The whole of society will be enriched if we make it possible for them to achieve all that they are capable of.

*Sir William Utting*
23 March 2005

# Acknowledgements

The studies included in this book were all carried out at the Thomas Coram Research Unit at the Institute of Education, University of London. The views expressed belong to its authors, but the research on which it is based was made possible by the support of a variety of funders to whom we express our thanks: the Department of Health; the Department for Education and Skills; the Social Exclusion Unit and the Frank Buttle Trust.

The authors would like to thank all the children and young people who participated in the research projects covered in this book and who provided unique insights into their lives and experiences. Without them none of this work would have been possible. Thanks also go to the professionals and carers across the various research sites who gave generously of their time, and to all the experts from both voluntary and statutory agencies who have provided support in an advisory capacity to the various research projects.

For the book as a whole, special thanks must go to Peter Aggleton for his editorial support; to June Statham and Elizabeth Monck for their helpful suggestions about the book proposal; and to Jenny Stratford and Sean Jennings for their administrative assistance.

Finally, we would also like to acknowledge the contribution of another book, edited by Janet Boddy, Claire Cameron and Peter Moss, Care Work: present and future, London: Routledge, 2005. This was written by some of the same contributors to this book, and explores both national and European perspectives on care work from those who provide care in different settings. The books complement each other, providing important illustrations and discussion of how public care work is perceived by those who are looked after and those who provide care.

# 1 Introduction

## Towards a positive perspective

*Elaine Chase, Sonia Jackson
and Antonia Simon*

In recent years, a growing emphasis on research with children and young people in public care has to a large extent informed the policy and legislative agenda for the UK generally. A major impetus for changes in policy in England and Wales has also come from the strength of voluntary and non-statutory agencies that for many years have taken a lead in lobbying for change on behalf of young people in the care system. The work of the Who Cares? Trust, the National Children's Bureau, Barnardo's and A National Voice, among others, has influenced the highest echelons of policy making.

Whether commissioned by external bodies or conducted internally within organisations, this research, by concentrating more intensely on the needs and experiences of these young people, has uncovered some of the many shortfalls in services and support available to them. In consequence, there is a fairly strong body of research depicting the relative disadvantages young people in public care face compared to their non-looked-after peers. Such disadvantages affect their education, their life opportunities and their physical, mental and social well-being.

The idea for this book was developed within an interdisciplinary group in the Thomas Coram Research Unit (at the Institute of Education, University of London) composed of researchers working on a range of projects all focusing on young people in and leaving care. The aim of the group was to support each other's work and share experiences of research in this field. It soon became apparent, however, that distinct research projects faced very similar challenges in pursuing a common research agenda and hence the idea emerged to document some of these challenges. The strength of this book lies in its pulling together the experiences and perspectives of researchers from a wide range of academic disciplines including social care, education, economics, health promotion, pedagogy, sociology, psychology and statistics. Authors are united by the shared goal of conducting research which helps to promote the well-being of children and young people in public care. Throughout the book the terms 'in care', 'looked after', and 'in public care' are used interchangeably.

It is hard to refute research findings illustrating the extent to which systems and services have let down children and young people in public care, and that is by no means our intention. As researchers and/or former practitioners in the field of social care, we have firsthand experience of these failings and the devastating impact they can have on young people's lives. However, there is a risk that the poor track record of service provision begins to determine the lot of young people and makes it seem impossible that, having spent time in public care, they can actually achieve anything at all. By presenting young people in and leaving care solely as 'victims' of systems that fail them, we risk ignoring and undermining the role they themselves play in determining their own futures, and the resilience and resourcefulness that many possess.

Over recent years, a conceptual framework for social care has evolved that focuses more on what is working well rather than what is going wrong. The so-called 'strengths perspective' in social work practice (Weick and Saleeby 1995; Saleeby 1996) adopts a different way of looking at individuals, families and communities, and encourages empowering practices that seek actively to support family strengths and capacities rather than concentrate on their shortfalls and inadequacies. The impetus for this change in approach has emerged from an acknowledgement that much social care work is still based largely on 'individual, family and community deficits, problems, victimization and disorder' (Saleebey 1996: 296).

Similarly, the notion of 'resilience-led practice' (Gilligan 2001) has come to define an approach to child and family social work that resists overly bureaucratic child protection systems and instead takes greater account of relationships, strengths and the social context of the child or family. It acknowledges that resilience, or an ability to adapt positively to adversity, can be nurtured through supportive contexts and as such needs to be an important focus of social work practice. Resilience-led practice is based on a belief in the self-healing and self-righting capacity of children and young people as they grow up; in other words, in the strengths and attributes that they have (Gilligan 2004).

Proponents of strengths or resilience-led approaches do not seek naively to ignore risks and weaknesses but aim to look at these in relation to strengths and protective factors. They also acknowledge that any therapeutic relationship may have its origins in wider social networks and may not only be related to the intervention of the professional (Gilligan 2004). The role of social work, therefore, should be about helping to release positive processes in this wider context that might support the child or the family. The practical implication is that the nurturing of resilience and the ability of children and young people to cope in the face of adversity may be more important than securing an ever elusive state of permanence in child placements (Gilligan 1997).

Importantly, concepts of promoting strengths and resilience are not confined to the realms of social care. Similar developments have taken place in the field of psychology with the evolution of the notion of positive psychology, concerned with the promotion of happiness or well-being (Seligman and Csikszentmihalyi 2000; Seligman 2002). Particularly for young people who are rendered vulnerable either genetically or through their life experiences, Seligman (1998) claims that mental ill-health, depression, injury and avoidable illnesses can be prevented by systematically promoting the competence of individuals, rather than emphasizing their deficits.

There are other important aspects of this conceptual framework that have relevance to promoting the well-being of children and young people in and leaving care. One such aspect lies in enabling a balanced time perspective (Boniwell and Zimbardo 2003) or encouraging a view of the world that is neither overly biased towards negative past experiences nor towards a perspective on the present that is either hedonistic or fatalistic. Rather, a balance is required that allows an individual to work towards future goals and rewards and to see a future for themselves.

The tendency to focus on the negative influences of the past can influence attitudes of professionals towards children from disruptive backgrounds and limit their perceptions of them. We have all come across young people with experience of public care who feel that others have low expectations of them. One young woman, in the study described in Chapter 6 of this book, remembered moving school and the comment made by one of her new teachers when she arrived: 'I suppose you'll need special needs being in care and everything.' The young woman went on to say, 'It was just because I was a foster child they think you can't be good.'

The Who Cares? Trust (WCT), in particular, has done much in recent years to advocate for providing appropriate educational and other support to young people in care, which recognises their circumstances but also encourages their full potential. A range of resources to both directly support looked-after children and young people and to guide local authority practice have been produced. *Right to Read* (WCT/Paul Hamlyn Foundation 2001); *Who Cares about Education?* (WCT 2001); *Believe in Me* (WCT 2003a); *Education Matters* (WCT 2003b); and *Measuring Progress* (WCT 2004), among others, all assume a standpoint on supporting children and young people that expects the most of them and provides them with the greatest possible opportunities to succeed.

This book emerges during a time of great change in government policy in England and Wales affecting children and young people. It witnesses an unprecedented level of legislative and policy initiatives to promote and sustain the health and well-being of all children and young people. Indeed it is published at a time that has been described as 'the start of the most ambitious cross-government policy agenda for children ever attempted anywhere in the world' (Aynsley-Green 2004). Central to this agenda, and perhaps a reflection of broader academic discourses in social care and psychology, are the notions of holistic care, of attainment, of achieving, of safety and security and of opportunity. More than ever before, there appears to be a consistent emerging framework designed to redress the many imbalances in terms of access to care, security and life opportunities that have up until now disadvantaged many children and young people, those in and leaving care being a stark example.

The Children's Green Paper, *Every Child Matters*, launched in 2003, outlined five key objectives considered essential to allow all children and young people to progress successfully to adulthood: being healthy; staying safe; enjoying and achieving; making a positive contribution; and securing economic well-being. The Green Paper envisaged the fulfilment of these objectives through a number of linked strategies: supporting parents and carers; early intervention and effective protection; clear accountability; partnerships; integration of health, social care and education; and workforce reform.

An overall strategy for delivering the framework followed in 2004, with *Every Child Matters: next steps*. This outlined the findings from the public consultation on services for children, young people and families following *Every Child Matters*; the government's response to the consultation proposed in the Children Bill; and the first steps taken in implementing the Green Paper through strong and effective partnership working.

The *Children Act* (2004), the legislative instrument for implementing the Children's Green Paper, proposed widespread changes including the introduction of a national Children's Commissioner for England (following the example of Wales which appointed the first Children's Commissioner), local authority directors of children's services and the further development of Children's Trusts. The National Service Framework (NSF) for Children and Maternity Services (2004) set out a ten-year strategy to improve the lives and health of children. Recognising the specific needs and contexts of children, it called for responses that were appropriate to their distinct circumstances. Importantly, it placed children and young people at the heart of services, and adopted a holistic approach to supporting them through strengthening the integration of health, social care and education services.

As a whole, this new 'change for children' agenda is underpinned by the recognition of inequalities that diminish the health, social and economic prospects of some children and young people. While policies aspire to the same outcomes and achievements for all, they now concede that the starting points are so variable that attention must be paid to reducing the gap between those who thrive and those who struggle. At a policy level at least, all children and young people stand to gain a great deal from these developments. The key point is that those historically left on the margins of policy advances should now be central to the shared agenda for reducing inequalities and making 'every child matter'. There is clearly some synergy between the combined strengths, resilience-led and positive psychology perspectives as they relate to social care and the change for children agenda that promotes the best possible outcomes for all children and young people.

Together with policy developments concerned with improving the prospects of all young people, in 2001, one of the most significant pieces of legislation affecting children in care, the Children (Leaving Care) Act, 2000, came into effect. By extending the duties of local authorities to care for and support young people during their transition from care up until the age of at least 21 years, the act undoubtedly represented a radical shift in social policy, contrasting starkly with previous policies which envisaged that young people at the age of 16 could simply go forth and survive on their own. As a whole, the current policy and legislative framework should mean that the outcomes for children and young people currently in and leaving care should be better than ever before.

Throughout this book, we have attempted to provide examples of how notions of strength, resilience and resourcefulness may be applied to various aspects of work with children and young people, and how research, as well as highlighting problems, may be used effectively to document children's and young people's strengths, attributes and capacities. We draw on experiences that demonstrate the importance of nurturing the skills of young parents rather than assuming their failures, a process at worst culminating in child protection proceedings. We show how a belief in what children and young people in care can achieve academically will enable them to go on to experience and benefit from higher education. A key chapter provides insights into the importance of the quality of residential care and the adoption of a pedagogical approach to looking after children that provides holistic care and support and encourages their personal growth and development, and hence builds resilience and a positive outlook on life and their personal potential. A chapter on advocacy highlights the importance of approaches that affirm young people's views and opinions, provide them with a voice and believe in what they are saying.

In contrast to the rather bleak picture drawn from previous research findings, we as editors and authors have assumed a positive and optimistic perspective in which we focus less on the failings of social care systems and more on the factors that enable some young people to achieve a great deal despite the disadvantages they have faced. By doing so, we do not in any way intend to undermine research that has highlighted the stark inadequacies of previous policy and practice and provided the impetus for change – after all, we are among its authors. Rather, our intention is to begin to identify and unpack what it is that makes or might make a difference to the outcomes for young people. To do this, we have as far as possible asked young people themselves to define what helps and what hinders them in realising their aspirations, however grand or modest they are.

In presenting our collective experiences of research, we cover a lot of ground and pull together a large information and research base on a variety of aspects of the lives of children and young people in public care, and during their transition from care. The content of the book was however determined by the studies carried out at the Thomas Coram Research Unit and, as such, is a diary or log of empirical research completed or nearing completion at the time of writing. We are aware that there are some serious gaps.

For example, a major cross-national study on foster care, parallel with the one on residential care reported in Chapter 8, was in progress at the time that the book was conceived but the findings were still being analysed and not ready for publication. As a result, although we have included a chapter on one of the most unexamined aspects of out-of-home care – private fostering – mainstream foster care does not have a chapter of its own. Most of the people interviewed for the private fostering study were of West African origin, but apart from this, the issue of the high representation of minority ethnic children in the care system has not been specifically addressed. Any astute reader will recognise other evident gaps in key areas of social care such as adoption, the care of children and young people within secure settings, issues around providing care to unaccompanied children and young people arriving in local authorities, and other facets of care that relate to the broader planning and configuration of care services. What we do offer, however, is a unique set of insights into the work we have done and the various processes we have been through along the way.

We hope that this book speaks to a range of audiences. As well as the empirical research findings, it provides important reference material, for example, about how care services have historically evolved and, in an accessible form, how their progress is monitored over time. It also offers much food for thought in relation to research approaches, particularly those that give children a voice and a say in the issues that affect them. We believe that these insights will be relevant to students, other researchers, policy-makers and practitioners from a range of professional backgrounds.

Chapter 2 provides an historical overview of government policy over the past century. It plots the evolution of present-day policy and practice, and underlines the fact that in many respects policy-makers are still grappling with the same issues as they were at the turn of the twentieth century. Given the embryonic stages of comprehensive legislation and policy to support children and young people through and after care, we cannot help but pose the question: Why has their conception taken so long?

Chapter 3 goes on to provide an overview of what we know and indeed do not know about the lives of young people in and leaving public care. For the benefit of the reader, we summarise the key literature and available factual data, and identify gaps in the knowledge necessary to support effective policy and practice. The chapter highlights the difficulties in researching a large cohort of young people who are so dissected in terms of how they are presented in published datasets that they cease to be seen as people but rather as educational, health or place-ment 'outcomes'. Although data-collection systems have improved substantially through the introduction of performance assessment frameworks (PAFs), there is still much to be done if we are ever to be able to trace the long-term outcomes for those young people with experience of the care system.

Chapter 4 opens the theme of education and reports on the first attempt ever made to calculate the economic benefits of bringing the educational attainment of children in care up to the same level as the rest of the population. It illustrates the cost, in both financial and human terms, of our past failure to treat education and care as complementary rather than separate services, and shows how a relatively small investment in measures which have been shown to be effective could result both in a better quality of life for care leavers and huge savings in public expenditure.

Chapter 5 explores the experiences of a group of young people who, against the odds, have managed to access higher education. It plots their lives prior to and since the beginning of their university careers and highlights the main reasons why they, unlike the vast majority of care leavers, have managed to enter higher education. The chapter goes on to outline the factors that enable them to succeed at university and the types of support that are central to keeping their education sustainable. It finishes by summarising key policy implications. Importantly, the chapter highlights the contribution that being in public care can make to the educational opportunities for some young people.

Chapter 6 explores the lives of young people in and leaving care who become parents during their teenage years. Against the backdrop of policy aimed at controlling and reducing the numbers of teenage parents, it argues that for some young people, given the extent of disadvantage and marginalisation they have experienced, pregnancy may in fact have some positive consequences. It goes on to outline from the perspectives of the young women and men themselves what the key factors are that enable them to assume their roles as parents successfully and the types of support that are most important to them.

Chapter 7 provides a rare insight into the hidden world of private fostering through the retrospective accounts of adults who were fostered as children. It examines their experiences in detail and explores both the potential benefits as well as risks of these types of care arrangements and their long-term impact on the health and well-being of children. The chapter raises questions about the appropriateness of imposing stricter regulations on private foster care and highlights the need for further research to fully understand the complexities surrounding private fostering arrangements and how they change over time.

Chapter 8 introduces an international dimension by comparing the quality of care in residential settings for children in England, Germany and Denmark. It suggests that a key factor is the pedagogical approach to care that is more commonly adopted in other parts of Europe. It illustrates the stark contrast between the approach to professional development and retention of staff in residential care in these other countries and the experiences of low-paid and undervalued workers in the UK who have limited education and training and few opportunities for professional development. The chapter underlines the importance of looking to other countries to see what may be learned and adapted for policy and practice for care services within England and Wales.

Chapter 9 introduces the reader to the world of advocacy. It provides important insights into the personalised support that can be provided to children and young people through advocacy services. The diverse roles of advocacy are presented including giving children and young people a voice, and encouraging professionals to re-examine and reflect on their practice. Overall, the chapter presents a highly positive appraisal of the potential of advocacy in promoting and sustaining the well-being of children and young people. It discusses the concepts of children's rights and children's welfare, how these are often polarised, and explores the extent to which advocacy can strengthen their integration. The chapter subsequently highlights some of the challenges facing advocacy services including negative attitudes on the part of some mainstream social care professionals and organisational structures, and economic constraints that limit children's access to an independent advocate.

Chapter 10 discusses some of the challenges of conducting research with young people in and leaving care and promoting their full participation. A study examining care leavers' access to and use of health and other services is used by the authors to illustrate these points. It explores difficulties in conducting research with a highly mobile and transient population, such as the often unavoidable use of opportunistic rather than scientific sampling processes. It presents ways of challenging the scepticism among practitioners and policy-makers about the potential of research in informing practice. By drawing on other research projects conducted within the Thomas Coram Research Unit, the authors demonstrate that these difficulties and challenges are not unique and are commonly faced in conducting research of this type. As a whole, this chapter provides important yet rarely documented information about research processes and the types of strategies that may be employed to overcome difficulties.

In conclusion, we summarise the lessons to be learned from this body of research as a whole and discuss the implications for future research in this field.

There are a number of questions that we would encourage the reader to bear in mind and that we seek to address in this book. First, is the overall shift in policy and practice in relation to social care moving in the right direction to provide a more supportive and nurturing environment for children and young people in public care? To what extent are local authorities, in their capacity as 'corporate parents', assessing their provision for children and young people against what well-informed and adequately resourced birth parents would offer their own children, as opposed to simply aiming to meet government targets? Second, what types of services and support enable young people in care to feel that they have succeeded or at least had a chance to succeed in whatever they aspire to? Third, how could the strengths or resilience-led perspective be more readily translated into social care practice? Fourth, how could research in this field provide a more robust and intact picture of the experiences, positive as well as critical, long-term as well as immediate, of young people who enter and leave the care system? In the chapters contained within this volume, we have attempted to provide some answers to these questions. We believe that the findings reported on here have important implications for commissioning and supporting future research that encourages enlightened policy and ultimately improves the lot of all young people in and leaving care.

## 2  Looking after children away from home

### Past and present

*Sonia Jackson*

> We were sure we were building the new Jerusalem. We improved material conditions, we cut down numbers, we treated children as individuals, they got individual clothing instead of going to the local school in a pauper uniform. We eliminated the Masters who kept the cane in the corner, we got more staff and set up new, smaller homes. But at the end of ten years we had not built the new Jerusalem . . . we did not get to the heart of it and haven't now.
>
> Sylvia Watson, Children's Officer for Hertfordshire,
> quoted in Holman (1998: 102–3)

The innocent optimism of that moment in 1948 when the National Assistance Act announced that the existing Poor Law would cease to have effect and the new children's departments were set up now seems very distant. Fifty years on, despite many volumes of legislation and guidance and innumerable government circulars, a substantial body of research shows that there are still serious deficiencies in the care we provide for children who cannot live with their families.

Understanding the way that child welfare policy in Britain has evolved over time can enable us to see how the spotlight shifts from one aspect of children's care and development to another, without identified problems necessarily being resolved (Jackson, 1989). Approaches that were once standard practice are often reinvented as new initiatives. Major changes usually occur in response to critical incidents or 'scandals' and their impact on public opinion. This chapter identifies some of these 'turning points' and considers how they have helped to shape children's services in the present.

### What drives child care policy and legislation?

Reviewing the origins and development of child care policy does much to explain why some aspects of the service are so resistant to change and why damaging preconceptions persist. For instance, stigmatization and low expectations of children in local authority care can be traced back to nineteenth-century attitudes to parental authority and responsibilities. Comparisons with other countries with a different history highlight this point. Matthew Colton and his colleagues have shown that having a child looked after away from home in Spain or the Netherlands

LIVERPOOL JOHN MOORES UNIVERSITY
LEARNING SERVICES

is not a cause for shame or concealment, whereas in this country, even when parents are satisfied with the service they are receiving, they feel a deep sense of inadequacy for needing to use it (Colton *et al.*, 1997). Similarly, attitudes to residential care and to the education of children in care may be shown to have deep historical roots.

It is clear from reading contemporary accounts that many of the issues debated today were quite familiar in the past. For example, education was regarded by the Poor Law Authority as the most effective means of breaking the cycle of pauperism, or what we would now call 'welfare dependency'. The Poor Law Board Order of 1870 made very detailed regulations to govern arrangements for the education of boarded-out children. Placements were not to be more than one and a half miles from a school; school attendance was compulsory (before this applied to the general population), and the schoolmaster was required to provide quarterly reports on the child's progress (Parker, 1990).

However, Heywood notes that 'one of the arguments which at first discouraged the Local Government Board from giving its approval to the practice of boarding out was the difficulty of ensuring an interest in education among the sort of people thought most likely and suitable to offer homes for the children' (1964: 79). It was well over a hundred years before education once more rose to the top of the official child care agenda (see Chapter 4), and the idea that an interest in education should be an important criterion in the selection of foster carers is still not widely accepted (Jackson and Sachdev, 2001).

The separation of child care from education is a feature that differentiated Great Britain from many other European countries. Parker attributes the persistence of this division, which was to have such damaging effects on the quality of care and life chances of separated children, to the deep sectarian divisions between the main children's societies (Parker, 1990). Successive governments were anxious not to revive the bitter controversies that had accompanied the introduction of compulsory elementary education in 1870. The one real opportunity to reunite the systems was in 1944 with the enactment of the Education Act which introduced universal secondary education. However the Ministry of Education, preoccupied with drafting and negotiating the provisions of the Act, left it too late to bid in competition with the Home Office for child care responsibilities, and it was not until 2003 that the care and education of children away from home were finally reunited in England under the Department for Education and Skills.

The history of child care in Britain falls into a number of distinct phases. Turning points may often be identified with the publication of an official report, evoked by an event causing public concern or, more recently, by an influential piece of research leading in time to legislative or organizational change. These will be discussed in turn, beginning with the first landmark, the 1948 Children Act which laid the foundations of the child care system that exists today.

### From Poor Law to children's departments

During the nineteenth century there were three parallel streams of provision for children away from home, the vestiges of which may still be seen. The basic form of public provision was laid down by the Poor Law of 1834 which had as its prime objective the limitation of expenditure and discouragement of able-bodied adults from becoming a burden on the rates. 'Outdoor relief' – subsistence payments to those with no other means of supporting themselves or their family – gave way to the workhouse. The regime of the workhouse was designed to be less attractive than living outside it, on however minimal an income, the application of the principle of 'less eligibility'. Long after workhouses – at least under that name – had disappeared, the idea of 'less eligibility', that provision for children in care should never be better than they might have enjoyed in their family and class of origin, maintained a strong influence on the thinking of policy-makers and administrators. A senior civil servant in the Department of Education told me in 1982: 'It is no business of ours to do better for these children than their own parents could have done.'

Another form of public institution for children was the system of reformatory and industrial schools which evolved into 'approved schools', later renamed Community Homes with Education (CHEs). The kinds of children and young people who were locked up in these so-called 'schools' now find themselves in 'secure accommodation', young offenders' institutions or sometimes adult prisons. As Chapter 3 shows, children in care are at much higher risk than other children of being drawn into the criminal justice system.

The third stream of care was provided by the large voluntary organizations that grew up during the late nineteenth century, each identified with a different church or religious grouping. Their aims were broadly similar. They all aspired to protect children from the corrupting influences of their families of origin and the living conditions of inner-city communities, to indoctrinate them in their own particular religion, and to equip them to earn their living in the kinds of employment that were available to young people in their level of society. For girls this meant domestic skills such as sewing and laundry work; boys were generally expected to join the forces, an assumption that continued well into the twentieth century (Curtis, 1946).

Most of the larger charitable societies survive today under different names. The Waifs and Strays became the Children's Society (having dropped the Church of England from its masthead along the way); National Children's Homes became NCH Action for Children; Dr Barnardo's kept its name but without the title; the Crusade of Rescue became the Catholic Children's Society. Until the 1950s they continued as major providers of residential care for children, either in large institutions or in grouped 'cottage' homes managed by a house mother. The 'cottages' might accommodate up to thirty children so that their regimes were still quite institutional, and the idea that they could provide individualized care remained largely a myth. As provision of residential care passed increasingly to local authorities the voluntary organizations in England changed their function to filling in perceived gaps in public child care and piloting new forms of provision, setting up family centres and a variety of projects such as leaving care schemes (Stein, 1986). Coram Family, which provides supported housing and education services for care leavers as well as day care, nursery education and a range of projects to help disadvantaged families, is a direct descendant of the first residential home for children, the Foundling Hospital set up by Captain Thomas Coram in 1739 (Oliver, 2003a).

## Child care up to the Second World War

Throughout the nineteenth and first half of the twentieth century the people who made decisions had a clear perception of parents who were unable to provide adequate care for their children as worthless and untrustworthy (Parker, 1990). This applied even when there were obvious practical reasons for the need for care away from home. For example, single mothers, especially if they had never been married, had no way of supporting themselves except through domestic service, which normally involved living in, with no possibility of taking a child with them. Many of the children accepted for care by the charitable societies fell into this category, although the societies, particularly Dr Barnardo's, liked to present themselves as rescuing ragged and hungry children from the streets.

Once received into care, children at that time rarely returned to their parents. This was partly because the parents' circumstances were unlikely to change, but also because distance, cost and the policies of the homes discouraged visiting so that gradually contact was lost and the parents, even 'deserving' ones, were labelled irresponsible and uncaring. There was also a strong suspicion that parents who asked to have their child back were motivated by the hope of profiting by that child's labour once he or she was old enough to work. In the large voluntary homes the children's work was essential to the economy and maintenance of the establishment, providing a strong deterrent to returning children to their families. There were also many hundreds of small homes or orphanages run by religious communities or informal committees which, until the Children and Young Persons Act (1933) imposed registration, were entirely unregulated.

Many of the children's societies continued to pursue active policies of severance right up until the 1960s, most notoriously in the practice of 'emigrating' large numbers of children by sending them to Canada or Australia. Only much later did evidence emerge of the abuse and exploitation to which many were subjected in their 'new lives'. The requirement for the child's agreement to be sought was frequently swept aside, and if parents were informed at all it was often when the child was already on board ship, never to be seen again (Wagner, 1982; Bean and Melville, 1989; Humphreys, 1994).

## The Curtis Report and the 1948 Children Act

During the second half of the nineteenth century there was widespread charitable concern about the condition of orphaned and abandoned children, but this was succeeded by a long period of public indifference to the whole issue (Holman, 1998). It was the mass evacuation of children during the Second World War that started to draw attention once more to the needs, both psychological and material, of those separated from their families (Winnicott, 1957). Not only the basic form of the present child care system but also the principles that underlie it may be dated back to the Curtis Report, published in 1946. Like so many turning points in child care policy the impetus resulted from a child homicide, the case of Dennis O'Neill, who, having been removed from his parents for his own protection, was placed in a rural foster home. There he and his brother were treated with such brutality that Dennis died from beating and starvation. The subsequent inquiry by Sir Walter Monckton found that the system for inspecting foster homes was seriously deficient. The job was often carried out by volunteers and in this case the lady visitor did not make any attempt to talk to the boys on their own or to investigate their living conditions. In fact she did not even bother to dismount from her horse (Monckton Report, 1945).

As a result of the report on this tragic case, two committees of inquiry were set up in 1945: the Clyde Committee for Scotland and the Curtis Committee for England and Wales, the latter chaired by Dame Myra Curtis, Principal of Newnham College, Cambridge. Her inquiry ranged over all the forms of substitute care for children and revealed the abysmal conditions for children looked after in workhouses under the Poor Law (Curtis, 1946). The report is still profoundly moving to read and many of its recommendations were far ahead of its time. It laid great emphasis on the need to treat each child as an individual: 'Throughout our investigation we have been increasingly impressed by the need for the personal element in the care of children' (p. 146), in contrast to the institutional nature of most child care at the time. The aim should be for children to be brought up in a way that resembled as closely as possible life in an ordinary family. The Committee came down firmly in favour of foster care as preferable to children's homes and urged local authorities to make a 'vigorous effort' to extend the system (p. 179). Scotland already had a long-established system of fostering, mainly in the form of boarding out pauper children to work in rural crofts and farms, and there was some complacency about the fact that 60 per cent of separated children in Scotland were already in foster care. As the Clyde Committee pointed out, there was a high risk of exploitation if supervision was inadequate (Clyde, 1946).

Many of the issues discussed in the Curtis Report sound familiar: the importance of stability; the shortage of good-quality foster homes; neglect of education; lack of recreational facilities and private space in residential care, low expectations and stereotyped work destinations. It was even suggested that children in care should have the opportunity to go on to further education or university, a startling suggestion for that time. The most important recommendation was that every local authority should set up a children's department, headed by a highly quali-fied children's officer, who would 'know and keep in personal touch with all the children under her care', either directly or through her deputy (p. 147). It was assumed that this post would be held by a woman, although about one-third of those subsequently appointed were men (Brill, 1991).

The time was propitious for a change, a necessary condition, as Butler and Drakeford (2003) point out, for a major shift in social policy. The children's departments were set up, as recommended, under the 1948 Children Act. The central authority was the Home Office, but responsibility for the care of separated children remained with local authorities. An alternative proposal considered by Curtis was that child care should be transferred to a single central department, and it is interesting that the similar suggestion put forward in the Climbié Report (2003) in relation to child protection was also rejected by the government of the day.

## The children's departments and the 1963 Act

Although many problems remained in the child care system, there is no doubt that the establishment of the children's departments represented a great step forward. Bob Holman's book *Child Care Revisited* (1998), based on interviews in the mid-1990s with the surviving children's officers, provides a vivid description of the early days of the service. In the beginning the children's departments were quite small organizations, consisting of the chief officer and a few child care workers, mostly unqualified. The hierarchy was very flat with easy access to the top, and the children's officers took a keen personal interest in every child in care, most of whom they knew individually. At first the service was primarily reactive, responding to requests for care from parents, often coming via family doctors, or to reports of maltreatment, but increasingly child care officers began to look for ways to avoid the necessity for separation, and in 1952 the Association of Children's Officers added to its objectives 'to encourage and assist in the preservation of the family' (Holman, 1998).

In most areas the new children's departments inherited a ramshackle system with relatively few children boarded out and the majority accommodated in very large, impersonal children's homes, memorably described by Jean Packman (1975) as 'mouldering bastions'. To add to the problems, the number of children requiring care was rising very rapidly, by 15 per cent in the two years 1949 to 1951.

Then, as now, children were received into care for a wide variety of causes. A common reason for short-term admissions was that the mother was having a baby in hospital – a man could not be expected to look after a house and a young child on his own. Moreover, the concept of paternity leave was far in the future; taking time off work would mean losing wages and might create severe financial problems. Many young women entered care and were even sent to punitive institutions because they stayed out later at night than their parents thought desirable and were labelled as being 'beyond parental control'. The great fear was that they would bring disgrace on their families by conceiving a child out of wedlock. Truancy and minor delinquency were also frequent reasons for being sent away from home. Underlying many of the ostensible reasons for reception into care were poverty and poor housing.

Approved schools were run on the same lines as independent public schools, reproducing all their worst features, such as beating and bullying. I remember visiting one as a student where the Headmaster showed me with pride the shields of Oxford and Cambridge colleges, painted by the boys, displayed around the dining-hall. It struck me at the time as a terrible irony, since none of the inmates had the slightest chance of attending university or receiving any but the most basic education. The practice of using the boys as unpaid labour (for example, building or decorating staff houses with the excuse of teaching them a trade) was an obvious relic of the industrial schools (Parker, 1990).

As mentioned above, there was an agreed view in the children's departments that every effort should be made to avoid the need to separate children from their families. A few forward-looking children's officers, notably Barbara Kahan in Oxfordshire and Sylvia Watson in Hertfordshire, were already experimenting with different approaches to this end despite doubts that it was a legitimate use of public money. The 1963 Children and Young Persons Act for the first time authorized local authorities to spend money, including giving assistance in cash, in order to avoid the need to receive children into care. At first this was on a very small scale, consisting of nothing more sophisticated than a petty cash tin from which families in need could be given money to buy food on a weekend or a small sum to pay rent and avoid eviction — since homelessness was a common reason for children to come into care.

Reunification of separated families, or rehabilitation as it was then called, received much less attention. Although the 1948 Act should have ended an active severance policy, the question of contact between children in care and their parents continued to be given low priority. Research in the 1960s and 1970s showed that children who stayed in care for more than six months were very unlikely to leave before they grew up (Rowe and Lambert, 1973). As in the past, this was often put down by carers and child care officers to indifference and irresponsibility on the part of parents. In fact there were numerous factors which prevented parents who cared deeply for their children from keeping in touch with them. One was the requirement that they should pay for their children's upkeep in care. Since poverty was usually one of the factors that had led them to relinquish the child in the first place, this was not only unrealistic but meant that parents were often afraid of visiting or even making contact in case they were pursued for arrears of payment. When children were in residential care the homes were often unwelcoming to visiting parents and provided nowhere for them to meet and talk in private. Research by the Dartington Social Research Unit showed that some children who had lost contact with their families found themselves entirely alone in the world once they left care (Millham *et al.*, 1986).

## From children's departments to Social Services

The children's departments lasted for just over twenty years before they were absorbed into the Social Services departments created in 1971 as a result of the Seebohm Report (Seebohm, 1968) which brought together adult services, mental health and child care into a single local authority department. The rationale was that children's welfare could not be considered in isolation from that of their families and that the existing system often resulted in large numbers of different workers knocking on the same door, each in ignorance of what the others were doing. There were frequent disputes between departments about whose responsibility it was to deal with a particular case but also a strong tendency for them to defend their own territory and resist intrusion. I had a personal experience of this as a welfare officer when, visiting a family threatened with eviction for nonpayment of rent, I found a mother who had just given birth, four other unattended children and one little girl tied to her bed and clearly a victim of serious neglect and abuse. When I rushed back to the office and reported the need for urgent action to the child care officer on duty I was rudely told that the family was well known to their department and it was none of my business.

It was not the intention of the Social Services Act that all social workers should immediately take on the tasks of former specialists, but that was how it was interpreted at the time. The result was a disastrous loss of expertise, perhaps most seriously in knowledge of child development, and this is a consistent factor emerging from child abuse inquiries (Reder *et al.*, 1993). In time specialist teams re-emerged in Social Services and, although there was a rather short-lived fashion for 'patch' work, the trend, as a glance at job advertisements shows, is for social work posts to become increasingly specialized. Ironically this creates its own problems. As Stroud and Pritchard have argued, many child homicides could be avoided if children and family workers knew more about mental health and mental health professionals were more aware of the needs of children (Stroud and Pritchard, 2001).

Most of the children's officers had been women, as envisaged in the Curtis recommendations, but they usually failed to secure the top job of Director of Social Services. Within the new departments children's services had a much lower profile and were in a weak position to compete for resources. Social workers now formed only a small section of the workforce and slipped down in the hierarchy and in public esteem. The previous detailed knowledge of each child in care was lost and perhaps this was the beginning of the process by which child care social work became increasingly administrative and depersonalized, a cause of frequent complaint from the 1990s onward. It is interesting to note that the children's officers interviewed by Holman, some of whom had been strongly in favour of the Seebohm recommendations at the time, had almost all changed their minds thirty years later (Holman, 1998).

## Maria Colwell and the 1975 Children Act

A tension that runs right through the history of child care is between the aim of protecting children and young people from ill-treatment and undesirable influences and the ideal of family preservation and reunification. Sometimes the first objective is uppermost, sometimes the second, in a process that has often been likened to the swing of a pendulum (Fox Harding, 1997).

During the later years of the children's departments the idea of keeping families together whenever possible was gaining ground, but two events caused the pendulum to swing in the opposite direction and led to the Children Act of 1975.

One was the publication of the book *Children Who Wait* (Rowe and Lambert, 1973), which showed the large number of children 'drifting' in residential care who could have been placed in foster or adoptive families. The other was the horrific life and death of Maria Colwell, an 8-year-old girl killed by her stepfather after being returned to the care of her mother (Colwell, 1974). The inquiry that followed filled the newspapers for weeks and set a pattern of exposing social workers to public shame that was to continue for the next thirty years. This in turn led to child protection becoming increasingly dominant in the work of child care social workers (Dartington Social Research Unit, 1995; Sanders et al., 1996).

The other influence on the 1975 Act was the publication three years earlier of the Houghton Committee Report on Adoption (Houghton, 1972). This proposed reform and updating of the 1926 Adoption Act to make adoption more easily available. The campaign for a new Act was led by Mia Kellmer Pringle, the founder and Director of the National Children's Bureau, who pressed strongly for abused and neglected children to be more easily freed for adoption without parental consent. It was given support by findings from the 1958 National Cohort Study which showed very good outcomes for adopted children (Seglow et al., 1972). At a more theoretical level Anna Freud and her colleagues argued that 'psychological parents', those providing daily care for a child, should take precedence over birth parents, and indeed that birth parents were best excluded from the picture altogether if they could not provide stable long-term care (Goldstein et al., 1973).

The 1975 Act required local authorities to become adoption agencies, outlawed private adoption placements, made it easier to dispense with parental consent and gave greater security to long-term foster parents. However, it was only implemented in part. Many sections were deferred 'until resources become available' and it had much less impact on the lives of children in care than its advocates had hoped. It did raise the profile of adoption in the voluntary sector, which saw finding homes for hard-to-place children as an alternative to its declining residential provision.

Almost before the Act became law the pendulum was swinging back again. The idea of placing more children for adoption was attacked on the grounds that in practice this meant removing children from impoverished parents and giving them to childless middle-class couples when what was really needed was more support for families and anti-poverty measures (Holman, 1980). The Act was also attacked by black activists because at the time black and mixed-parentage children were often placed with white adoptive parents. Local authorities were never very enthusiastic about adoption (Morgan, 1998; Jackson and Thomas, 2001), and it was not until the Prime Minister ordered an inquiry as a result of the Waterhouse Report on abuse in residential homes in North Wales (Waterhouse, 2000) that attitudes began to change.

## Assessing outcomes

Throughout the 1980s there was growing concern about the impact of the care system on children and families. The report of the Select Committee of the House of Commons on children in care and a number of research studies, some already cited above, pointed to fundamental weaknesses in the system (Short, 1984). Among those which caused most concern were:

- The failure to plan effectively for separated children (Rowe and Lambert, 1973; Vernon and Fruin, 1986).
- The neglect of education for children in care and their poor attainment (Jackson, 1987).
- Disregard of parents' rights and of their legitimate interest in their children living away from home (Millham *et al.*, 1986).
- Excessive and unnecessary use of coercion (Packman *et al.*, 1986).
- Multiple problems of care leavers (Stein and Carey, 1986).
- The absence of any perceived link between services and outcomes for children.
(Parker *et al.*, 1991)

Driven partly by the Conservative government's drive for efficiency and effectiveness, the Department of Health and Social Security, as it then was, set up a working party, chaired by Professor Roy Parker, with the objective of creating a system for assessing outcomes in substitute care for children separated from their families. Following an initial meeting attended by most leading UK researchers in the field, a smaller group went on to develop the Looking After Children (LAC) system (Parker *et al.*, 1991). The original focus on research measurement shifted in the course of the next eight years to the production of a practical tool that would be acceptable to social workers and their management. The complete system, consisting of administrative forms and age-related Assessment and Action Records (AARs), together with a research report, Reader and Training Pack, was launched by the Department of Health in 1995 (Ward, 1995; Jackson and Kilroe, 1995, 1996) and was adopted by most local authorities in England and Wales, and subsequently in Scotland, Northern Ireland and a large number of overseas countries.

The principle behind the AARs was that many of the weaknesses of the care system could be attributed to the absence of any one person to oversee the child's developmental progress and the failure of social workers and caregivers to undertake the kinds of action that ordinary parents take for granted as necessary to safeguard and promote their children's welfare. The domains covered by the system were related to deficits in care identified by previous research, and consisted of health, education, identity, family and social relationships, emotional and behavioural development, social presentation and self-care skills.

At the same time a committee of senior civil servants, chaired by Rupert Hughes, Assistant Secretary at the Department of Health, was conducting a fundamental review of child care legislation, which had remained essentially unchanged since

1971. The result of these two strands of work, which interacted with each other, was the Children Act 1989 and its associated volumes of Guidance and Regulations (Department of Health, 1991a, 1991b). The Children Act coincided with the United Nations Declaration on the Rights of the Child and is informed by its provisions, although it pre-dates ratification by the UK government.

## The Children Act 1989

Unlike the 1975 Children Act, the 1989 Act was implemented in full in 1991, and the implementation date was preceded by an intensive publicity campaign and training programme designed to familiarize child care social workers and their managers with the new legislation. It is probably no exaggeration to say that the authors of the Act hoped to bring about a paradigm shift in the concept of public care for children. At the same time the politicians and civil servants responsible for getting it through Parliament had to steer a careful course if it were to continue to command all-party support. They achieved this partly by keeping a low profile, by avoiding any hint that the new law would involve an increase in public expenditure, and by compromising on some issues, mainly by *authorizing* local authorities to spend money for certain purposes but not *requiring* them to do so.

### The Children Act: underlying principles

The Children Act 1989 introduced a number of important principles which continue to exert a powerful influence on child care practice today (Department of Health, 1989). Care was reconceptualized as a service to parents rather than a punishment for inadequacy. This was symbolized by a change of terminology. 'In care' would in future refer only to children subject to a court order. Others were to be 'accommodated' or 'looked after' by the local authority. A second important principle was the least possible use of coercion, inspired by Jean Packman's research showing the widespread and often unnecessary use of Place of Safety Orders (Packman *et al.*, 1986). The ideal of working in partnership with parents, though not in the Act, was strongly promoted in all the associated literature and training materials (Jackson and Kilroe, 1995, 1996). Court action was in future to be a last resort, to be avoided whenever possible. Parental rights were replaced by the concept of parental responsibility, only to be extinguished by adoption, even when children are in care under a court order. Along with this went an emphasis on promoting continued contact with parents and other family members. Of all the provisions of the Act this is probably the one with the most lasting impact on practice.

A third change was the introduction of a new administrative category, 'children in need', defined as 'children whose health and development is likely to be significantly impaired without the provision of services'. The Act lays a duty on the local authority in whose area the children live to provide such services. Day care and family centres are given as examples of the kinds of provision, short of accommodation, that might be offered to children in need. For political reasons there is no reference to poverty in the Act or in the Guidance, despite the fact that poverty and the social ills which accompany it continue to be the main reason why children come into care (Pritchard, 2004); thus, paradoxically, poverty in itself does not count as 'need' under the Act.

## How far has the Children Act 1989 fulfilled its intentions?

### Positive changes

In line with the UN Convention on the Rights of the Child, the Act reaffirmed the right of children to be consulted on matters which concern them, depending on their age and understanding. However listening to children, still more taking their views seriously, is such an alien concept in the UK that relatively little progress has been made until very recently (Thomas and O'Kane, 1998; Thomas, 2000; Westcott and Jones, 2003).

The Act brought together and rationalized a large body of fragmented laws and regulations concerning children, most of which are outside the scope of this chapter. There is no doubt that it had a significant impact on social work practice and produced some improvements. The idea of working in cooperation with parents and avoiding unnecessary conflict is firmly established in contrast to the antagonistic relationship which was previously common. The number of Care Orders fell steeply in the early 1990s, though the trend is now upwards again (see Chapter 3). Overall, more effort now goes into maintaining contact between looked-after children and their birth families, and there is more general recognition of the importance of ethnic and cultural identity.

### Continuing weaknesses

The Children Act also had a number of serious weaknesses, the consequences of which shaped the direction of services throughout the 1990s. No extra money was provided to enable local authorities to carry out the additional duties contained in the Act, and in recognition of this many of the provisions were enabling rather than obligatory, and were often left deliberately vague. This was particularly true of the definition of 'need'. Although giving local authorities responsibility for providing a service, not simply to prevent reception into care, was an important step forward, in practice they were each left to define 'need' in the light of local circumstances. There was a strong financial incentive to draw the definition as tightly as possible so as to exclude children and families who might qualify and make demands on resources.

The second factor which distorted the good intentions of the Act was the increasing dominance of child protection throughout the decade. A number of reports on child abuse fatalities pointed to failures of communication and co-operation as causative factors (Reder *et al.*, 1993). The government responded by issuing guidance in *Working Together under the Children Act*, which laid a strong emphasis on the role of Area Child Protection Committees and the development of detailed procedures for investigating allegations and the operation of the Child Protection Register (Department of Health, 1992).

A series of research reports commissioned by the Department of Health questioned if this enormous effort was well directed. In particular Jane Gibbons and her colleagues showed that only 5 per cent of children were removed from home as the result of a child protection investigation. A higher proportion was placed on child protection registers, but even this did not necessarily lead to any action other than monitoring (Gibbons *et al.*, 1995). Many investigations concerned families with a high level of need, often well known to social services already, but few received any effective treatment or support as a result. Other studies found that the investigations themselves had a devastating effect on parents and rarely resulted in any benefit to the children (Cleaver and Freeman, 1995; Colton *et al.*, 1995; Farmer and Owen, 1995).

The Department of Health studies were summarized in a widely disseminated publication, *Child Protection: messages from research* compiled by the Dartington Social Research Unit (1995), generally regarded as one of the most influential reports to appear during this period. The authors argued for a greater emphasis on family support and initiated what became known as 'the refocusing debate'. The Department of Health urged Social Services departments to adopt 'a lighter touch' and to refrain from invoking formal child protection procedures unless it was really unavoidable.

However, the expected revised guidance did not materialize at that time (it was eventually issued in 2001), and the refocusing debate was swiftly overtaken by another wave of child abuse scandals (Utting, 1997; Waterhouse, 2000). There was little change on the ground. Child protection or the investigation of abuse allegations continued to dominate child care work within Social Services departments to the detriment both of family support and ongoing active work with children looked after away from home. Even within child protection services far more effort went into investigation and registration than into prevention or after care. Refocusing at either policy or practice levels seemed to carry too high a risk for professionals (Colton *et al.*, 1996; Sanders *et al.*, 1996; Parton, 1997). Social workers and managers failed to take on the idea that family support *provides* child protection and persisted in treating them as alternatives. Moreover the concentration on the youngest children, those in most danger of serious injury or death, moved the spotlight away from adolescents, who continued to make up the largest group of children looked after by local authorities.

In relation to children in care, some important topics were relegated to non-statutory guidance. Adoption was left out altogether due to lack of time, and this resulted in a fifteen-year delay in the updating of adoption law. There is much evidence that large numbers of children who could have been adopted were left to drift into care (Ivaldi, 1998; Morgan, 1998; Jackson and Thomas, 2001). Another major area which was left to local authorities' discretion was arrangements for young people leaving care and for supporting those wishing to continue in education. The Guidance to the Act states clearly that children in care have the same entitlement to further and higher education as do all other children (Department of Health, 1991a, 1991b), but in the absence of any duty to provide financial support this element of the guidance was widely disregarded. Provision for leaving care remained seriously deficient and even deteriorated through the 1990s, with all the emphasis on 'preparation for independence' and an increasing tendency to throw young people on their own resources as early as 16 years (Broad, 1998).

## Development of child care services through the 1990s

As mentioned above, the Department of Health invested heavily in the Looking After Children materials which were designed to provide the missing link between service inputs and outcomes. Subsequent research on their implementation suggests that their impact on practice, though generally beneficial, was somewhat limited (Ward and Skuse, 1999). This seems to be due to structural problems in the child care system, such as shortage of suitable foster homes and understaffing in Social Services departments, rather than to weaknesses in the system or the materials. The Assessment and Action Records have been criticized as 'middle class' and likely to encourage form-filling at the expense of direct work with children (Knight and Caveney, 1998), but this is strongly disputed (Jackson, 1998; Skuse and Evans, 2001).

Apart from the LAC system there were few significant developments in children's services under the Conservative government. The dominant attitude was described by a senior policy-maker as one of 'benign neglect', though the term 'benign' might be disputed. There was a resolute refusal, politically motivated, to recognize the effects of the enormous increase in child poverty resulting from monetarist economic policies. The suggestion in the Children Act 1989 that local authorities should provide day care for children in need was largely ignored, and expansion of childcare for working parents took place almost entirely within the private sector at a cost far beyond the means of the average family (Moss and Penn, 1996; Goldschmied and Jackson, 2004). The number of community family centres increased but these were usually run by the voluntary sector with support and funding from local authorities. There is evidence that resources were shifted from children's services to community care for adults and, within child care teams, child protection continued to take priority.

## 'Quality protects'

The election of the Labour government in 1997 was the most obvious turning point since the 1948 Children Act. Probably for the first time ever children rose to the top of the political agenda.

The previous government had commissioned Sir William Utting to undertake a review of safeguards for children looked after away from home. Although sparked by concerns about child sexual abuse in residential care, Utting ranged much more widely in his highly influential report *People Like Us*, pointing out significant weaknesses in the child care system and the neglect of many aspects of children's development, in particular education and health (Utting, 1997).

At the same time the voluntary bodies were moving from simply providing services to plug the gaps in the public care system to becoming campaigning organizations and pressure groups. They began to appoint policy officers and to seek to influence legislation and service provision at a national level. For example, the National Foster Care Association (later becoming the Fostering Network) pointed out that the traditional supply of foster carers was drying up as working outside the home became the norm for women as well as for men. The only solution, they argued, was increasing professionalization, including foster care allowances that paid a reasonable salary, not simply covering the direct costs of looking after the child (National Foster Care Association, 1997). The successful campaign for a Children's Commissioner with wide-ranging powers, following the publication of the Waterhouse Report (Waterhouse, 2000), was led by a voluntary organization, Children in Wales. Scotland and Northern Ireland followed closely in appointing their own Commissioners, though England had to wait longer.

The Who Cares? Trust (WCT), founded by Tory Laughland in 1992, exposed the many taken-for-granted practices that stigmatized children in care and prevented them from realizing their potential. From the first the Trust emphasized the vital importance of education for children separated from their families. The Gulbenkian-funded Equal Chances project involved working closely with two local authorities where education and Social Services departments undertook to collaborate to improve the experience of school and attainment of looked-after children (Firth and Fletcher, 2001). The findings of this project, and the pioneering work of the Trust in seeking children's views directly, informed the first joint guidance issued by the two responsible government departments, and later the work of the Social Exclusion Unit, discussed in Chapter 4 (Department for Education and Skills and Department of Health, 2000; Social Exclusion Unit, 2003).

The government responded to the Children's Safeguards Review with the 'Quality Protects' programme, launched in September 1998 (Department of Health, 1998e). This was the most ambitious attempt since the 1948 Act to improve the care and future life chances of children in public care. For the first time it laid down specific aims and set outcome targets for all aspects of children's lives. It adopted Roy Parker's concept of the 'corporate parent', the whole local authority, being responsible for the well-being and progress of the children in its care (Parker, 1980; Jackson and Sachdev, 2001). Frank Dobson, then Secretary of State for Health, underlined this point by writing personally to every local councillor to introduce the initiative. The idea of 'safeguarding children' was developed beyond merely protecting them from abuse to enhancing the quality of their lives, and this was reflected in consultation documents such as the Framework for the Assessment of Children in Need and their Families (Department of Health, 1999c) and the joint guidance referred to above.

How far has Quality Protects improved the lives of looked-after children? The initiative (and the money) were widely welcomed, but there were obstacles which made it difficult to achieve its ambitious aims. The targets were negotiated with local authorities and were intended to be 'achievable' – that is, they were set extremely low – but even so only a minority of areas managed to meet them. The targets are still very far from what average parents would hope for their children. There are also structural problems in the care system which Quality Protects does not address. Many of the difficulties in delivering good-quality services and the resulting poor outcomes for children arise from these underlying factors, the same as have frustrated previous efforts.

## Leaving care

Throughout the 1990s research on the experiences of care leavers showed consistently poor outcomes, with a high proportion of young people living in poverty and inadequate housing, not in education, employment or training and in poor health. Up to a quarter of girls leaving care were pregnant or already had a child, usually with little support from the baby's father. The incidence of addiction and mental health problems was also very high (Stein, 1997; Broad, 1998).

So for young people who remain in care throughout their childhood, the Children (Leaving Care) Act 2000 (CLCA) could be seen as even more important than the Children Act 1989. In the first place it reasserted 18 as the expected age of leaving care for young people who cannot return to their families. In many areas during the previous decade it had become age 16 by default, and to this may be traced some of the negative findings discussed in Chapters 3 and 4. What parent other than a corporate one would consider throwing out their child to sink or swim at such an early age? (Action on Aftercare Consortium, 1996). In addition, the Act lays a duty on local authorities to keep in contact with young people formerly in their care up to the age of 21 and to provide financial support and accommodation to those continuing in full-time education up to the age of 24. As we show in Chapter 5, this has opened up a multitude of opportunities from which care leavers were previously excluded.

## Conclusion

In this chapter I have tried to trace some of the recurrent themes that run through the history of child care policy in Britain. Many of the problems that persist were recognized as far back as the beginning of the twentieth century. So often, it seems, we have to keep rediscovering what was well known by earlier workers in the field: for instance, the enduring nature of kinship ties, the destructive effects of instability, the crucial importance of education for children's long-term future and the need for continuing support into adulthood. Residential care in particular has proved stubbornly resistant to all attempts at improvement and, as Chapter 8 shows, the problems of today's small units are not dissimilar from those already identified in the large institutions of the 1940s (Archer *et al.*, 1998; Sinclair and Gibbs, 1998).

Despite all this, looking back offers grounds for hope; it only needs a brief dip into the Curtis Report to realize how far we have come in the past sixty years. Although there are still many issues that we have yet to tackle effectively, in most ways our present system of out-of-home care for children represents a great improvement on the past.

# 3 Outcomes for children in care

## What do we know?

*Antonia Simon and Charlie Owen*

In 1998, the government White Paper *Modernising Social Services* (Department of Health 1998c) shifted the focus away from who was providing welfare services towards closer scrutiny of the quality of those services. In order to encourage a more rigorous approach to the management of social services departments, the Personal Social Services Performance Assessment Framework (Department of Health 1999a), commonly known as the PAF, was launched.

The PAF sets targets for 'improving the life chances of children in care' and measures the levels of education, training and employment outcomes of children in and leaving care. While statistics on children in care had been routinely collected for over thirty years, the idea of using them in a planned way as a tool to bring about improvements in services and outcomes was new. Thus, the PAF transformed the way in which statistics were collected and placed greater importance on using statistics to measure outcomes. Joint DfEE/DH *Guidance on The Education of Children and Young People in Public Care* (2000) stressed the importance of data as a necessary and powerful tool for improving services and outcomes.

Increasingly, comparative targets have been set to measure outcomes for children in and leaving public care against those of all children in the population. For instance, in the light of a series of publications drawing attention to the persistently low achievement of children in the care population (Fletcher-Campbell 1997; Borland *et al.* 1998; Goddard 2000; Jackson 2001), in 2003, the government for England announced a target to 'substantially narrow the gap between the educational attainment and participation of children in care and that of their peers by 2006' (Social Exclusion Unit 2003: 71).

One consequence of these reforms is that statistics are now routinely collected and published on a number of significant outcomes for children in public care, such as their educational attainment, their health and whether or not they have committed criminal offences. This chapter presents an overview of what is known statistically about such outcomes and highlights some of the inadequacies of the available information. By 'outcome' we mean a measure of the quality in people's lives after they have entered or left care. These include factors such as school performance, quality of health status and the likelihood of being homeless or in prison. Where appropriate, these outcomes are compared with the outcomes for all children and young people, although it should be noted that even where there are evident differences in outcomes, these are not necessarily a consequence of the care experience, since we cannot know with any certainty what would have been the outcomes for children and young people had they not been taken into care.

Here, emphasis is first placed on data that may be obtained from routine statistical collections in England on children in and leaving care and the reforms that have taken place in recent years, including the introduction of outcome measures. The chapter then explores what is known from other sources such as findings from focused research studies. Finally, the limitations of both small-scale research and of large-scale statistical returns, in providing an accurate and complete national picture of the circumstances of young people within the care population, are discussed.

## Performance measurement

Public Service Agreements (PSAs) were introduced following the 1998 government Comprehensive Spending Review (CSR) and set out, for the first time, clear public targets to show what departments aimed to achieve in terms of public service improvements. The 2000 CSR further developed the concept of PSAs, making the targets more clearly focused on key governmental priorities and outcomes. At the same time, to complement the *Quality Protects* initiative (Department of Health 1998e), the government undertook a significant review of social care, publishing the White Paper referred to above and, as part of this agenda, introduced wide-ranging performance measures for Social Services departments (Department of Health 1998c).

In February 1999, a consultation exercise produced a list of fifty indicators which made up the Performance Assessment Framework. Four of these are recognised as national strategic objectives: the CF/A1 measure of the stability of placements for children and young people in care; the CF/A2 measure of educational qualifications of children looked after; the CF/A3 measure of re-registrations on the child protection register, and the CF/A4 measure of employment, education and training for care leavers (Department of Health 1999a). Apart from the benefits they brought to achieving national targets, the PAF indicators were also designed to enable local authorities to benchmark themselves against other authorities and to help them identify areas for local improvement. Taken together, the performance assessment arrangements were intended to enhance the provision of care and support to vulnerable people requiring Social Services (Department of Health 2003).

## Performance targets

The annual Autumn Performance Reports provide an overview of progress towards meeting the relevant performance targets. An understanding of these targets is important for recognising the basis of the outcome measures for children and young people in and leaving care.

For care leavers, essentially only one main PSA target was set, 'improving the level of education, training and employment outcomes for care leavers aged 19 so that levels of this group are at least 75 per cent of those achieved by all young people in the same area by 2004' (DfES 2003a: 13).

For young people in care, several targets were established. In terms of education, the PSA aimed to:

- Improve 'outcomes for 11-year olds in English and Maths so that they are at least 60 per cent as good as those of their peers' (DfES 2003a: 13).
- Increase the proportions of those leaving care aged 16 who get qualifications equivalent to five GCSEs graded A*–C by 15 per cent by 2001.
- Increase the proportion of those leaving care aged 16 with at least one GCSE equivalent qualification graded A*–G by 50 per cent by 2001.
- Increase the proportion of those leaving care aged 16 with at least one GCSE equivalent qualification graded A*–G by 75 per cent by 2003.
- Reduce 'the proportion that become disengaged from education . . . so that no more than 10 per cent reach school leaving age without having sat a GCSE equivalent exam' (DfES 2003a: 13).

In terms of youth offending, the PSA target was defined as 'narrowing the gap between the proportions of children in care and their peers who are cautioned or convicted' (DfES 2003a: 13), requiring a reduction of 3.6 percentage points from the September 2000 baseline by 2004 (DfES 2003a: 14).

One further PSA target relevant to this discussion is the reduction of the under-18 conception rate among all young women in the local authority by 50 per cent by 2010 (DfES 2003a: 14), a joint target with the Department of Health.

## Outcome data collection in England

In response to the Utting Report of 1997, the government set forth its National Objectives for Children's Social Services (Department of Health 1998f) and issued guidance in the form of *Quality Protects* (DoH 1998d). This set out eleven key objectives, three of which were directly relevant to outcome assessment. Although linked to the PSA targets, the *Quality Protects* objectives were set out separately from those targets. The three most relevant objectives were to:

1　Ensure that children in need gain maximum life chance benefits from educational opportunities.
2　Ensure that children looked after gain maximum life chance benefits from educational opportunities, health care and social care.
3　Ensure that young people leaving care, as they enter adulthood, are not isolated, and that they participate socially and economically as citizens.

A pilot exercise was conducted in 1998 by the English Department of Health in order to identify the most useful and reliable indicators of outcomes for children and young people in care. Subsequently, these indicators were sent to all 150 local authorities in England with a requirement for them to make their first statistical returns for these outcomes for 1999. Although *Quality Protects* has been superseded by *Choice Protects*, the set of indicators, known as the OC2 collection (DfES 2004b), has remained a routine requirement for local authorities. Local authority returns are compiled to form an annual national report that is available to the public. The OC2 collection includes a number of measures relating to educational attainment and school attendance, juvenile offending rates, and a series of indicators monitoring the health care received by children and young people in care.

In parallel with these outcome indicators, a new child-based collection, the OC1 collection, was set up in 1999 to collect data on the educational qualifications of young people leaving care aged 16 and over. This was in order to provide new statistical information for one of the Department of Health's key targets for children's social services. The collection was also designed to enable educational outcome data to be linked with other data on the care histories of children, and to permit the Department of Health to conduct further analysis of these data. In the same year, a new collection, the OC3 collection (DfES 2003b), began to gather data on young people with respect to their latest period of care, the date they ceased to be looked after and whether they were in education, training or employment on their nineteenth birthday.

These collections were in addition to the pre-existing SSDA903 return (a child-level return) routinely made by local authorities to provide a national annual picture of the numbers of children in care and leaving care; the numbers of children in care being accommodated in different settings; the legal status of children; and the reasons why they are taken into care. In 1998, major changes were introduced to this collection in order to streamline and speed up the process of data collection and dissemination. From the year ending 31 March 1998, authorities were asked to complete a new aggregate statistical return (the CLA100) to provide basic headline data for rapid publication.

The SSDA903 provides a detailed annual analysis of the looked-after population, which is used with the total figures provided on the CLA100 to estimate the full national picture. Such annual returns have been regularly collected over many years for monitoring purposes. The data have also been used, for example, to inform the performance assessment frameworks aimed at improving the life chances of children in and after care.

## Numbers of children in care and leaving care

Statistics on the numbers of children and young people in care (called 'children looked after') in England have been collected and published by the Department of Health at least since the Children and Young Persons Act 1969. Similar arrangements have been in place for the Welsh Office, the Scottish Office and the Northern Ireland Office. It is therefore possible to examine change in the numbers of children and young people in care over a long period of time.

Figures for 2003 are shown in Table 3.1, compiled from data published by the Department for Education and Skills for England, the Scottish Parliament,

*Table 3.1* Children looked after by local authorities, year ending 31 March 2003

|  |  | England | Wales | Scotland | Northern Ireland |
|---|---|---|---|---|---|
| Looked after at 31 March | Number | 60,800 | 4,219 | 11,388 | 2,446 |
|  | Per 10,000 | 55 | 49 |  |  |
| Looked after at any time in year | Number | 83,200 | 75 | . . . | . . . |
|  | Per 10,000 |  |  |  |  |
| Started to be looked after | Number | 24,100 | 1,651 | 4,513 | 1,152 |
| Ceased to be looked after | Number | 24,000 | . . . | 4,034 | 1,068 |
| Ceased aged 16+ | Number | 6,500 | 327 | . . . | . . . |

Source: DfES (2004a): Forms CLA100 and SSDA903; Local Government Data Unit – Wales (2004): Form SDSA903; Scottish Executive (2003); Department of Health, Social Services and Public Safety (2003): Forms LA1, LA6 and LA8.

the Welsh Assembly and the Department of Health, Social Services and Public Safety in Northern Ireland. The table shows the numbers of children looked after, numbers starting to be looked after, and numbers ceasing to be looked after. Across the UK in 2003, there were almost 79,000 children looked after. This number has increased fairly steadily since the mid-1990s while the numbers starting to be looked after over the same period have been falling. At the same time, the numbers ceasing to be looked after have been falling more rapidly, so that there is a continuing slow growth in the total number of children looked after (Statham *et al.*, 2002).

## Outcomes for children in care and after: what is known?

There are two major difficulties in attempting to present any comprehensive national picture of what is known statistically about the outcomes for children in and after care. First, an analysis of national data for children and young people in care is problematic because the constituent parts of the United Kingdom do not coordinate their data collections. Sometimes different data are collected and published, making it difficult to draw general conclusions about the UK as a whole. Although some comparable data are also published for Scotland, Wales and Northern Ireland, only statistics for England will be presented here. Second, there are only statistical data on some of the possible outcomes for children in and leaving care. Since 2004, statistical returns for 'outcomes' for children and young people in care in England have been collected by the DfES. These cover academic performance, employment and training, youth offending and some health-related outcomes. All other knowledge on outcomes for young people both in and leaving care derives from other non-statistical, small-scale research studies.

### Outcomes covered by the statistical collections

*Education*

The OC2 return brings together data on the educational attainment of children and young people in care at Key Stages 1, 2 and 3 and for GCSEs. These key stages are approximately equivalent to the ages of 7, 11, 14 and 16. Results for Key Stages 1, 2 and 3 for 2003 are shown in Table 3.2.

From the returns shown for 2003 it is clear that older children and young people in care performed worse than younger children. At Key Stage 1, around half of children were performing at the expected level for their age; this dropped to about one-third at Key Stage 2 and a quarter at Key Stage 3. Since the care population is constantly changing, with new children and young people entering care and others leaving care, these data do not indicate a deterioration in the performance of any individual child, since the children taking the three tests are different. Most of the children who were in care at Key Stage 1 will have left care before they are assessed again at Key Stage 2 or 3, and will be replaced by other children.

The relatively poor achievement of children and young people in care compared to all children, even at Key Stage 1, is striking. For all children, scores for older children were worse than those for younger children. However, the difference was much smaller for all children and young people than for those in care. For all children, over 80 per cent were performing at the expected level for their age at the Key Stage 1 assessment; this fell to just under 80 per cent at Key Stage 2 and 70 per cent at Key Stage 3. For children in care, the corresponding figures were over 50 per cent, over 40 per cent, with a fall to around 25 per cent at Key Stage 3. Even allowing for inaccuracies in these percentages since three assessments are involved at each age and not all children took all tests, there are conspicuous differences between the two groups.

Most children took GCSE (General Certificate of Secondary Education) or GNVQ (General National Vocational Qualification) examinations in Year 11, at around the age of 16. Table 3.3 shows that only just over half of young people in care sat these examinations at that time.

Overall performance for young people in care was also markedly below that for all children. Just over half of young people in care achieved at least one pass at any grade. Since many children sat no examinations, this means that nearly all the young people in care who sat the exam gained at least one pass. However, applying stricter criteria gives a worse picture. Taking five GCSE passes at any grade, the middle criterion for overall performance, this was achieved by just over one-third of young people in care but by 89 per cent of all children. Yet it is the strictest criterion, namely five passes at grades A*–C, that highlights the greatest

Table 3.2 Eligibility and performance of looked-after children in Key Stage tasks and tests, school year ending 30 September 2003

| | Looked-after children | | All children |
| | Number | % | % |
|---|---|---|---|
| Year 2 | | | |
| Number eligible to sit Key Stage 1 tasks and tests | 1,900 | … | … |
| Number who obtained at least level 2[a] in the following tasks: | | | |
| • Reading task/test | 970 | 50.8 | 84 |
| • Writing task | 930 | 48.5 | 81 |
| • Mathematics test | 1,200 | 61.0 | 90 |
| Year 6 | | | |
| Number eligible to sit Key Stage 2 tasks and tests | 3,000 | … | … |
| Number who obtained at least level 4[a] in the following tasks: | | | |
| • English | 1,100 | 37.1 | 75 |
| • Mathematics | 1,000 | 34.8 | 73 |
| • Science | 1,600 | 52.9 | 87 |
| Year 9 | | | |
| Number eligible to sit Key Stage 3 tasks and tests | 3,800 | … | … |
| Number who obtained at least level 5[a] in the following tasks: | | | |
| • English | 850 | 22.3 | 69 |
| • Mathematics | 890 | 23.3 | 71 |
| • Science | 890 | 23.2 | 68 |

Note: [a] Target level for age group.
Source: DfES (2004b): Table B, Form OC2.

discrepancies. In 2003, this level was achieved by just 8.7 per cent of young people in care but by more than half of all children.

The *Quality Protects* Indicator 8 is defined as the proportion of young people in care obtaining at least five GCSEs at grades A*–C during the most recent school year, as a ratio of the proportion of all children in the local authority achieving these standards. In 2003 this indicator was 0.16. While the achievement of young people in care has improved slightly since the figures started to be collected in 2000, so too has the achievement of all children; thus little actual progress has been made in terms of reducing the gap in performance between those in care and the general population.

Data on the educational qualifications of all care leavers aged 16 and over are also collected by local authorities. Results for 2003 are detailed in Table 3.4 which shows that more than half left care with no qualifications.

*Table 3.3* GCSE performance or equivalents of looked-after children in Year 11, school year ending 30 September 2002

| | Looked-after children | | All children |
|---|---|---|---|
| | *Number* | *%* | *%* |
| Number in year 11 | 4,200 | . . . | . . . |
| Number who sat at least one GCSE or GNVQ | 2,600 | 56.8 | . . . |
| Number who obtained at least: | | | |
| • 1 GCSE at grade A* to G or GNVQ | 2,400 | 52.9 | 95 |
| • 5 GCSEs at grade A* to G | 1,700 | 36.8 | 89 |
| • 5 GCSEs at grade A* to C | 400 | 8.7 | 53 |

Source: DfES (2004b): Table C, Form OC2.

*Table 3.4* Children who ceased to be looked after during the year ending 31 March 2003 aged 16 or over, by level of qualification received

| | Looked-after children | |
|---|---|---|
| | *Number* | *%* |
| Number of care leavers | 6,400 | . . . |
| Number who obtained at least: | | |
| • 1 GCSE at grade A* to G or GNVQ | 2,800 | 44 |
| • 5 GCSEs at grade A* to G | 1,800 | 28 |
| • 5 GCSEs at grade A* to C | 370 | 6 |
| • No GCSEs or GNVQs | 3,600 | 56 |
| • No qualifications | 3,400 | 54 |

Source: DfES (2003b): Table 4, Form OC1.

*Employment*

Another important outcome concerns the education and employment status of young people immediately after finishing Year 11. Data on education and employment are collected on the forms OC2 for children in care and OC3 for care leavers.

Form OC2 includes the employment and education status on 30 September for all young people in care who had been in Year 11 in the previous school year (i.e. who could legally have left full-time education). One of the aims of *Quality Protects* was to reduce the number of young people in this group who are 'Not in Education, Employment or Training' (NEET). These are shown as 'unemployed' in Table 3.5. Fifty-seven per cent of children who were looked after in Year 11 were in full-time education on 30 September 2003. This is less than the 72 per cent for all children, but it still represents more than half of young people in full-time education beyond the compulsory school-leaving age. Adding in part-time education, training and employment with training indicates that 71 per cent of young people who had been looked after received some form of education or training: this is lower than the 92 per cent for all children, but is still a positive achievement. On the more negative side, 23 per cent of young people who had been looked after were unemployed, compared to 7 per cent of all young people.

Local authorities are expected to maintain contact with care leavers and to collect some further outcome data from them on their nineteenth birthday. Form OC3 collects data about activity on their nineteenth birthday for those who were looked after at age 16. The results for 2003 are shown in Table 3.6. By age 19, almost half of those who had been in care when they were 16 were known to be in education, employment or training, and one-third were not in education, employment or training (NEET). However, these figures need to be treated with caution since 19 per cent of care leavers were not in touch with the local authority. The percentage of young people who had been looked after and were not in education, employment or training could therefore be as high as 50 per cent.

*Offending*

Information on whether or not young people commit criminal offences is only currently collected for those young people in care, and not for care leavers. The same is true of the small-scale research studies, which also seem to present data only about those in care. Such studies commonly report that contact with the police for children in care is three times that of other children in similar age groups who are not in care (e.g. Jackson *et al.* 2000; Courtney *et al.* 2001).

The OC2 form collects information on the number of young people in care aged 10 or over (and looked after for at least twelve months) who were convicted or subject to a final warning or reprimand during the year. In 2003, this amounted to 9.5 per cent of the relevant group, as shown in Table 3.7. This was nearly three times the rate for all children (so is very similar to the information gleaned from the small-scale research studies), and does not indicate a positive outcome.

Table 3.5 Education and employment status at 30 September 2003 of looked-after children in Year 11 in 2002/2003 school year

| | Total number of children in Year 11 | Position at 30 September 2003 as a percentage of the total | | | | | |
| --- | --- | --- | --- | --- | --- | --- | --- |
| | | Full-time education | Full-time training | Full-time employment with planned training | Full-time employment with no planned training | Part-time employment, education or training | Unemployed |
| Looked-after children | 4,600 | 57 | 8 | 3 | 3 | 6 | 23 |
| All children | 608,800 | 72 | 7 | 5 | 3 | 1 | 7 |

Source: DfES (2004b): Table D, Form OC2.

Table 3.6 Activity on nineteenth birthday of care leavers who were looked after on 1 April 2000 aged 16 and over, by activity

| | All care leavers aged 16 and over | Council in touch with young person | | | | Not in touch |
| --- | --- | --- | --- | --- | --- | --- |
| | | In education, training or employment | Of which | | Not in education, training or employment | |
| | | | In education | In training or employment | | |
| Number | 4,900 | 2,400 | 1,000 | 1,400 | 1,600 | 940 |
| Percentage | 100 | 49 | 21 | 28 | 32 | 19 |

Source: DfES (2003b): Table 7, Form OC3.

*Table 3.7* Offending by looked-after children aged 10 or older and looked after for at least twelve months, ending 30 September 2003

| | Looked-after children | | All children |
| --- | --- | --- | --- |
| | Number | % | % |
| Number of children aged 10 or older looked after for at least twelve months | 29,100 | . . . | . . . |
| Number convicted or subject to a final warning or reprimand during the year | 2,800 | 9.5 | 3.3 |

Source: DfES (2004b): Table E, Form OC2.

Hobcraft (1998) does, however, offer some additional information about what happens to young people who have been in care but who subsequently leave care, in terms of offending. He reported that when looked-after children are followed up some time after leaving care, they are more likely to have had further contact with the police or probation services than other young people who have not had an episode in care, and this likelihood is three to four times higher for males than for females. Commonly, studies on crime that present data on children in care or who have left care draw on samples from the prison population rather than samples from the care population. Therefore, we only know about those young people who have committed a crime and have been convicted of that crime and who also happen to have had an episode in care. We do not have information about those who have had an episode in care but who do not go on to commit a crime. Such studies report high figures of between 25 per cent and 50 per cent, which equates to around twelve to twenty-five times that of the general population (Jackson *et al.*, 2002). Sampling biases may mean that these figures are very unreliable.

*Health*

A limited number of health outcomes for children in care are routinely collected through the annual medical assessment, to which children entering care have been subjected since 1948. Data on these annual medical assessments are also collected on the OC2 form, so they apply only to children and young people looked after for at least twelve months. There are three indicators collected for all children and young people in care: the number with immunisations up to date, the number who had their teeth checked by a dentist during the year, and the number who had an annual health check. For children aged 5 or under, there is a further indicator: the number whose developmental assessments were up to date. The results for 2003 for all these indicators are shown in Table 3.8.

These figures indicate that a high proportion of looked-after children and young people have had health checks, but there are no available comparable data for all children. For instance, the PAF indicator C19 is the percentage that both had

*Table 3.8* Health care of children looked-after for at least one year, twelve months ending 30 September 2002

|  | Number | % |
|---|---|---|
| Number of children looked after for at least one year | 44,900 | ... |
| of these: | | |
| Number whose immunisations were up to date | 32,300 | 71.9 |
| Number who had their teeth checked by a dentist | 33,800 | 75.3 |
| Number who had their annual health assessment | 33,700 | 75.0 |
| Number of children aged 5 or younger at 30 September | 7,100 | ... |
| of these: | | |
| Number whose development assessments were up to date | 5,700 | 80.7 |

Source: DfES (2004b): Table F, Form OC2.

their teeth checked and a health assessment in the past year: for 2003 this was 75.2 per cent. A case-controlled study of looked-after children in Wales found that children living at home were much more likely to be taken for regular dental check-ups, twice as likely to return for follow-up treatment and twice as likely to have orthodontic treatment (Jackson *et al.* 2000). The indicators for health care have been showing consistent improvements since data on them were first collected in 2000. It is unfortunate, however, that data on a wider range of health indicators are not as yet routinely collected, including information on mental health and well-being, and pregnancy and parenthood.

*Independent living*

The OC3 form also collects information about the living arrangements of care leavers on their nineteenth birthday. While not strictly an outcome in itself, the type and quality of accommodation is likely to greatly influence young people's lives. As may be seen in Table 3.9, 11 per cent were living with parents or relatives, 15 per cent were in supported accommodation and 4 per cent in a community home, with 37 per cent living independently. Nineteen per cent of young people who were looked after were no longer in touch with their local authority, hence their accommodation status is unknown. There are no comparable data for all children from these statistical collections.

**Outcomes reported from other research studies**

Official statistical collections are constraining in that they contain information about a very limited range of outcomes and are largely restricted to providing information about short-term rather than longer-term outcomes. For instance, in terms of health outcomes, while we can find information about the numbers of children and young people *in care* who have been inoculated, there is nothing in

*Table 3.9* Accommodation on nineteenth birthday of care leavers who were looked after on 1 April 2000 aged 16 and over, by accommodation

|  | Number | % |
| --- | --- | --- |
| All young people | 4,900 | 100 |
| Council in touch with young person: |  |  |
| • With parents or relatives | 530 | 11 |
| • Community home | 200 | 4 |
| • Supported accommodation | 710 | 15 |
| • Lodgings | 270 | 6 |
| • Independent living | 1,800 | 37 |
| • Other | 300 | 6 |
| • In custody | 120 | 2 |
| Not in touch | 940 | 19 |

Source: DfES (2003b): Table 8, Form OC3.

the statistical returns to provide important information on other aspects of health such as mental health. For young people leaving care, there is a complete absence of health outcome measures.

Neither do the outcome statistical returns cover important indicators of social exclusion such as the numbers of people sleeping rough and the numbers of young people in prison, although some figures on conviction rates may be derived from the Home Office collections. Consequently, to date, research studies remain the only way of seeing how looked-after young people and care leavers fair on a range of important outcomes compared with other children and young people. Although such studies have limitations, since findings are often small scale and spread over time, they are still valid since they persistently highlight the same issues for children in care and care leavers.

While annual health assessments have a very narrow conceptualisation of health and well-being, small-scale studies have provided unique information about the types of health issues affecting children in and leaving care including some lifestyle measures on drug and alcohol use. For instance, Broad (1999a) reported that 48 per cent (twenty-three) out of a sample of thirty-three care leavers in one research project had long-term illnesses or conditions such as asthma and eczema, 81 per cent drank alcohol (26 per cent heavily) and two-thirds of the young people interviewed reported that they had used drugs. Similarly, a Department of Health study (1997) also reported that young people in care were more likely to become involved in substance misuse than were young people in general. A study comparing looked-after children with a matched sample of children living with their own families found that those in care were seven times more likely to have used illegal drugs and over a quarter of those under age 16 were regular smokers compared with none of the sample not in care (Williams *et al.* 2001). Numerous other studies have shown that looked-after children and young people experience significant disadvantages with respect to their health (Saunders and Broad 1997; Utting 1997; House of Commons Health Committee 1998; Skuse and Ward 1999; Wyler 2000).

Several small-scale studies have also provided important, albeit limited, information on the lives of disabled young people who comprise an estimated 25 per cent of young people in care (Department of Health 1999b). This is a somewhat misleading figure since it includes a large number who have been assessed as having emotional and/or behavioural difficulties as well as those with learning disabilities. Nevertheless, these young people form a distinct subgroup of young people in and leaving care who are likely to experience very different outcomes to their peers without disabilities (Rabiee *et al.* 2001). Yet, to date there are no routine statistics on such outcomes for young disabled people either in or leaving care.

Through research conducted into the transitions to adulthood for young disabled people in care in England and Wales, Priestley *et al.* (2003) estimated that on average eleven young people would leave care in any given local authority each year. The study interviewed a sample of these young people and revealed that in terms of educational attainment, although most expressed an interest in further education they felt they had been prevented from accessing appropriate education and training due to disabling barriers. In terms of their health, many reported frequent contact with medical practitioners and some had very significant and complex health needs.

There are no national figures about the nature or extent of mental health problems of children in care or leaving care and there have been very few UK studies looking specifically at the type and prevalence of mental health problems they face (Richardson 2002; Broad 2005). However, there are a number of small-scale studies that are indicative of these outcomes and it is widely documented that children in and leaving care are more likely to have mental health problems than the general population of the same age (Utting 1997; Arcelus *et al.* 1999; Buchanan 1999; Richardson and Joughin 2000; Williams *et al.* 2001). Similarly, Mount *et al.* (2004) found that carers perceived that 70 per cent of young people in their care had a significant mental health need. High rates of conduct disorder have also been reported among looked-after young people (Ward and Skuse 2001) as well as a high prevalence of self-harming and risk-taking behaviour, including suicide attempts, inappropriate sexual behaviour and involvement in prostitution (Richardson and Joughin 2000; Ward and Skuse 2001). Saunders and Broad (1997) reported that 17 per cent of a sample of forty-eight care leavers (mostly female) experienced long-term mental illnesses including depression, eating disorders and phobias.

Several studies have reported an incidence of early pregnancy and parenthood among young people in and leaving care up to three times the rate for the general 16- to 18-year-old population (e.g. Garnett 1992; Hobcraft 1998). Garnett (1992) reported that between 12.5 per cent and 25 per cent of young women were pregnant or already parents by the time they left care. Some studies claim that the likelihood of early pregnancy is even greater. Sinclair and Gibbs (1996), for example, reported that female care leavers were eight times more likely to be pregnant by the age of 19 compared to young women not in care, while the Department of Health (1999b) suggested that between 25 and 30 per cent of young women leaving care are teenage parents. However, the report by the Social Exclusion Unit, *A Better Education for Children in Care* (2003), gives a lower estimate, suggesting that those who have been in care are two and a half times more likely to be teenage parents. It should be borne in mind that all of these figures are derived from relatively small-scale studies from which broader extrapolations have been made. At the time of writing there are no data routinely collected by local authorities on the numbers of young people in their care who become pregnant or parents, although there are plans to begin collecting such information in the near future. Chapter 6 reports findings from a study conducted by the Thomas Coram Research Unit on teenage pregnancy and parenthood among young women and men in and leaving care. It highlights the lack of available data and includes an overview of what is known of the extent to which care leavers are likely to become fathers in their teenage years.

Estimates of the proportions of young people leaving care who experience homelessness are also reliant on small-scale studies. Various studies point out that young people more often than not leave care at a younger age than young people who leave home (Biehal *et al.* 1995; Stein 2002; Stein and Rees 2002). Indeed, Jackson *et al.* (2000) suggest that on average young people leave care three to five years earlier than the age at which young people typically leave their family home. One study found that one in ten young people in care had already experienced living independently before the official school-leaving age (Jackson and Sachdev 2001). Stephens (2002) reported that 30 per cent of young single homeless people had been in care and 20 per cent of care leavers experienced some form of homelessness within two years of leaving care. This figure is supported by the homelessness charity Centrepoint (2004), which reported that 21 per cent of the homeless people they assist had experienced a period of being in care. Many care leavers who are provided with local authority accommodation have been found to be living in unsatisfactory, temporary and/or social housing (Quinton and Rutter 1988; Randall 1988; Broad 1994; Warren and McAndrew 1997).

Somewhat more information on the employment outcomes for young care leavers is available from small-scale studies compared to statistical returns, although these are still limited and somewhat dated. Indeed, Jackson *et al.* (2002) point to the evidence by Quinton and Rutter (1988), which suggested that care leavers looking for employment (either full-time or part-time) were more likely to go into low-paid semi-skilled or unskilled work, than those who have never been in care; and to the work of Cheung and Heath (1994), which indicated that employment outcomes were far worse for those who entered the care system before age 11, who did not leave the system until after they were 11 years old and who spent much longer in the system (on average nine years). Slightly more recent studies, such as Biehal *et al.* (1995) and Sinclair and Gibbs (1996), indicated that unemployment figures for those leaving care during the mid-1990s ranged most commonly between 40 and 50 per cent.

Related to outcomes of unemployment and employment, but not covered by the statistical collections, is the outcome of claiming social security benefits. Hobcraft (1998) found that those who had ever been in care or fostered were 1.69 times more likely to receive any state benefits than those who had been brought up with their biological parents (Hobcraft 1998: table 14). However, as Jackson *et al.* (2002) point out, there is overall a 'paucity of research pertaining to the long-term benefit-claiming status outcomes of looked-after children' (p. 66). Yet it is not inevitable that children in or leaving care will remain so disadvantaged compared to all children and young people. Jackson *et al.* (2002) describe a US intervention programme to help aid independent living. This study suggested that after four to five years of aid through this programme, only 6 per cent of their sample of young people leaving care were claiming benefits, which compared very favourably to the general population figure of 5 per cent.

## Progress in meeting the PSA targets

As well as setting out the targets for children in care and after, the DfES *Autumn Performance Report 2003* provides an overview of the progress that has been made throughout the previous year in achieving the PAF for children's social services (DfES 2003a). It therefore provides an illustration of the sorts of changes that have taken place over time in relation to the PSA targets and which, if any, of the targets are showing positive signs of improvement.

The *Autumn Performance Report 2003* reported that, although there was an upward trend in the average performance of 19-year-old care leavers, the target remained 'challenging' (DfES 2003a: 13). Examination of the figures shows that overall there have been some increases in the average performance of 19-year-old care leavers over time. For example, in 2002, care leavers aged 19 enjoyed outcomes for education, training and employment comparable to 53 per cent of the achievement of all children. By the end of 2003, they had seen improvements in outcomes for education, training and employment comparable to 57 per cent of all children. However, this falls some way short of the PSA target of 75 per cent of all children. Indeed, in 2003, 'only 17 per cent of local authorities achieved this target compared with 13 per cent in 2002' (DfES 2003a: 13).

Young people in care have also seen improvements in their educational outcomes. The *Autumn Performance Report 2003* revealed that young people in care aged 11 achieved as well academically (in terms of English and maths results) as did all children. The report also showed that the proportion of young people in care qualifying with GCSE results (young people in care aged 16 achieving five or more 'good' GCSEs) was steadily improving.

The *Autumn Performance Report 2003* also discussed the progress that had been made with regard to reducing the proportion of looked-after children committing criminal offences. Importantly, the proportion of looked-after children convicted or cautioned in the previous year had fallen significantly since 2000, while the proportion of all young people convicted or cautioned had remained broadly the same (DfES 2003a). While the gap between the proportion of young people in care convicted or cautioned and the proportion of their peers convicted or cautioned had fallen from 7.2 per cent in 2000, to 6.1 per cent in 2002, this reduction of 1.1 per cent is significantly lower than the 3.6 percentage point reduction that was aimed for (DfES 2003a: 14).

Finally, the *Autumn Performance Report 2003* reported on the target to reduce the under-18 conception rate. This report revealed that the 'latest data for 2001 showed a 10 per cent reduction in the under-18 conception rate for all young women from the baseline year of 1998' (DfES 2003a: 14), still some way off the target of a reduction of 50 per cent by 2010. However, as mentioned above, there are no separate data available on the conception rates for young women in and leaving care.

## Conclusions

Recent reforms that have taken place in the collection of statistics by the government have to some extent increased the quality and quantity of outcome data being routinely collected nationally about children in care and care leavers. However, there remain a few notable shortcomings to this data.

First, many of these data are available only for England, not elsewhere in the UK. Second, the data are for short time periods only – they provide snapshots about young people for single years, and as the tables on education, employment and training show, the data only provide information about what outcomes occur immediately after Year 11 or immediately after a care leaver's nineteenth birthday.

Although the data do supply useful information about outcomes for children and young people in care from local authority returns published regularly by the DfES, they clearly have limitations. Some issues, such as mental health and well-being, are not covered at all and others not in sufficient detail. Furthermore, the data are all cross-sectional snapshots whereas longitudinal data would provide a much more informative overview of outcomes. There remain major gaps in information on the extent to which young people in and leaving care are likely to offend, use drugs, become homeless, claim benefits, become young parents or experience mental health or general health problems.

While the SSDA903 form collects data on individual children, until 2003/2004 data from successive years were not brought together. Consequently it has not been possible to link data on children between years. However, since 2003/2004 SSDA903 data are collected as a longitudinal dataset for all children in care, so that eventually it will be possible to look more closely at the life course of children and young people in care. That said, there are two limitations to these data. First of all, due to considerations of confidentiality and data protection, it may not be possible to gain access to the longitudinal dataset. Second, data collected on other forms will not be part of the longitudinal dataset. Despite these limitations, if the longitudinal SSDA903 data can also be linked to school performance data from the DfES Pupil Level Annual Schools Census (PLASC), it will be possible to get a more rounded picture of the outcomes for children and young people in care.

We have seen that where outcome figures are unavailable for care leavers and young people in care from the current statistical data, important small-scale research studies provide vital qualitative information about some or all of these outcomes. However, as with the statistical collections, these too have their limitations. For instance, the young people reported about in these studies may not always be representative of young people in and leaving care as a whole, and studies may fail to include those who are most vulnerable and marginalised. In addition, research often focuses on a 'problem' group – for example, we may know the percentage of young people with a statement of Special Educational Need (SEN) and who have been in care, or the percentage of young people who are homeless and have been in care, but we do not have comparative data for those without such problems. These issues are very much part of the research process and are important to understand when designing and conducting research with children and young people in or leaving care. The logistical and practical challenges of such research along with the complexities of promoting young people's participation are discussed in more detail in Chapter 10.

Overall, it may be said that the information base for young people in and leaving care is improving. Reforms have developed statistical collections and more data than ever before are now routinely available. The transfer of responsibility for children's services from the DoH to the DfES offers the potential for a more 'joined-up' approach to data collection between education and care, such as the possibility of linking children's care records with their education records. These steps are all moves in the right direction and as such should be applauded. Yet, given what we aim to achieve in this book, the greatest dearth of information relates not so much to where young people are disadvantaged and failed by services, but where they experience outcomes that are at the least comparable with their peers who are not within the care population. Available data rarely indicate where things are working well or where young people have flourished or excelled, information which would help guide further exploration into the factors that promote these more positive outcomes. Ironically, statistical returns, for the most part, measure reductions in inadequacies rather than actual progress. It is perhaps to this gap in information that policy-makers and statisticians need to turn their attention.

# 4   The costs and benefits of educating children in care

*Sonia Jackson and Antonia Simon*

Chapter 3 set out the statistical evidence on outcomes for looked-after children, supplemented by findings from research. In this chapter we draw together evidence from a range of disciplines – economics, demography, statistical modelling and sociology – to examine the link between educational attainment, outcomes and public expenditure.

We do not, of course, suggest that saving money should be our main motive for educating children better. However, social work and education services often claim that they know what to do but lack the resources to put their knowledge into practice. We aim to show that the sums required to support children's learning effectively when they are separated from their families are trivial compared with the costs incurred by failing to do so, and compared with the potential savings if the average attainment of looked-after children could be brought closer to that of the school population generally.

The research on which this chapter is based was commissioned by the Social Exclusion Unit as part of the inquiry ordered by the Prime Minister in 2001 into raising the educational attainment of looked-after children. It aimed to answer two questions:

1   What is the cost of looking after children in care and their education?
2   What would be the saving in overall public expenditure if the difference between life outcomes for children in care and other children were reduced or eliminated?

Although considering how this second objective might be brought about was not part of the original remit from the Social Exclusion Unit, in this chapter we go on to reflect on how it might be achieved. In order to do this we draw on information from four bodies of knowledge: theoretical and empirical work on the wider benefits of learning; published statistics from a number of different sources; research on the education of children in care and outcomes from care, some of which was reviewed in Chapter 3; and findings from the British birth cohort studies on adult outcomes for people who have been in care as children as compared with those who have not. The British Cohort Studies comprise data collected about the lives of up to 40,000 individuals across three post-war generations – people born in one week of 1946, 1958 and 1970 respectively. They enable us to assess the effects of changing social and economic circumstances and policies on subsequent education, employment, health and citizenship outcomes in adult life.

In addition, although there is a serious lack of empirical data on what works in raising educational achievement for children in care, there is a growing body of practice wisdom derived from the efforts of local authorities and schools and from the work of voluntary organizations such as Barnardo's, the Who Cares? Trust and the National Children's Bureau. We draw on some of this work throughout the chapter.

## Education and quality of life

We start by briefly reviewing the evidence on the long-term impact of educational attainment and lifelong learning on adult outcomes and quality of life. People who have achieved a good level of basic education are much more likely to continue to seek further education and learning throughout their lives (Sargant *et al.*, 1997). The impact of learning, and the potential effects of improving educational outcomes for looked-after children, are discussed in more detail below.

The Centre for Research on the Wider Benefits of Learning, established in 1999 at the Institute of Education and Birkbeck College, has explored links between levels of education and a number of other areas – health, crime, families and parenting, active ageing and civic engagement, drawing on evidence from the British Cohort Studies (Schuller *et al.*, 2001). This evidence will be reported below.

### Education and health

There is robust evidence for positive correlations between years of education and health status with respect to physical and depressive conditions (Hammond, 2002). Learning impacts upon health through its effect on economic conditions and social status and, in addition, affects access to and uptake of medical services. It appears that education affects health behaviours both through shaping attitudes and enabling individuals to behave in accordance with these attitudes.

There is consistent evidence that education, as measured by years of formal education and qualification level, is correlated with happiness, lower rates of depression and reduced risk of suicide. Very substantial effects have been reported. Results from the 1970 British cohort study show that respondents with no qualifications were by the age of 26 four times more likely to report poor general physical and mental health than those with the highest educational qualifications (Whitty *et al.*, 1998).

Outcomes of learning include improvements in self-esteem, self-efficacy, interpersonal trust, anti-discriminatory attitudes, access to a wider network of social support, and social and political engagement and activity. These outcomes not only change health-related behaviours but also increase resilience – the ability to cope with adverse conditions and stress-inducing circumstances. Individuals who are more resilient experience lower levels of stress in such circumstances, which in turn benefits their health.

Higher educational levels are strongly associated with self-efficacy, which US research suggests acts as a mediator between education and health-related behaviours (Ross and Mirowsky, 1999). Perceived self-efficacy has also been shown to be associated with educational success for children in care (Jackson and Martin, 1998), so it appears that the effect works both ways. It may be seen that all these positive outcomes of better education would be of particular benefit to looked-after children and care leavers, who typically have low self-esteem, have no feeling of control over their lives, are liable to be extremely mistrustful and are often isolated and lack supportive networks (Biehal *et al.*, 1995).

### Promoting resilience

The most important effects of learning for looked-after children may be the psychosocial outcomes in generating the behaviours, skills and personal attributes that have a long-term impact on both mental and physical health. As noted in Chapter 3, many studies have found high levels of mental health problems among looked-after children. There is also evidence that they experience poorer mental health than do other young people (Williams *et al.*, 2001). There is evidence from qualitative studies that higher education makes it more likely that mental health difficulties can be managed and overcome rather than carried into adult life (Jackson and Martin, 1998). This view is supported by quantitative and qualitative work at the Centre for Research on the Wider Benefits of Learning (2005) which shows the complexity of causal relationships between education and outcomes. While education may have important direct and transformative effects, one of its most significant effects, especially in the field of mental health and psychological well-being, is the contribution it makes to sustaining people during periods of stress (Schuller *et al.*, 2002). Both the transformative and the sustaining effects are relevant to looked-after children.

### Social and community effects

A further line of research demonstrates the effect of reducing inequalities in education on social capital and social cohesion which in turn improves the health of individuals and communities (Whitty *et al.*, 1998). In considering the benefits of better education for children in care it is important to recognize these wider outcomes.

Learning affects family life in a variety of ways (Blackwell and Bynner, 2002). Education levels shape fertility patterns and family formation, and play an important role in ameliorating the effects of family dissolution (though not in reducing the incidence of divorce). They influence maternal employment – better educated women are more likely to remain in full-time continuous employment, contributing to higher family income. Education can equip people to make cost/benefit analyses in decision-making – for instance, using contraception or postponing childbearing.

The effects are intergenerational. In the 1970 British Birth Cohort, the daughters of men in unskilled manual work were nine times more likely to become teenage mothers than were the daughters of fathers in professional occupations. Girls who were successful at school were less likely to become pregnant in adolescence but also more likely to return to education after the birth of a child. The protective effect of education is especially important for young women in care because they are at higher risk of teenage pregnancy.

There are also intergenerational consequences of negative educational outcomes, and looked-after children who fail at school are likely to transmit their poor experience of schooling to their own children. Bynner and colleagues (2000) found that parents' educational level at the time their respondents in the 1958 and 1970 birth cohorts were born were 'critically important factors in determining what was going to happen to them sixteen years later' (p. 61). Raising the educational attainment of children in care is therefore not just important for them and their own life outcomes but for their future children as well.

Some of the strongest associations between education and life course outcomes may be seen in relation to crime, though a number of writers have argued that poverty is a more important predisposing factor. These are not necessarily alternatives. Education and training reduces crime directly because it increases wages; conversely the lack of education and training increases crime because it leads to unemployment and increased poverty (Ward, 1995).

Young people who lose interest in education, often because it offers them no chance of success, can become caught up in a vicious cycle of cumulative disadvantage, including low aspirations and achievements, dropping out of school, problems with their parents and ultimately second-generation delinquency (Hagan, 1997). Many male care leavers with no educational qualifications fall into this category.

## Educational outcomes for chldren and young people in care

As we have shown in Chapter 3, it was the publication of national statistics on the educational performance of looked-after children when compared with the school population as a whole that highlighted the enormous gap in achievement between looked-after children and others. Prior to that, children in care were known to do less well in school than children generally but the extent of the difference could not be quantified. On the basis of statistical analysis it was argued that most of these effects could be explained by the fact that the children were drawn from a highly disadvantaged population rather than being the result of their care status.

The first suggestion that neglect of their educational needs might be a major factor in their poor performance was made in a position paper commissioned by the Social Science Research Council, forerunner of the Economic and Social Research Council (ESRC), in 1982 (Jackson, 1983). The paper, which combined a literature review and small-scale original research, was not published at the time but was used by the ESRC as the basis for a call for research proposals.

### Research approaches

The ESRC programme resulted in two substantial bodies of work, by a group of researchers in Oxford, led by the sociologist Anthony Heath, and by the National Foundation for Educational Research (NFER). The Oxford study looked at the educational progress of a group of forty-nine children aged between 9 and 13 in stable long-term foster care at the start of the research. The research included standardized tests of reading, vocabulary and mathematics, and a questionnaire to carers and teachers. The control group consisted of fifty-eight children of the same age whose families were receiving help from the Social Services department but who had not been in care.

Even compared with this disadvantaged group, the foster children were found to be performing poorly. Tested again two years later, the study children were found to have made progress, but not enough to catch up with their age group. The foster families were considered by the researchers to have provided good-quality care and were described as 'mainly middle class'. The two children who made better than average progress in reading (though less progress in mathematics) were both in foster families where the father was a graduate. The groups who made least progress were those who came into care as a result of neglect or abuse.

It is interesting to note that in the first report of the study the emphasis was on the finding that the children's low attainment could be attributed mainly to the social background of their birth families (Heath *et al.*, 1989). The second report also concluded that children's early histories before entry into care have a profound effect on their educational attainment, but responded to criticism that no account was taken of the failure of the care or education systems to compensate for the children's earlier disadvantage. The paper, entitled 'Failure to Escape', comments that:

> When 'average' educational inputs are given to children with 'above average' educational needs they fail to make 'greater than average' educational progress. Given their low starting point, greater than average educational progress would have been needed for these children to have caught up with the national average.
>
> (Heath *et al.*, 1994: 57)

The NFER report took a very different approach, consisting of a study of local authorities and their policies, with an emphasis on social work practice (Fletcher-Campbell and Hall, 1990). The authors also interviewed a number of children and young people about their experience of education. Their conclusion, in line with the earlier ESRC report (Jackson, 1987), was that the educational problems of children in care were caused more by the failure of social services and education to work together and by social workers' ignorance and neglect of educational matters than by any characteristics of the children themselves. The report comments that even when joint training was arranged for teachers and social workers (an uncommon event in any case), the agenda was that of social services, usually focusing on child abuse and protection. Promoting children's educational attainment was not considered relevant, since expectations of what they could achieve were so minimal.

These two streams of research represent two different ways of conceptualizing the educational failure of looked-after children and set the tone for the sparse literature on the subject throughout the early 1990s, until the launch of the *Quality Protects* programme in 1998 (Department of Health, 1998d). One line of thinking argues that most children who come into the care system are so damaged by their previous experience that it is unrealistic to expect them to achieve educationally at anything like average levels. The other side of the argument is that provision for the education of looked-after children has been so deficient in the past that we can have no idea what they might achieve unless local authorities as corporate parents put the same kind of effort into educating the children in their care as do well-informed and adequately resourced parents in the community.

### Effects of early disadvantage

There is no doubt that there is some truth in the first proposition. Increasingly, children are accommodated only when they are at serious risk of neglect or abuse in their own homes. The number of children who enter care as a result of drug or alcohol misuse by their parents is rising rapidly. There is a large body of evidence from the USA that substance misuse in pregnancy can affect the child's ability to learn (Barth *et al.*, 2000; Harbin and Murphy, 2000). Neurobiological research has shown that neglect and under-stimulation in the early weeks and months of life can have long-lasting effects.

Our estimates of the benefits that may be expected from bringing outcomes for children in care into line with the average for the population take account of the probability that looked-after children will have suffered many adversities before they come into care. However, this could be taken as an argument for intensifying remedial efforts and support mechanisms rather than lowering expectations. Moreover, the finding that children who begin to be looked after early do better in primary school but fail to make predicted progress at secondary level (Evans, 2000) suggests that it is something about the care system itself rather than simply the characteristics of the children or their background that results in the enormous gap in attainment by the time they reach Year 11. The study reported in Chapter 5 provides powerful new evidence that young people can recover from very harmful experiences in childhood and do well educationally given strong personal motivation and a stimulating and supportive care environment.

In order to take account of both points of view, we have included in our calculations of benefits *upper bound estimates* which make no allowance for the fact that looked-after children are an atypical population and compare them with the average child in the community, and *lower bound estimates* which compare them with children from other disadvantaged families. The higher estimates represent what might be attainable as the result of a generously funded national initiative

local authorities with commitment and determination. The lower
e account of the difficulty of overcoming earlier adversities,
ially for those who come into care as teenagers.

### Ability and attainment

In the past there was resistance to the idea of obtaining or publishing information
on the educational attainment of looked-after children on the grounds that
it would be too discouraging for them, or too critical of their carers (Ward, 1995).
There was also a misconception that the majority of looked-after children have
learning difficulties and could not be expected to achieve at average levels. In
fact, the proportion of children in care who have a severe learning disability
due to congenital or organic causes is not very much higher than in the general
population – 3 per cent as against 2 per cent. Mittler (2000) has argued that social
and economic disadvantage is the main determinant of moderate and mild
learning difficulties. This would be in accord with research previously cited which
suggests that children are already behind their peers at the point when they enter
care, due to the highly disadvantaged population from which they originate
(Bebbington and Miles, 1989). We do not yet know how far this is remediable,
although Mittler and colleagues suggest that a commitment to inclusivity could
produce much better results than in the past (Mittler *et al.*, 2002). The picture
is confused by the fact that around a quarter of children in the care system are
classified as disabled or having special educational needs, but this is due primarily
to behavioural and emotional problems rather than to learning disability.

Although the poor educational performance of children in care was acknowledged prior to 1999, it was usually expressed in rather vague terms. It is important
to know the precise size of the gap in attainment between the looked-after
population and other children in order to estimate what would need to be done
to begin to close it. The targets set by *Quality Protects* and detailed in Chapter 3
have been criticized both for being too low and for laying too much emphasis
on examination results. The first criticism has some validity but, from a position
where 70 to 80 per cent of care leavers had no qualifications at all, the target did
at least offer a starting point. It is all the more disappointing that, as we showed
in Chapter 3, most local authorities still fell far short of achieving even these very
modest goals.

The second criticism is a variant of the argument about discouragement.
Examination results at the end of compulsory schooling are the best single measure
of educational attainment and the key to further education and employment.
Children who leave school and care without qualifications are at high risk of
becoming 'NEET' (not in education, employment or training), as we show below.

The figures shown in Chapter 3 (Table 3.4) detailing the low educational
achievement of children leaving care demonstrate that the comment in the
preamble to the Department of Health Statistical Bulletin that 'on average looked
after children do less well in school than other children' is a serious under-
statement. The table illustrates the size of the gap that needs to be bridged to bring

their attainment as a group up to the average of the population. It has to be borne in mind that this is not likely to be achieved quickly or easily. The seeds of success or failure in GCSE are sown at least four years earlier so that any measures put in place now are unlikely to change the figures significantly for the group of children currently in school years 10 and 11. Since many looked-after children are starting from a long way back there is an argument for setting intermediate targets designed to improve basic skills such as literacy and numeracy, which in the longer term may benefit them more than one or two low-grade passes at GCSE level.

It also has to be noted that even if the average educational level achieved by looked-after children were the same as that of children living with their own families, this would not automatically lead to their obtaining employment at the level which would currently be expected for that qualification. Other obstacles, such as lack of social skills, discrimination and the absence of a supportive network, are still likely to put them at a disadvantage in the job market. As Sally Power and her colleagues have shown, class factors continue to play a large part in determining occupational outcomes, irrespective of educational achievement (Power *et al.*, 2003). However, as compared with other care leavers, those with recognized educational qualifications are in a much better position to obtain and keep employment with all the benefits that brings.

### Lack of quantifiable data

One problem in making cost and benefit calculations is the continuing lack of reliable evidence on school progress and educational attainment for looked-after children. For example, earlier estimates of the proportion of looked-after young people in post-16 education varied between 12 per cent and 19 per cent (Biehal *et al.*, 1995; Broad, 1998) and the official figure is 17 per cent, but part of the problem is that although more children in care are staying in education after age 16 the drop-out rate is very high; indeed one estimate puts it at 75 per cent (Dixon and Stein, 2002). Even official statistics are not always consistent and education statistics, as we show below, do not include looked-after children as an identified group either in information on use of different kinds of educational provision or in cost data.

Local authorities have been required to collect information and submit returns on test and examination results for looked-after children only since April 1999. Although there are now numerous local initiatives to address some of the deficiencies identified by earlier research, there is almost no outcome data on their effectiveness. The only exception is the evaluation of the National Children's Bureau 'Taking Care of Education' project, which found modest improvements in attendance, attainment at early Key Stages and young people's self-esteem and attitudes to education (Harker *et al.*, 2004). The Social Exclusion Unit report gives many examples of good practice in local authorities and in voluntary and independent agencies, but these tend to be patchy and depend too much on key individuals rather than being embedded in standard practice (Social Exclusion Unit, 2003). There is some evidence of greater awareness at managerial level of

*nd benefits of education*

*rtance* of education for looked-after children, although it appears to be *filter* down to the field (Jackson *et al.*, 2002).

## Explaining the low attainment of looked-after children

What factors other than birth family background might help to explain the low educational attainment of looked-after children? The main findings from research and literature reviews are remarkably consistent (see Borland *et al.*, 1998; Goddard, 2000; Jackson and Sachdev, 2001; Social Exclusion Unit, 2003).

Among the most significant adverse factors to be identified in the research reviews are:

- The failure of corporate parenting at policy and individual levels.
- Low expectations.
- Placement instability.
- The care environment and the educational level of carers.
- Exclusion of looked-after children from mainstream schooling.
- Bullying and discrimination in the school setting.
- Insufficient emphasis on basic skills such as literacy at the point of admission and during the period in care.

### Corporate parenting

Education and Social Services departments still find it difficult to work together and share information (Firth and Fletcher, 2001). Children in care are seen as mainly the concern of Social Services despite the emphasis in the Children Act 1989 on the responsibility of the whole local authority for looked-after children. It is too soon to know how this will change as a result of the transfer of responsibility for children's services to the Department for Education and Skills and the requirement for every local authority to appoint a Director of Children's Services with responsibility for education as well as care. More importantly, local authorities now have a legal duty to promote the educational achievement of children they look after, under the Children Act 2004.

A continuing problem is that when a child is living apart from his or her birth family no one person has an overview of the child's developmental progress. The Department of Health's Looking after Children system was intended to address this issue, but research indicates that it has had a limited impact, especially in relation to education (Ward, 1995; Skuse and Evans, 2001). Turnover of social workers often results in failure to implement plans or to take remedial action until a crisis arises.

### Low expectations

Children in care are often not expected to do well at school either by carers or teachers. Instead of carefully monitoring progress and taking immediate action to overcome difficulties they simply accept low achievement as inevitable. The annual report of the Chief Inspector of Schools (OFSTED, 2002) remarked that some local authorities automatically assign all children in public care to a stage on the Special Educational Needs Code of Practice, irrespective of their level of attainment. Attention is often focused on attendance and behaviour rather than on learning. Unlike children with good home support, many looked-after children do not see public examinations or university as goals to aim for and therefore lack motivation, especially in the later years of secondary school.

### Placement instability

Most children who stay in care for many years are likely to experience several changes of placement (over ten for about 10 per cent). These often involve changes of school frequently disrupting preparation for exams. The practice of moving children at age 16 in the run-up to GCSE to 'independent living' is especially damaging to their chances of success (Evans, 2000; Jackson and Thomas, 2001; Jackson et al., 2003, 2005). However, the association between instability and poor education outcomes is not simple. Placement breakdowns or changes are certainly damaging to educational opportunities, but school difficulties are also an important cause of placement problems or of needing to be looked after in the first place (Francis, 2000). A planned placement move to a home that provides more encouragement and support for school attendance and achievement can be beneficial (Harker et al., 2004).

### The care environment

Many traditional foster homes and children's homes fail to offer an educationally stimulating or supportive environment (see Chapter 8; Goddard, 2000). Social Services departments do not pay attention to educational background in selecting foster carers; nor do they give them a clear understanding that educating the children is as important a part of their role as caring for them (Jackson and Sachdev, 2001). Foster homes often lack suitable facilities for homework and are not able to provide help. Foster carers are also confused about their responsibilities *vis-à-vis* social workers and birth parents, and are not given clear guidance (Borland et al., 1998).

The education and training of residential care workers is generally at a very low level (Boddy et al., forthcoming) They often consider education the business of the school, but on the other hand do not succeed in promoting school attendance (see Chapter 8). Facilities and equipment for study, including books, in most children's homes are still extremely poor. Computers may be reserved for staff use or available to the residents only for limited periods (Berridge and Brodie, 1998; Rees, 2001; Jackson et al., 2005). Chapter 8 illustrates the limited understanding UK residential workers have of their educational role compared with their counterparts in other European countries, although there are some signs of improvement, especially in relation to provision of facilities for study (Harker et al., 2004).

## Exclusion or diversion from mainstream schooling

Children in care are twenty times more likely to be excluded from school than other children, but are also much more likely to miss school for other reasons (Jackson, 2000, 2001). Despite the Guidance (Department for Education and Skills and Department of Health, 2000) which requires care and school placements to be planned together and an education place to be found within twenty school days (now incorporated into the Guidance to the Children Act 2004), many children still experience long gaps in their education. An education place may be in an alternative provision such as a pupil referral unit where the focus is on social learning and which offers limited opportunities for academic achievement. Such provision is also experienced as stigmatizing by children (Galloway *et al.*, 1994). Looked-after children are five times more likely to be allocated to special schools than those living with their families, even when their disabilities are less serious than those of other children in mainstream schooling (Gordon *et al.*, 2000).

Missing periods of schooling due to family turmoil or not having a placement cause children to fall even further behind and make reintegration very difficult. Few succeed in returning to mainstream schools, though further education colleges sometimes offer a lifeline. Attendance at school for young people from children's homes is particularly poor, with outcomes markedly worse than from foster care (Berridge and Brodie, 1998). Furthermore, there is a strong association between exclusion from school and offending behaviour, especially for boys (Social Exclusion Unit, 1998a; Berridge *et al.*, 2001) and, as we show below, reducing the amount of crime accounted for by the care and ex-care population could produce very substantial savings in public expenditure.

Regular, continuous school attendance is one of the few factors that distinguishes care leavers who are relatively successful in education from looked-after children generally (Martin and Jackson, 2002). This finding is confirmed by the *By Degrees* study described in Chapter 5.

## Bullying and discrimination

Looked-after children are at high risk of victimization by other pupils if their care status is known and bullying is a major problem faced by many (Borland *et al.*, 1998). In the case of disputes arising from taunting or insults from other children the looked-after child is much more likely to be blamed, having no parent to come to the rescue (Who Cares? Trust, 1999; Brodie, 2001). This is a common cause of school exclusions (Blyth and Milner, 1994; Brodie, 2001). Some local authorities have a policy that all permanent exclusions of looked-after children should be appealed but this is not likely to be successful unless an independent advocate is involved or unless the child happens to have a confident and well-educated foster carer (Blyth and Milner, 1994). Social workers may lack the time, knowledge and commitment to argue the child's case effectively.

*Inattention to literacy*

Research on higher achievers from care shows that reading early and fluently is a strong predictor of later success (Jackson and Martin, 1998). Most pre-school children who enter care have had little acquaintance with books and are ill-prepared to learn to read (Ward, 1995; Evans, 2000). Those who enter the care system later may already have serious literacy problems. A few may have specific learning difficulties, such as dyslexia. Others have just not been taught to read (Griffiths, 2000). Either way immediate remedial action is required but is often delayed for many months, during which the child has increasing problems at school which may manifest themselves as difficult behaviour. The care environment is not often conducive to literacy or developing a love of books (Bald *et al.*, 1995; Griffiths, 2000; Who Cares? Trust, 2001).

## Estimating the cost of educating children in care

Cost data relating specifically to the education of children in care are extremely hard to find. The fact that no cost information is published illustrates something of the past invisibility of this group of children within the education system. The cost of their education can only be calculated by combining and reanalysing statistical information on children in care with educational cost data for all children.

### Types of education costs

In the process of estimating the expenditure on the education of children in care, we identified seven different types of educational costs for children in care in addition to the ordinary costs of educating children living with their parents on the one hand and the cost of substitute care on the other. Some of these costs would also apply to children living with their own families, but to a much lesser extent, and others would be borne by parents.

The different categories of cost are:

1  Standard costs associated with underachievement or behavioural problems: pupil referral units, learning support assistants, educational psychologists' time, and home tuition for excluded children.
2  Costs associated with placement instability: for example, taxi transport to avoid a change of school.
3  Costs associated with equipment for learning: books, stationery, project materials, computers, internet access.
4  Costs associated with 'corporate parenting': for example, leisure activities, music lessons, sports equipment and school trips.
5  Costs associated with residential care: training for care workers on supporting education, employment of teachers for school liaison or homework support, building modifications to create study space.

6   Costs associated with foster care: educational support and training for foster carers, teachers employed to visit foster homes.
7   Miscellaneous costs such as school uniform.

In addition to these direct costs, there are large indirect costs at operational level related to educational difficulties. Placement breakdown is strongly associated with problems of school attendance whatever their cause (Francis, 2000; Jackson, 2000). Dealing with formal and informal exclusions and negotiating for alternative education placements takes up a great deal of teacher and social work time. In future work, it would be valuable to estimate the extent of these largely hidden costs. However, such a task is beyond the scope of this chapter.

The last resort, when a child with significant educational difficulties cannot be placed in a school or local alternative provision, is an out-of-authority placement in an independent residential home or school. In this case the cost for a single child can be over £150,000 a year. One authority in 2001 was reported to be spending over £500,000 per annum for eight children placed outside the borough for educational reasons (Walker, 2002). In recognition of the high cost of these placements, many authorities are now instituting a policy of bringing back children placed outside the borough or county. In some cases this could be counterproductive if it means ending a stable and otherwise satisfactory placement.

While it was possible to make some estimates of costs in Category (1) by extrapolation from published sources, none of the other cost information is available except directly from local authorities, although we did have some information on expenditure related to higher education from the *By Degrees* project reported in Chapter 5. These costs are very low due to the small number of care leavers who go to university at present, but would be expected to rise if the aim of substantially raising attainment is achieved, and as more local authorities recognize their responsibilities under the Children (Leaving Care) Act 2000.

## Calculating the cost

It is relatively simple to estimate the direct public expenditure on looked-after children by type of accommodation status. Such figures, previously published by the Department of Health and now by the Department for Education and Skills, include the gross expenditure on children's homes and on fostering services (which for 2000 to 2001 was £690m and £550m respectively), and on secure accommodation and other residential accommodation (which for the same period was given at £30m and £50m respectively).

However, in order to convert these figures from unit costs per child per week to annual costs per child requires information on how many weeks a child spends in each type of accommodation in a year, and this is less straightforward. Data are collected on the total numbers of days children spend in each form of care, but not on how many children that represents. Rather, on 31 March each year, local authorities report how many children are currently being looked after in each of these care settings. However, it is a reasonable assumption that the number

*Table 4.1* Public expenditure on the care of looked-after children (LAC) (2001)

| Type of care | Number of LAC | Annual cost per child | Total annual expenditure (£m) |
|---|---|---|---|
| Foster care | 41,800 | £14,600 | £550 |
| Children's homes | 7,720 | £99,300 | £690 |
| Secure units | 180 | £40,000 | £50 |
| Other | 9,300 | £5,700 | £53 |
| Total | 58,900 | – | £1,343 |

present on 31 March will be much the same as the number present on every other day in the year. Although there tends to be a small increase in the number of looked-after children over the year, making the 31 March figure a slight over-estimate, the difference is very small (less than 2 per cent in 2000) and so makes little difference. Therefore, the annual cost was estimated as fifty-two times the weekly cost, even though different children might be accommodated during different weeks. On that basis, the annual costs per child together with total annual expenditure are shown in Table 4.1.

In addition to the direct public expenditure on the care of looked-after children, we also aimed to obtain an estimate of the average lifetime cost of care per child. The lifetime cost of care for looked-after children depends both on the type of care they are receiving and the length of time they spend in that care. However, estimating how long a looked-after child spends in care during his or her childhood is also not straightforward.

It is not possible to estimate the total time in care by multiplying the average duration of an episode in care by the total number of episodes, since there is so much variation in the number of times different children enter care and the length of time they stay there. It cannot be assumed, for instance, that for the majority of children ceasing to be looked after at any one point, this was their only period of care. No data have been published on the lifetime care histories of individual children, which also makes it difficult to estimate how long, on average, a looked-after child spends in care during his or her childhood. This total will only be known once children reach the age when they can no longer be looked after by the local authority. The average amount of time a child was looked after during the year to 31 March 2001 was 711 days. Some of these children will continue to be looked after over coming years, so this average probably underestimates the mean duration in care. Taking into account the average number of care episodes and the average length of each episode – both of which are likely to be underestimates – we calculated an average duration of 1,350 days, or 3.7 years. It seems reasonable, therefore, to estimate that any one child taken into care is likely to spend at least four years of his or her life being looked after.

Obtaining an estimate of the annual public expenditure on the education of looked-after children is even more complicated than calculating the expenditure on public care, since none of the required data to do this are published. In the absence of such data, a reasonable estimate of such costs therefore meant that a number of assumptions had to be made (see Jackson *et al.*, 2002).

Allowing for these assumptions, the total public expenditure in 2000 to 2001 on the education of looked-after children was estimated to be around £251 million, making the average expenditure on each child's compulsory education in that year £5,192. If we include 16 to 18-year-olds, the average cost falls to £4,442 since only 17 per cent or so of looked-after young people continue with post-16 education (Department for Education and Skills and Department of Health, 2002). In order to estimate the additional public expenditure on education due to these children being in care, the education expenditure for these children if they were not looked after needs to be subtracted from the overall total of £251 million. This would give an annual net saving of £76.7 million. This is the amount, according to our calculations, that is spent on various forms of special educational provision which are designed mainly to contain problems rather than making any contribution to raising attainment.

## Estimating the savings

We now go on to look briefly at the cost benefits of raising the educational attainment of looked-after children to the average level achieved by those in the general population. The calculations on which these estimates are based are extremely complex and technical, so we will not repeat the details here but refer interested readers to our report to the Social Exclusion Unit (Jackson *et al.*, 2002) where they are set out in full.

Earlier in this chapter we showed the very negative effects of being looked after by a local authority on adult outcomes, even taking into account the socially disadvantaged backgrounds from which most looked-after children originate. Many of these effects have large social and economic costs as well as personal costs for the individuals themselves and those with whom they form relationships. They are likely also to be transmitted to their own children. These personal, intergenerational and wider relationship costs have not been estimated on a pound-for-pound basis. However, we have attempted to estimate the public finance and resource costs in some more accessible areas.

The first method adopted was to estimate effects of care status on particular outcomes for which information is available and to model the implications of negative outcomes in those areas where reliable cost information could be obtained. For many areas this information was not available so that the survey of outcomes considered had to be limited to crime, health and worklessness.

The second method was to use available work on the costs of being not in education, employment or training (NEET) (Social Policy Research Unit, 2002) and to match in the effects of care status on being NEET. This uses more robust and wide-ranging cost data but underestimates the care effect which is greater than that of being NEET.

We note that a whole range of potential savings are excluded by the first method due to a shortage of evidence. Primary among these are forgone earnings and benefits due to unemployment, wider benefit costs including the costs of teenage parenthood, peer effects in schools and communities, costs in terms of personal well-being and inter-generational effects. The result of these omissions is that our figures, although we believe they give a good indication of the kind of savings that are feasible, err very much on the side of caution. Further work on these issues would almost certainly show that far greater reductions in public expenditure are possible, whereas the benefits in quality of life for the individuals concerned are incalculable.

The two methods give very different results, since the second method is based on the benefits for the flow-out of looked-after status (young people leaving care year by year) whereas the first method necessarily considers cost effects of the numbers of people in the community who have previously been in care. The first method also obtains a better estimate of the likely cost of crime.

Overall, by using the first method we find a benefit in terms of reduced crime, better health and higher levels of employment of between £9bn and £16bn per annum if the outcomes for the ex-care population could parallel those who have never been in care. This is largely made up of effects on criminality, for which young men in and after care show very high propensity not explained by their prior circumstances and which carry a very high cost. Health and worklessness costs are smaller but none the less extremely substantial given the kinds of expenditure involved. Because a high proportion of crime is committed by teenagers and men in their early twenties, the effect of improved education in reducing criminality would be seen quite quickly and would have cost benefits within a relatively short space of time.

The second method suggests that current costs from the yearly flow resulting from the high proportion of looked-after children who are not in education, employment or training are between £43.2m and £60.5m per annum. The resulting, discounted lifetime costs are between £388m and £543.2m. These are the savings that could be achieved if young people in and leaving care could be helped to attain the same outcomes as the non-NEET population. In other words, an additional £50 million would be released annually for constructive expenditure on children's services and further improving educational outcomes.

## Changing the picture

There is no shortage of diagnosis and prescription on the poor educational outcomes for looked-after children but very little hard evidence of what actually works to raise attainment. One reason is the relatively small numbers in any one age group within each local authority, so that the performance of one or two children can make percentage results fluctuate from year to year with the result that any effects of particular measures can be seen only over a long period of time. The evidence on what contributes to poor outcomes is much stronger and has already been reviewed. Putting right some of the well-recognized deficiencies in the care and education systems should change outcomes for the better, but as yet there is no clear evidence that it will do so.

The Social Exclusion Report *A Better Education for Children in Care* (Social Exclusion Unit, 2003) gives many examples of good practice. It lists thirty-nine measures to be taken by the DfES aimed at raising attainment and another thirty-nine recommendations for local action, but provides no evidence on improved outcomes. As noted above, the only substantial intervention study that has been systematically evaluated so far is the 'Taking Care of Education' project by which three local authorities were provided with additional funding by the Gatsby Foundation to be spent on the education of children in care (Harker *et al.*, 2004). This enabled the authorities to appoint lead officers at senior level and to introduce various practice innovations designed to lead to better school experiences for looked-after children and to raise attainment. The improvements achieved related more to attitudes and self-perception than to measurable achievements, partly for the reasons given above, but the study provides useful information on the most effective ways of using resources. Encouraging findings were also reported by Gallagher and colleagues in a study of one residential home where a strong focus on education markedly improved attendance and attainment among a group of residents with high levels of emotional and behavioural disturbance (Gallagher *et al.*, 2004).

It is noticeable that discussion of the education of children in care draws on a quite narrow range of research and publications and largely ignores the huge body of literature on education more generally. Two consistent and universal findings on educational attainment are that the children who do best, controlling for other factors such as housing, family income and employment, are those who have parents with higher levels of education themselves and those whose parents take a keen interest in their schooling (Halsey *et al.*, 1980). There is great resistance to recognizing the implications of the first finding which are, that if we seriously wanted to close the gap in achievement between looked-after children and others, the best way of doing so would be to ensure that they are placed with well-educated carers. This in turn would mean greatly raising the status, educational qualifications and remuneration of those who provide the care. The research reported in Chapter 8, and the forthcoming comparative study of foster care in France, Denmark and the UK, shows that this is perfectly feasible.

As witnessed throughout this book, a lack of attention to education is only one of the failings of the care system and it is important to acknowledge that educational achievement also depends on many other factors such as the general quality of care provided, relationships with carers and family members and the level of placement stability. Thus, even if dramatic improvements in support for education were put in place, certain problems may still persist. Nevertheless, there is a strong body of evidence, as discussed above, to show that educational experiences profoundly influence the rest of a child's life.

All the negative factors listed above (and well supported by research evidence over many years) could be overcome, given the political will and adequate resources. Since the education of children in care has been neglected for so long, it will be necessary to tackle it at all levels and by all possible means to make any impression on the problem. It is important to recognize this because if the obstacles to improved attainment levels for children in care were immutable the potential cost benefits discussed above could not be achieved.

## Conclusion

The government's aim of bringing the educational attainment of looked-after children closer to that of children generally is to some extent a moving target, since educational standards have been steadily rising, particularly between 2000 and 2003. This means that, if anything, the gap between children in care and others has widened in that time. As we showed above and in Chapter 3, outcomes for children who spend any length of time in care are extremely negative and are likely to persist throughout their adult lives. On the other hand, the work of the Centre for the Wider Benefits of Learning is demonstrating the benefits of better education, both for individuals and the community, with the greatest benefits occurring at the top end. For children in care who start from such a disadvantaged position, we should not therefore be satisfied with average performance but aim for them to achieve the highest level of education of which they are capable (which is after all the aspiration of most parents).

In Chapter 5 we show that some children who have been in care, even those who have suffered the most painful experiences, including severe abuse and neglect, are capable of going to university and completing their courses successfully. At present only one in a hundred care leavers has this opportunity, compared with 43 per cent of the school population. It would not be an unreasonable ambition to aim for every young person who achieves five good GCSE passes to go on to higher education. This is not to say that we should be satisfied with 6 to 8 per cent participation, but at least it would be a start. Although five GCSEs at grades A*–C is no more than an average level of attainment for those who have not been in care, it represents a great achievement by the standards of the care population and indicates much higher than average ability and motivation. The evidence from the British Cohort Studies shows that each step up the educational ladder has benefits in every sphere of adult life, but the greatest differences are between those who have graduate-level qualifications and those who do not.

In recent years, considerable progress has been made in raising awareness and creating structures to facilitate collaboration between social services and education. The numerous education initiatives introduced by the government since 1997 have the potential to benefit looked-after children as much as any other disadvantaged group. The transfer of responsibility for children's services from the Department of Health to the Department for Education and Skills in 2003 made an important statement about the central importance of education for children in care. The Children (Leaving Care) Act 2000 opened up realistic opportunities for looked-after children to continue into post-16 and higher education, providing them and their carers with new goals to aim for, and a few, as we demonstrate in Chapter 5, are already achieving them.

The Children Act 2004 for the first time lays a specific duty on local authorities to promote the educational achievement of children they look after. Increasingly, local authorities are appointing lead officers for the education of children in care, crossing education/social work boundaries. Every local authority must now have a Director of Children's Services, and most of the people appointed to these posts so far have come from an education rather than a social work background.

All this provides grounds for optimism. At present, as we have shown, large sums are spent on the care and education of looked-after children, with very poor results. We are certainly not arguing for saving in expenditure on services. There will be no way of transforming the chronic underachievement of looked-after children without substantial extra resources and seriously questioning our current assumptions about how they should be spent. We do suggest that the most cost-effective way of targeting those resources is to focus clearly on providing intensive support for education, both in and out of school, from the first day that children begin to be looked after and throughout their care career (which may include several separate episodes and periods when they return to their families). There is little doubt that very substantial changes in the care system are necessary if the education of looked-after children is to improve significantly. Our reading of the evidence is that such changes are achievable with sufficient funds and commitment.

Our estimates of the potential savings in expenditure that could result can only be approximate due to the lack of reliable data. We have been extremely cautious and even the upper bound figures probably underestimate the likely benefits. It is clear, however, that if we could make coming into care a path to educational success, as it is in some other countries (see e.g. Feuerstein and Krasilowsky, 1967; Dumaret, 1988), we would not only transform the lives of the children concerned but save immense amounts of public money.

## Acknowledgements

This chapter draws extensively on research commissioned by the Social Exclusion Unit and cited in its report to the Prime Minister, *A Better Education for Children in Care* (SEU, 2003). We thank our co-authors Leon Feinstein, Rosalind Levacic, Charlie Owen and Angela Brassett-Grundy for permission to use this material. We also thank Tom Schuller of Birkbeck College, and Tim Walker, Chief Executive of the National Teaching and Advisory Service, who acted as consultants to the project.

# 5  By degrees

## Care leavers in higher education

*Sarah Ajayi and Margaret Quigley*

In this chapter we focus on a group of young people who could be considered the successes of the care system, the very small number who move on from school or college to higher education. There are no reliable figures but the best estimate is that they make up less than 1 per cent of the relevant age group in the care population (Social Exclusion Unit, 2003).

Little was known about university students coming from a care background until the Frank Buttle Trust, set up after the Second World War to support children and young people in need, decided to commission this research. In the light of the knowledge gained through their grant aid programme for students and trainees about the challenges faced by care leavers in higher education, the Trust wished to examine their experiences in more detail. The study was unusual in several ways. First, it was designed to have a five-year time span, instead of the more common two or three years. Second, it built in an action component, providing for grant aid and advice to individuals in need, and third, it incorporated a strong policy element directed at government and local authorities. The research proposal, building on earlier work by Sonia Jackson (Jackson and Martin, 1998; Jackson and Roberts, 2000) was for a longitudinal project, tracking three successive cohorts of young people from public care, through all or part of their university degree courses.[1]

As was shown in earlier chapters, the average attainment of children in local authority care falls far behind that of others in their age group. This chapter shows how, despite difficult and traumatic childhoods and the shortcomings of the care system, some young people manage, against the odds, to pursue successful academic careers. It begins by describing the research design and then traces the paths of the research participants into and through university, while illuminating the factors that have been influential in their success. For the few young people who, in spite of their great achievement in accessing higher education, ended up not starting or completing their studies, the chapter highlights how this loss of opportunity might have been avoided.

## By Degrees: a longitudinal study

The limited previous research into the lives of young people going to university from a care background had identified a number of recurrent problems. These included: a lack of information and guidance for care leavers aiming to continue in education after leaving care; low expectations and little encouragement from social workers; unwillingness by Social Services to provide a realistic level of financial assistance; difficulty in finding accommodation, particularly during vacations; problems in meeting educational expenses, and the absence of any system of continuing personal support (Jackson and Martin, 1998; Martin and Jackson, 2002). It was not known, however, if these experiences were common, since previous studies had been on a very small scale.

For the purposes of this study, three successive cohorts of research participants were recruited, mainly through local authorities, though some volunteered independently or were referred by the Frank Buttle Trust. The first cohort was tracked throughout their university career, the second group for two years and the third group for their first year. Since at the time of writing data analysis from the third cohort was not complete, findings discussed in this chapter are from interviews with the first and second cohorts of young people only.

The By Degrees Study was established at a time when the *Quality Protects* programme, with its strong emphasis on education, was in its third year, a factor that ought to have been reflected in the care experience of the participants. Moreover, new government initiatives (as detailed in Chapters 1 and 2) have followed each other with bewildering speed and have had a direct bearing on elements of the study and on research participants, both as care leavers and as university students.

Just before the main study began in January 2001, the Children (Leaving Care) Act (CLCA) 2000 completed its passage through Parliament. Since it was not implemented until the following year, this provided an opportunity to compare the services received by the first cohort (C1) to whom the Act did not apply, with what local authorities provided for the second and third cohorts (C2 and C3) who started their courses after the Act came into force. In order to do this, a postal questionnaire was sent to all local authorities in England and Wales in the first year of the project and again in the fourth year. In addition, twelve authorities agreed to act as an ongoing reference group. These were selected using a purposive sampling strategy. We used the percentages of young people leaving care with five or more GCSEs Grades A*–C as our selection criterion, and chose four authorities with low percentages, four with comparatively high percentages and four where attainment was average. Representatives from this core group of authorities were interviewed at yearly intervals.

One further strand of the project was a survey of all universities, Oxford and Cambridge colleges, and other higher education institutions. This aimed to find out whether any were aware of applicants and students with a care background as a discrete group who might need special consideration, and to identify any special initiatives designed to support them. Significantly, the survey was conducted in the context of the government's agenda of widening access to universities for young people from areas or families with no tradition or experience of higher education. A full account of the first local authority survey and the response from the higher education institutions has been documented elsewhere (Jackson *et al.*, 2003). In this chapter we will focus on the experiences of the young people who took part in the study.

All the research participants in the study were volunteers and were recruited initially either through local authority leaving care and after-care teams, or by contacting lead officers for the education of looked-after children. The criteria for inclusion were that they had been in local authority care at the age of 16 and that they had obtained a conditional or confirmed place on a degree-level course.

Based on estimates from an earlier feasibility study, the project aimed to identify fifty participants among students entering higher education in each of the academic years 2001 to 2002, 2002 to 2003 and 2003 to 2004. Although an ambitious target, with the cooperation of the leaving care and post-16 teams, it was possible to recruit above this target number in each year. Despite many difficulties in sustaining contact with participants, the final research sample of 129 (all three cohorts) is by far the largest group of educationally successful young people in care that has ever been studied. In addition, being able to follow the first group through a full three years provided a unique insight into the way the impact of care, and of the experiences that led up to it, continue to resonate during young adulthood.

### Research method

A similar approach was adopted with all three cohorts, whereby each participant was initially sent a brief questionnaire to collect basic information. Subsequently, several contacts by telephone and letter were made before researchers met participants for the first time.

The first interview was unstructured and involved researchers asking the young person to tell the story of his or her life. An interview guide was used only to ensure that all relevant areas were covered. The interviewer attempted to follow the unfolding narrative rather than asking a series of questions. Some interviewees needed more prompting than others, but in general they were eager to talk about themselves and their experiences. Interviews sometimes lasted up to three hours, and many of the young people remarked that they had never before had the chance to tell their story without interruption, despite numerous encounters with social workers.

In most cases the information relevant to the research study emerged spontaneously. This included: what lay behind their exceptional achievement in accessing higher education; their experiences in care; the reasons for the separation from their families; the extent to which being in care had been a help or an obstacle to their educational progress; their five most important sources of support; how much they knew about the Children (Leaving Care) Act (2000) and its implications; and the details of financial support provided by their local authorities.

Interviews were tape-recorded, transcribed as far as resources allowed, and analysed using SPSS and the NVivo qualitative data analysis package. Each participant was allocated an assumed name which was used for all recording purposes and publications, with the information kept under secure conditions.

All the participants were interviewed twice more using a semi-structured questionnaire, once at the end of their first academic year and again during their second year of study. Those who began their degree courses in 2001 were also contacted after they had completed their courses. In addition to face-to-face interviews, much useful information was obtained from informal telephone conversations throughout the progress of the research and through two focus group discussions. The project culminated for the participants with a celebratory party hosted by Lord Laming of Trewin at the House of Lords, which provided an opportunity for the young people to meet each other and exchange experiences, both of care and student life.

## Findings

### The participants

Since it was not possible to select the research group to form a representative sample of looked-after children, it was important to find out if the participants in the project were unusual in some way. We looked at geographical distribution, gender, ethnicity, family background, reasons for coming into care, age of entry, and educational qualifications. Where possible we compared the characteristics of the students in Cohorts 1 and 2 with those of the care population generally.

The largest single group of students in both cohorts came from London boroughs but there was a good spread of participants from all over England. Outside London a majority of students in the first cohort were drawn from northern authorities, whereas in the second cohort they came predominantly from southern authorities. There was no obvious reason for this although it may possibly have been due to the larger number of participants coming from outside the UK in the second cohort, who were more likely to be placed in southern counties. Although students from Wales were eligible to take part we did not have any participants from Welsh unitary authorities.

In both cohorts women outnumbered men and this was true across all ethnic categories. There were twice as many women as men in the first cohort and three times as many in the second. There are probably a number of reasons for this. Studies relying on volunteers almost invariably find women over-represented (Jackson and Martin, 1998). Girls do better than boys educationally, both in the care and non-care populations (National Statistics Bulletin, 2003). A third factor is that girls have a higher chance of being fostered than boys, and foster care is more likely to offer an environment conducive to educational success, as we show below.

*Ethnicity*

The most striking difference between our research group and the care population generally was the high proportion from minority ethnic backgrounds, which was even more marked in the second cohort. Table 5.1 shows the ethnicity of C1 and C2 participants.

*Table 5.1* Ethnicity of participants by gender for Cohorts 1 and 2[a]

| Ethnic background | Males (N) | Females (N) |
|---|---|---|
| White British | 12 | 27 |
| European | 2 | 3 |
| Black African | 7 | 11 |
| Black Caribbean | 0 | 3 |
| Black British | 2 | 2 |
| Asian | 0 | 1 |
| South East Asian | 0 | 2 |
| Mixed Heritage | 4 | 7 |
| **Total** | 27 | 56 |

Note: [a] N=83 (Cohorts 1 and 2).

In some cases, young people described their own ethnicity in a way that did not correspond with the information they gave during their interview. This may have been due to a wish to distance themselves from an absent or abusive parent, or to a sense of not belonging to a particular culture or ethnic group.

As in the care population generally, the majority of participants (47 per cent) fell into the category White British. Yet, although the number of children entering the care system from minority ethnic and mixed ethnicity families is growing, they were still over-represented proportionately in the study sample. The majority of Black students in the study were of African rather than Caribbean origin. Importantly, a significant number of participants had come to Britain as refugees or asylum-seekers and were often unaccompanied. Most of them were African but there were also a number of young people from other European countries. The characteristics and experience of this group differed markedly from those of young people who were born and brought up in the UK.

*Family background*

It was often difficult to obtain precise information about the birth families of participants. Either they were very young when they came into care and social workers had not been assiduous in constructing life story-books, or the interviewees preferred not to dwell on unhappy experiences. Young people were asked about the occupations and educational qualifications of their fathers and mothers at the time when they were first separated from their family. Young people from overseas were more likely to have parents who had completed a higher education qualification than those born within the UK, of whom only a small minority had passed any examinations (36 per cent of mothers from overseas compared to 19 per cent of other mothers, and 18 per cent of fathers from overseas compared to 4 per cent of other fathers).

The general picture presented by the participants' accounts of their birth families was one of extreme volatility, with many house moves, changes of partners, new people joining or leaving the household, constant turmoil and upheaval. The abuse and conflict which was a feature of many accounts was most often associated with stepfathers, though one young woman had spent six months in hospital as a 4-year-old as a result of being dropped into a hot bath by her mother as a punishment. Emotional abuse and scapegoating were also common. Other parents were said to be well-meaning but unable to function effectively due to mental illness or drug and/or alcohol problems. Many of the young people displayed remarkable understanding and compassion for their parents and continued to feel affection for them. A young man whose mother's alcohol addiction eventually led to her death told us:

'We always knew she loved us and she cared very much about our education whenever she wasn't drinking.'

A few of the participants had made a deliberate decision to have nothing more to do with either of their birth parents and had not seen them for many years, but they were in a minority. Most of the UK students had contact with one or more birth relatives (not necessarily parents) and were on reasonably good terms with them, though they usually made it explicit that they did not want to live with them. Birth relatives were named as an important source of personal and emotional support by 22 per cent of the sample.

In summary, there were no obvious differences in the family background of By Degrees participants from what is known of the care population generally (Bebbington and Miles, 1989).

*The care experience*

In order to ascertain whether participants had experiences of care that were very different from other looked-after children's experiences, they were asked to describe their time in care in as much detail as possible, starting with the circumstances that had led to the need for them to leave their families. Overall, participants had mixed responses to discussing these often distressing or difficult aspects of their lives. While some preferred to put unpleasant experiences as far behind them as possible, others related the facts as they knew them without apparent emotion. A few broke down in tears and occasionally felt they could not go on with the interview.

The reasons for coming into care for both cohorts corresponded closely with those given for the care population in official statistics and are presented in Table 5.2. For those who first came into care in their teenage years, self-referral was quite

*Table 5.2* Reasons given by participants for being admitted into care

| Reasons for admissions into care | % of admissions for each factor | | |
| | Cohort 1[a] | Cohort 2 | Amalgamated % |
| --- | --- | --- | --- |
| Family breakdown | 52 | 19 | 37 |
| Mental ill-health of parent/relative | 37 | 16 | 27 |
| Physical and emotional abuse | 52 | 32 | 43 |
| Sexual abuse | 17 | 11 | 14 |
| Addiction (drugs/alcohol) | 22 | 11 | 17 |
| Death of parent(s) | 24 | 11 | 18 |
| Physical illness of parent/relative | 9 | – | 5 |
| Self-referral | 17 | 5 | 12 |
| Unaccompanied to the UK | 9 | 11 | 10 |
| Sample | N=46 | N=37 | N=83 |

Note: [a] Cohort 1 figures are comparatively higher than figures in Cohort 2. This is due to participants indicating more than one reason for entry into care as opposed to the main reason, as was the case with Cohort 2.

common, and some young people reported making several attempts to escape from abusive families before they were accepted for care by Social Services. In total, 57 per cent had suffered some form of abuse compared with the national average of 62 per cent (National Statistics Bulletin, 2005). Nine per cent of Cohort 1 and 11 per cent of Cohort 2 had come to the UK unaccompanied or had been rapidly abandoned by the adult who came with them.

For each participant, a full care history was obtained and more detailed questions were asked about the first and last placements, or the most important placement from the respondent's viewpoint. The majority of participants had spent over five years in care, so their care experience could be considered to have made a positive contribution to their educational success. Almost all acknowledged this explicitly, reporting that they would never have gone to university if they had remained with their birth families. The exceptions were those who had come from overseas, who in general said that their parents had impressed on them the importance of education and had given them support and encouragement up until the time of their separation. However, although their motivation may have come from their families, the practical means to continue their education depended on the local authority in which they found themselves.

The research evidence with regard to how much placement stability contributes to educational attainment is somewhat unclear (Jackson and Thomas, 2001). It did seem, however, that these students enjoyed relatively stable care careers, with just over half having one or two placements, of which at least one lasted several years. Since the peak ages for entry into care for the research group were 14 and 15 years, and placement breakdowns occur most frequently during adolescence, this degree of stability was unusual (Treseliotis *et al.*, 1995). From the participants' own accounts there was no doubt that a stable long-term foster home was a great advantage, both educationally and emotionally, even when they came to it relatively late and after a series of less successful placements. For example, Boris and his elder brother had a particularly traumatic family history and went through seven different foster homes before they were eventually placed with a single woman with a grown-up family, where they settled happily and from which they both went on to university.

Stability is obviously helpful but does not seem to be essential for educational success. One young woman, who persuaded Social Services to take her into care at the age of 14, lived with six different foster families, in three hospitals, a children's home, a semi-secure unit, an adolescent psychiatric unit, a women's hostel, and finally supported lodgings, staying for short periods with various relatives in between. Despite all this, she obtained excellent GCSE and A-level results, was offered places by three prestigious universities and did well academically at university. However, not surprisingly with such a history, she continued to suffer recurrent mental health problems.

Only one participant went directly from residential care to higher education – further testimony to previous research demonstrating that the majority of children's homes offer a poor educational environment and little encouragement to do well at school (Utting, 1997; Brown et al., 1998; Berridge and Brodie, 1998; Brodie, 2001). For most participants, residential care was a transient experience. They usually differed from other residents in wanting to do well in their school work. Steven spoke warmly of the head of the home where he spent three years but had nothing good to say of it otherwise:

> 'I was the only child in the home who went to school. I had work to do and the other kids would be kicking off, sometimes all night, and I had to go to school in the mornings. The others had no motivation. The staff didn't push them. . . . The only person who helped me was the only educated one, the one with a degree.'

Fiona's experience was similar:

> 'My problem was just, like, I was doing A levels, everyone else was on the dole. They played their music full blast and didn't care about me studying. And then we had to share the kitchen and cleaning duties and I was the only one who did my bit.'

Foster care however presented a very different picture to residential care. In many, though not all cases foster carers were said to have provided consistent support and encouragement for education. Perhaps most importantly they usually had high expectations for the young people they looked after. They insisted on regular school attendance, advocated for the young person if trouble arose, provided congenial study conditions, supervised and helped with homework, and often contributed to purchase or upgrading of computers and other equipment. Several interviewees expressed appreciation of the discipline and structure provided by their foster home, but on the other hand made a point of saying that they did not feel pressurised and that their foster parents always made it clear that they were free to make their own decisions, offering advice when asked.

Foster parents who had higher educational qualifications themselves invariably gave education top priority. However, there seemed to be little difference in attitudes or behaviour between these carers, who were in a minority, and those who, as far as the participant knew, had left school with minimal qualifications. It is noteworthy, however, that in Cohort 2, 22 per cent of foster mothers and 27 per cent of foster fathers had university degrees. This contrasts with what we know about foster carers generally (Triseliotis *et al.*, 2000; Pithouse *et al.*, 2004).

Some of the participants had many problems at school and were seriously behind their age group in academic attainment until they went to live in the foster home which they identified as their most important placement. They had often missed a great deal of school in their early years as a result of the chaotic lifestyle and frequent moves of their birth families. It was moving to foster care that seemed to have launched them on an upward trajectory, of which regular school attendance was an essential component.

In cases where relationships were good, the commitment of the foster carers and the strong emotional bond that formed between them and the young people was probably more important than anything else. Foster parents were almost always named among the five key people in the young person's life. Many participants commented on the closeness of the relationship: 'I class them as my real family'; 'They are my real parents'; 'I call them Mum and Dad'; 'My foster mother is a true friend – I can always talk to her'. Foster siblings were often referred to as brothers and sisters.

*Educational attainment*

Although coming into care was generally seen as helpful to their education, young people still faced many obstacles before achieving success. For some, the weakness of their early educational experience created longer-term problems in achieving their academic potential. In a few cases, young people described carers who were not supportive of their wish to go to university, suggesting that they should get a job or take a vocational course instead. At times, they were made to feel by social workers and carers that they were putting too much pressure on themselves, perhaps a reflection of the low expectations of children in care. In some placements, carers reportedly showed more interest in their birth children's education than in that of the foster child.

Not surprisingly, the By Degrees participants had done much better in the later stages of their school career than the majority of the care population. On average the C1 young women obtained nine GCSE passes compared with eight for the young men, and the differential increased with the number of subjects taken. Overall, their performance was close to the national picture, though they achieved fewer passes in the A*-C range. All the students had continued in education after age 16 but over 40 per cent had moved into further education colleges rather than staying at school to take A levels. They were also more likely to have taken vocational GNVQ or BTEC courses. This is significant given that, although they are supposed to be equivalent, a much lower proportion of young people with vocational qualifications than those with A levels go on to university (Newby, 2004).

## Aiming for university

### Motivation

For some of the participants who attended schools where a high proportion of pupils stayed until age 18 and moved on to higher education, going to university just seemed the natural thing to do. Their friends were all going and they assumed they would do the same. They described themselves as swept along the academic path to higher education without necessarily having a great deal of personal motivation.

A second group was responsive to the views or experiences of others. They were encouraged by family members and other people they respected, or followed in the path of older brothers and sisters. Being in a family where foster-parents' birth children already had experience of university also encouraged some participants to see it as a normal progression. In particular, refugee and asylum-seeking young people tended to come from backgrounds where education was highly valued.

A third group were strongly self-motivated. They wanted to make other people proud of them or to prove that schoolteachers or others who doubted their ability were wrong. Most of all, they had a clear perception that going to university would unlock career and lifestyle opportunities that would not otherwise be available to them. They often saw this as a means of escape from their family background and the route to a better way of living than their parents.

Motivation proved not only important in getting to university but also in staying there and succeeding. Those who made a conscious decision to go on to higher education for well-thought-out reasons were much more likely to stay the course. Those who wanted to please others or who were simply following in someone else's footsteps were more likely not to complete their courses.

For those young people who were successful not only in accessing but also staying in higher education, friends were the most important source of continuing support, followed by foster families. Foster-mothers were mentioned more frequently, but foster-fathers also played an important role, particularly in helping with homework and providing transport. In two cases single women provided supported lodgings for young people over age 16 when a previous foster placement broke down. For both, their 'landladies' became friends, and provided educational support and encouragement at a crucial time.

*Applying for courses*

Young people living independently or in families with no experience of higher education depended heavily on the careers service, websites, leaflets and brochures for prospective students for their information. University open days also played an important role, and some of the participants commented that it was either during or after an open day that they made the decision to go to university. Making their application was not easy without adequate advice from knowledgeable adults. They often had to be very determined to obtain the information they needed about universities and courses, and were in danger of choosing subjects or institutions that were unsuited to their interests and abilities, again putting them at risk of dropping out later.

Filling in the all-important UCAS (Universities and Colleges Admissions Service) form was another hurdle. The personal statement would have provided an opportunity for the applicant to inform the admissions staff that he or she had been in care, but few of them did so. This was partly because they were uncertain if it would help them or work against them, but also because they were often anxious to leave their care status behind and afraid that the stigma they had experienced in the past might follow them into their new life. However, when asked if they would have been prepared to tick a box on the form if it had been available, 78 per cent answered yes.

*Problems*

Care leavers faced two major problems which students living at home do not have to worry about. Some local authorities automatically terminate foster placements on the young person's eighteenth birthday. One young woman was told that she must find her own accommodation in the middle of her A-level course at a further education college when she was just 17. For others, moves arranged by Social Services just before examinations were sadly common. Foster carers often wanted the young person to stay with them but could not afford the loss of income when the fostering allowance was abruptly withdrawn. Some, however, protested strongly and managed to successfully oppose inappropriate moves suggested by Social Services.

Another major problem, especially for the first cohort, was that most local authorities had no agreed policies relating to care leavers in higher education and simply made decisions on an ad hoc basis. This often meant referring matters up the hierarchy and waiting for authorisation, which could be slow in coming. Some young people could get no information about what financial support would be forthcoming until a few days before they were due to start their course. In some cases this resulted in their losing the chance of getting a place in a hall of residence and being forced to settle for more expensive and less satisfactory private accommodation. There was some evidence that this was less of a problem for the 2003 entrants. By that time many local authority leaving care teams had devolved budgets and were able to use them to support care leavers in higher education under the CLCA (2000).

*Falling at the first fence*

Several young people who volunteered to take part in the By Degrees project never made it to university. There were three main reasons for this. Some did not obtain the required grades and there was no one available to advise them either to apply for admission through clearing, or retake their examinations. Some were offered a promotion in their vacation job with a higher salary and better prospects, and were unable to resist the temptation. A common reason, however, was that their local authority would give them no guarantee of financial support or accommodation during vacations, a risk they did not want to take. One young man in the second category had a place to read law at a prestigious university but had accepted a post as manager of a shoe shop instead, a decision which by the time of interview he bitterly regretted. Those who were afraid to take up their university place in case they found themselves destitute were mostly, but not exclusively, in the first cohort, before the CLCA 2000 was implemented.

## The university experience

The majority of the By Degrees participants completed their university courses successfully, or obtained good enough results (as is shown in Table 5.3) in their first or second year to go on to the following year. However, twelve students in Cohort 1 dropped out at some point during their university course, compared with five in Cohort 2. Two of these students later returned to university.

*Table 5.3* Completion and drop-out rates for Cohorts 1 and 2

|                     | Cohort 1 (%) | Cohort 2 (%) |
|---------------------|--------------|--------------|
| Completed course    | 43           | 0            |
| Still on course     | 24           | 84           |
| Dropped out         | 26           | 13           |
| Whereabouts unknown | 7            | 3            |
| Total               | 100 (N=46)   | 100 (N=37)   |

For purposes of analysis, young people were grouped depending on what they told us about what it was like to go to university from a background in care. The categories are not mutually exclusive but they may help to define the types of support that need to be in place for care leavers attempting to enter or stay in higher education. The following section describes the broad types of experience with illustrative examples.

*Flourishing*

This group consisted mostly of young people who were placed in an educationally supportive foster home between the ages of 10 and 14 and remained there until they went to university, usually returning for vacations in their first year and continuing to visit regularly thereafter. They stayed at school to take A levels or went to colleges of further education, were given appropriate help and advice by teachers or tutors, and applied and were accepted by the universities of their choice. After some initial trepidation they settled into university life, made new friends, established study and social routines that enabled them to do their academic work without undue strain, and completed the year with respectable grades. They were well supported by their local authorities, supplemented by help from foster families, and usually only worked during vacations, when they lived at home and were able to save some of their earnings. Being relatively secure financially, they applied early enough to obtain university accommodation in their first year and moved to shared houses or flats for their second and third years. They gave the impression of thoroughly enjoying their time at university. A typical comment from a young man interviewed during the first summer vacation was:

> 'In the first year you get used to the lifestyle and meet people. The academic work does give you the background but because it doesn't count towards the degree you don't feel you have to work so hard, so there's time for other things. I enjoyed it a lot, socially and academically.'

These young people were well aware that they had been fortunate compared with other care leavers. Dahlia's view was representative of this group:

> 'I think I've had quite an easy ride I'd say, compared to other people in my position, I have really. Everything has gone smoothly. I haven't had any problems at all regards education, everybody has been very supportive and has urged me to go to university. I haven't encountered any problems – yet, touch wood!'

*Surviving*

Some young people, although their path into and through higher education was much less smooth, showed exceptional determination from an early stage. Monica, for example, despite a chequered school career, decided at the age of 10 that she was going to university. Having been steered into a scientific path by her school, she decided at the last moment to switch to English. After receiving a formal rejection, she telephoned her chosen university and so impressed the Head of Department that she was offered a place, although her A-level results were well below the expected level, mainly because her foster placement had broken down a few weeks before the exams. She was quite unhappy during her first year and desperately short of money, but gradually adjusted to university life, was successful in obtaining better financial support from her local authority, and emerged after three years as a confident young woman with an Upper Second Class degree, planning to continue into postgraduate study.

Academic problems were more common among those who had come via the further education route, where they were used to having the work broken down into relatively short assignments. Consequently, they sometimes struggled initially to complete extended pieces of writing and to plan their work over a longer period of time. However, they were able to develop these skills as they went along, and apart from having to resubmit one or two pieces of work, completed their year successfully.

For others, the main problem was learning to budget, especially if they had to rely entirely on the student loan. A few ran into serious debt during their first year but were able to pay most of it off by working throughout the summer vacation.

### Struggling

In contrast to the first two groups, some students had a less happy experience. Denise's A-level results were so good that she was offered a place at one of the most popular and competitive universities. She loved the high-quality teaching and the stimulating academic programme but found the social aspects very hard. She felt that she had nothing in common with the other students, many of whom had attended well-known independent schools. She missed her boyfriend and her foster family acutely and went home frequently at weekends, running into financial problems as a result. At the end of the first year she decided to transfer to a much less prestigious home university and returned to live with her foster-parents.

Another example was Rushie. She was told, while still at school, that she would be financially supported by Social Services throughout her time at university. However, she received no financial help during her first year and had no allocated social worker to advocate for her. When a new social worker was appointed, Rushie was told that she was entitled to an allowance in her first year after all, but the local authority was only willing to backdate the money by four weeks. Rushie had to use all her own savings to survive. She described what a shock it had been to be suddenly 'dropped' when her Care Order finished. Despite struggling, Rushie has since completed her course, gaining an Upper Second Class degree, and is now working in the field she qualified in.

Vacation accommodation was a problem for those who had left care and had no homes to go back to, or who had been living independently and had been forced to give up their council flats. Some slept on friends' floors or former foster carers' sofas. Others had the soul-destroying experience of staying all alone over Christmas in empty halls of residence.

### Dropping out

Of particular interest to the study were students who decided to leave university before completing their courses. Given their achievement in entering higher education from care, their inability to complete their degrees was a particularly sad waste of potential that might negatively affect their future life chances. In some cases it happened when the students were quite near the end of the course when the cumulative strain appeared to simply become too much for them and they felt they had no alternative but to opt out. Researchers resisted, at times with difficulty, the temptation to take on a counselling role, but always urged the young person to contact the Frank Buttle Trust caseworker for advice before making any irrevocable decision.

Although the causes for giving up courses were diverse, many were attributed to a lack of adequate support. The constant anxiety of trying to manage on too little money, though not a concern exclusive to ex-care students, was far worse for them when there was no family to fall back on. On the whole, debt was a less common problem than we had expected, but one young woman who had set up house with a boyfriend instead of accepting a place in a hall of residence was left in severe difficulty when the relationship broke up. She took on three part-time jobs in an attempt to pay off bank loans and credit cards, dropped increasingly behind with her academic work, and finally became completely exhausted. Others committed themselves to long journeys in order not to lose their council tenancies, and in the end found the stress of hours travelling daily and the isolation this caused due to not being able to participate fully in student social life, too much for them to continue.

In a few cases the gaps in early schooling seemed to catch up with them as academic pressure and the demands of course work mounted. At many universities the academic load in the first year is quite light but increases rapidly in subsequent years. One young man obtained top grades for his practical assignments in applied art but found the theoretical work progressively harder and gave up in despair a few weeks before the end of his course.

There was also a small group of young people who did not complete their university course because of caring responsibilities. Three female students were looking after a child, and struggled to arrange adequate child care. One young woman decided to give up full-time study in order to care for her boyfriend who had been involved in a serious accident, with the intention of going back to study once he was well enough.

All in all, the most important cause of dropping out can probably be traced back to the individual's family and care history. As we showed earlier, the majority of the participants had experienced extremely traumatic experiences within their birth families, and sometimes also while in care. Problems sometimes manifested themselves as a difficulty in concentration or persistence. Dean, for example, passed ten GCSE subjects, six of them with high grades, but dropped out of his higher education course after a few weeks. After suffering many years of abuse from his stepmother, he had eventually run away from home, and had not seen his birth mother since the age of 3.

The majority of those who dropped out had endured severe physical, sexual or emotional abuse during childhood. While these experiences tended to be relegated to the backs of their minds while they were in the relatively protected environment of school and foster home, when out on their own they could resurface. At university, these young people often reported difficulty in forming new relationships and could find themselves quite isolated emotionally. Some told us that they experienced flashbacks or periods of severe depression. This could happen unpredictably so that they found themselves unable to study for long periods, and sometimes were unable to ask for help. Once they failed to submit assignments on time the work piled up into what they saw as an impossible load.

Very few found Student Support Services in their institution helpful and some had had no contact with personal tutors. For these young people the only available source of help when something went seriously wrong was the Social Services department. Yet accessing such support was by no means straightforward and, as illustrated by the comments of one young man, often caused intense frustration:

> 'You phone in today and tell the duty worker what the problem is, your duty worker goes "I'll get back to you". She doesn't get back to you that same day, so tomorrow you phone in again and now you meet a different kind of duty worker. So you've got to explain yourself through again. Again, all the way through again.'

Although once the CLCA (2000) was implemented this type of situation should have occurred less often, there were reportedly many cases where the student's named after-care worker or personal adviser had moved on without a successor being appointed.

### Coming from overseas

As mentioned above, most of the young people who came from other countries had a family background where a high value was placed on education as the key to future life opportunities. Many of their parents were reported to have had professional or administrative occupations. The young people had often suffered horrific experiences of wars and massacres and might be the only survivors in their families. On coming to England some found themselves in private foster homes of variable quality. However, they had their sights firmly fixed on going to university whatever the obstacles. Many of them displayed an extraordinary degree of determination and single-mindedness. It seemed that they had the kind of resilience that results from coming through extremely harsh experiences without being overwhelmed.

One young man had spent three years in a refugee camp in Africa before coming to the UK, speaking no English. After focusing entirely on learning the language for a whole year, he then went on to take A levels. At the time of interview he was in his second year at university reading law and living with his sister in a council flat. Both his parents, presumed dead, were highly educated professionals.

Muddah was also born in Africa and escorted to England at the age of 14 by a friend of the family to escape danger in his country. His escort left him to fend for himself and he found his way to a local hospital from which he was taken into care. He had three foster placements and took the initiative himself to ask for a move from the first two because they showed no interest in his education. His third placement he described as 'perfect'. Here, he felt welcomed and part of the family. His foster carers strongly supported his educational ambitions, their own children having gone through further and higher education. At the time of interview, Muddah was undertaking a marketing course at university. The financial package he received met the majority of his needs, and he had a good support network made up of friends, his social worker and his faith in the Muslim religion. However, he struggled with the academic work and attributed this to not having developed a routine of studying while in his two earlier foster placements.

Some of these students made a conscious decision to focus entirely on their studies at the expense of any kind of recreation or social life. One young refugee from China was living at the top of a tower block in an outer suburb of London, travelling an hour each way to university. He worked through every weekend to support himself, determined to achieve his ambition of becoming an architect.

## The role of the local authority

### Financial support

Students differed greatly in their ability to budget effectively and survive on a low income. Costs also varied from one university to another, so that an income that would have been sufficient at a campus university in the East Midlands was quite inadequate in London or Bath. Many local authorities offered very little financial support to their care-leaving students, or gave some arbitrary amount without attempting to calculate essential outgoings. Especially in the first cohort there was great inconsistency, not only between authorities but even between different social work teams within the same authority.

Samantha and Celia were in the care of the same county and attended the same university although they did not know each other. Samantha described her local authority as 'brilliant'. As soon as her university place was confirmed her post-care worker discussed her likely financial needs with her, and all her expenses were paid, including a generous allowance for food, stationery and internet expenses. At the end of the year these arrangements were reviewed and adjusted to take account of her changed requirements in the following year. Celia, on the other hand, received no help from Social Services, ended her first year seriously in debt and even considered discontinuing her course, despite her excellent academic record.

Some authorities gave living allowances equivalent to foster payments and met a range of other expenses such as transport, educational equipment and retainers for foster carers to ensure that young people had holiday accommodation. Others expected the young person to take out the maximum student loan and to do paid work, even during term times, to make up the shortfall, since the student loan by itself would not be sufficient. The Frank Buttle Trust benchmark figures for 2002 to 2003 estimated that the minimum requirement for a student at a London university for a thirty-eight week academic year (assuming that he or she would work through the summer) was £6,873 and £6,142 outside London (Jackson et al., 2003). However, some of the participants received far less. In some parts of the

LIVERPOOL JOHN MOORES UNIVERSITY
LEARNING SERVICES

country part-time or vacation work was very hard to find, which could create severe difficulties. Moreover, as we have shown, students who had to work long hours to support themselves often found that this was at the expense of their academic work, putting them at risk of falling behind.

Although under the CLCA (2000) local authorities are obliged by law to give financial support to young people who have been in their care up until the age of 24 if they are in full-time education, in practice they have wide discretion about how they interpret that duty.

## Conclusion

The evidence from this study so far points to some important conclusions. To start with, although some of the young people who participated in the research might be considered exceptionally resilient, the majority were quite similar in their background and personal characteristics to other children in local authority care. What mainly differentiated them was their good fortune in being placed with foster parents who became strongly committed to them and who gave high priority to education. It seems almost too obvious to say that this is the key to closing the attainment gap between looked-after children and those who live with their own families. Placement with foster parents who understand the importance of education and have the capacity to support it is crucial. Our findings challenge the assumption that children who come late into the care system or who have had a number of different foster placements are unsuited to living in a family and are better placed in children's homes. The evidence from this study is that much depends on the attitudes and understanding of the foster parents and the expectations on both sides.

What has also been demonstrated through this research is that consistent financial and personal support from the local authority is as important as the stability of the care placement. The first survey of local authorities conducted as part of this study did much to explain some of the problems these young people encountered on their path to higher education and during their time at university. A year after the enactment of the CLCA (2000), few authorities had worked-out policies or designated budgets for the support of care leavers in higher education. As we have shown, this resulted in a degree of uncertainty and stress that was highly damaging to the prospective students' chances and undermined their progress once they entered university. For those who did not have supportive foster homes, the absence of a named person to offer consistent emotional support posed even greater problems. However, interviews with second- and third-cohort students did suggest some gradual improvements to support provision as more post-16 and after-care teams became established, and social workers and managers grew familiar with the provisions of the CLCA (2000).

The interim report of this study details what a local authority, acting as a good corporate parent, should do to support a young person at each stage on the journey from school or college to graduation (Jackson et al., 2003). While the pattern of support will differ in response to the individual needs of each young person, the basic principle is that social workers and carers should offer the same level of support and guidance that well-informed and adequately resourced parents would give to their own children. This means establishing the idea of higher education as an attainable goal from an early age and paying for attendance at open days and summer schools. It means providing help with the process of application, being available and supportive on the day when examination results are announced, planning accommodation, making financial arrangements, providing help with budgeting, keeping in regular contact with the young person at university and being prepared to come to the rescue when things go wrong. It means keeping track of the student's academic performance, offering congratulations or comfort as appropriate, making sure that an appropriate person attends the degree ceremony and generally just being there for the young person.

Even young people who are fortunate enough to have spent the later years of their childhood in a secure and loving foster home still require the support and commitment of the local authority and its representatives. For those who have not had this kind of security, support from their local authority is even more essential to allow them to make the most of their great achievement in reaching higher education and to enable them to stay the course.

## Note

1   This chapter draws on findings from the project 'By Degrees – from care to university', commissioned by the Frank Buttle Trust. It is based at the Thomas Coram Research Unit, Institute of Education, University of London, and directed by Professor Sonia Jackson.

## Acknowledgements

The authors would like to thank Hugo Perks and the Frank Buttle Trust for commissioning the By Degrees research on which this chapter is based, as well as Gerri McAndrew and Karen Melton for their ongoing support. The chapter owes much to Professor Sonia Jackson, Director of the By Degrees study and to colleagues at the Thomas Coram Research Unit who read earlier drafts and assisted with statistical analysis, in particular Peter Aggleton, Peter Moss, Charlie Owen, Steff Hazelhurst, Jethro Perkins, Antonia Simon, Sharon Lawson and Tamara Boake.

# 6 Is early parenthood such a bad thing?

*Elaine Chase and Abigail Knight*

Research on young parents who have experience of local authority care is fairly limited, and to date has been somewhat preoccupied with the assumed negative impact of early pregnancy on life outcomes and prospects for young people in care. Yet the idea that pregnancy precludes other opportunities supposes that all young women (and indeed young men) have equal access to opportunities and life chances. However, there is a substantial research base which tells us that this is not the case and that young people in and leaving local authority care face significant disadvantages on many fronts. This chapter explores some of these issues in more detail, and draws both on the existing literature base and on more recent research conducted by the authors.

The chapter will discuss how, despite at times facing significant hardship, many young people in and leaving care manage to be successful and happy parents. Little has been written about positive outcomes for young people from care who become parents at a young age. For instance, there has been little, if any, acknowledgement that pregnancy and parenthood can provide a focus and stabilising influence for young people who perceive themselves to be caught up in chaotic and often harmful lifestyles.

To illustrate these points the chapter will draw on findings from a Department of Health-funded study of young parents in and leaving care, focusing on those young people who view parenting as a life-changing and worthwhile experience, and will highlight the factors that have enabled them to feel they have coped and succeeded. In so doing, it will demonstrate how current developments in policy and practice appear to have the potential to influence the level, type and acceptability of support available to young parents, thus improving outcomes for the mother, the child and, to a more limited extent, the father.

## Research on young mothers and fathers

International comparisons show that England has the highest rate of teenage conceptions in Western Europe (UNICEF, 2001). There is now a significant body of research identifying key contributing factors to early pregnancy and parenthood (Cheesbrough *et al.*, 1999; Kane and Wellings, 1999; Social Exclusion Unit, 1999; Swann *et al.*, 2003), and, while it can be a positive experience for some, research findings show that young parents (and their children) are more likely to experience long-term social exclusion and other poor outcomes compared to their peers (Kiernan, 1995; Botting *et al.*, 1998).

Limited research suggests that young people in, or leaving, care are at heightened risk of teenage pregnancy (Brodie *et al.*, 1997; Corlyon and McGuire, 1997, 1999). The 1958 Birth Cohort study found that at 33 years, young people who spent time in care were 2.5 times more likely to be mothers or fathers under 22 years than their peers (Hobcraft, 1998). Biehal *et al.* (1992) found that 25 per cent of care leavers had a child by age 16, and that 50 per cent were mothers within eighteen to twenty-four months of leaving care (Biehal *et al.*, 1995). However, the sample sizes in these latter studies were small, and research evidence to support a clear-cut association is still limited. At the time of the research and indeed at the time of writing, there were no official statistics on the numbers of young people in local authority care, or those leaving care who were pregnant or parents. A survey of local authorities, conducted in 2002 as part of the same research project, revealed that less than 40 per cent of local authorities surveyed collected any data on the young people in their care who became pregnant or parents.

As noted in Chapter 3, extensive research has, however, demonstrated the generally poor life outcomes for young people leaving care. These include a disproportionately high vulnerability to health problems, including mental health difficulties and substance misuse (Department of Health, 1997; Saunders and Broad, 1997; Utting, 1997; House of Commons Health Committee, 1998; Skuse and Ward, 1999; Arcelus *et al.*, 1999; Buchanan, 1999; Richardson and Joughin, 2000; Wyler, 2000). Limited access to education and a lack of educational qualifications or aspirations (Kiernan, 1995; Borland *et al.*, 1998; NCH, 2000; Jackson, 2001) have been linked to high levels of unemployment, poverty and homelessness (Biehal *et al.*, 1995; Social Exclusion Unit, 1998; NCH, 2000; Stein and Wade, 2000; Vernon, 2000). There is also an increased likelihood of running away (Wade *et al.*, 1998; Stein and Rees, 2002) and involvement with the criminal justice system (NCH, 2000; Courtney *et al.*, 2001).

Young people in and leaving care therefore exhibit a clustering of the risk factors associated with teenage pregnancy more generally. Furthermore, research illustrates that they are more likely to experience family relationship disruption (Musick, 1993; Sweeting and West, 1995); low self-esteem (Emler, 2001); a lack of access to good-quality sex and relationships education (Corlyon and McGuire, 1999; Health Development Agency, 2001; Wellings *et al.*, 2001) and difficulties in accessing health services (Social Services Inspectorate, 1998).

While there is only limited research on young women in and leaving care who become pregnant, still less is known about young fathers with experience of care (Coleman, 2001). Research on young fathers generally suggests that young men tend to become fathers at a slightly later age (around 18 or 19) than young women become mothers (Burghes *et al.*, 1997). Factors associated with teenage motherhood are also commonly associated with teenage fatherhood (Dennison and Coleman, 2000). Teenage fathers are more likely to have been involved in youth offending, with some estimates suggesting that more than a quarter of men in young offenders' institutions are already fathers or expectant fathers (Dennison and Lyon, 2003). They are also more likely to have engaged in truancy and to have left school at age 16 than young men who do not become fathers in their teenage years. However, there is limited evidence of a direct causal effect between educational 'drop-out' and fatherhood (Dearden *et al.*, 1995).

Teenage fathers, whether or not they live with the mothers of their children, have reported similar difficulties in parenting, including poor accommodation, unemployment and being benefit-reliant (Lalond, 1995); and receiving little or no encouragement or support to adjust to their role as fathers (Speak *et al.*, 1997; Quinton *et al.*, 2002).

Since the 1970s the concept of the 'new father' has evolved, as one who actively participates in the care of his child (Jackson, 1984; Haywood and Mac an Ghail, 2003). This has in turn created a starkly contrasting stereotype of fatherhood typified by feckless males who are uncaring about the child and the mother. Fathers from disadvantaged backgrounds appear to be most readily assigned to this latter category and this, in turn, may affect how professionals relate to them. In one recent study, professionals interviewed rarely saw work with young fathers as central to their roles and responsibilities (Quinton *et al.*, 2002). Yet some young fathers, especially those having experienced custodial sentences, while they strongly aspire to being the 'new father', require extensive support to enable them to take on their roles as fathers and avoid re-offending (Dennison and Lyon, 2003).

We now go on to describe and discuss our study of young parents who have been in care.

## The framework and methodology of the study

A preliminary review of relevant literature, together with a survey of a sample of local authorities in England, provided the contextual framework for the main qualitative study. This involved in-depth interviews with young parents (and those about to be parents), professionals and carers, in four contrasting sites across England. In total, seventy-eight local authority professionals and carers from a range of social care and support services participated in semi-structured interviews. Professionals were contacted in each site through the use of snowball-sampling, to identify those with experience of working with young parents.

In-depth semi-structured interviews, using a pre-tested discussion tool, were held with a total of sixty-three young people. Identifying young parents with experience of care to take part in the research and particularly young fathers, proved complex and time-consuming. Consequently, sampling of participants was largely opportunistic and where it was not possible to make appointments, it involved researchers just spending time in services in order to identify eligible respondents. This reflects the complexities of research with more marginalised young people, an issue discussed in more detail in Chapter 10.

Semi-structured interviews focused broadly, yet not exclusively, around a set of key themes that engaged young people in discussion: their own reaction and that of significant others to the pregnancy and subsequent decision-making; their views about and use of contraception; sources of information about sexual health and relationships; who or what had or had not helped them from when they or their partner had become pregnant up to the present time. There was also limited discussion of their care history, including the age at which they had entered care, and the number and type of placements they had experienced.

The study gave primacy to the accounts of young people themselves, and as such was located within the emerging tradition of childhood studies, in which young people's accounts of their social circumstances and experiences are regarded as valuable in their own right (Greig and Taylor, 1999; Lewis and Lindsay, 2000; Hallett and Prout 2003).

Interviews were normally tape-recorded and, when this was not possible, detailed fieldnotes were kept. Findings from interviews were analysed using the constant comparative method (Glaser and Strauss, 1967) to elicit recurrent themes identified by interviewees, and these are discussed below. Once each of these themes had been identified in a preliminary form, a search for 'negative instances' took place (Merriam, 2002; Seale, 2002), prior to confirmation of the principal themes structuring respondents' accounts of their own experiences.

## Research participants

Forty-seven young women, between the ages of 15 and 22, and sixteen young fathers between the ages of 15 and 23, were interviewed. Although seven young women were older than 20 at the time of the research, all had become parents for the first time at a young age (at 14, 14, 15, 16, 17, 17 and 18 respectively). All but one of these women had had more than one child. The young women who had their first child at age 14 had had three and four children respectively by the time the study was conducted. Likewise, young fathers interviewed in their early twenties had all become parents in their teenage years, and a number were the fathers of several children. Two had become parents at age 16 and had four and three children respectively.

At the time when the young people were interviewed, the majority of the fifty-one who were already parents were living with their child or children. However, the children of four parents interviewed had been taken into local authority care; one was at the time of the research due to attend a child protection conference to decide if she could retain custody of two children, one had had a baby taken into care and was later reunited with the baby, one couple had placed two of their three children in foster care voluntarily but maintained contact, and at least three others had experience of their children being placed on child protection registers. One young man was trying to gain custody of one of his children who had been living in another authority with his former partner and had ended up in care within that authority. Of the thirteen young men interviewed who were already fathers, only two were living with their child(ren) and the child's mother, although one of these had lost contact with two of his other children; seven said they had some regular contact with at least one of their children, although two had lost contact with another child; three reported having no contact at all with their child(ren); in one case the children had been taken into care. All three young men who had pregnant partners were living with their partner and envisaged staying together with that partner.

Of the forty-seven young women interviewed, four were in part-time work, seven were at college and three were about to re-enter education, all through specialist provision for teenage parents. A total of thirty-three were in receipt of income support (including one receiving a job seekers allowance). Of these, many had plans to re-enter education and/or training or employment in the near future. The London site reported the largest proportion of young parents currently on an education programme, with five out of the ten young women interviewed at this site currently studying. Prior to their pregnancies many reported having left school or having ceased to attend school early, often as young as 12 or 13 years old. One young woman in the study reported not being able to continue at school through her pregnancy on the grounds of 'health and safety'.

Of the sixteen young men interviewed, seven were in receipt of income support (including one receiving a job seekers allowance), three were on training programmes, two were in full- or part-time employment, three were in custody and one was at university. Again, the majority of young men reported early disaffection with education.

## Influences on early pregnancy

While the focus in this chapter is primarily on young people's experiences of parenthood, it is important to outline the range of factors identified by the young people themselves which rendered them vulnerable to pregnancy at an early age. These factors included a breakdown in family relationships, often preceding going into the care system, a lack of continuity in care, not trusting others, feeling rejected, lonely and stigmatised. Although the vast majority of pregnancies in the sample were unplanned, many young people spoke about their wish to continue with their pregnancy because they wanted 'someone to love' and to ensure that their children were not rejected in the way they had been. In addition, many young people had missed out on sex and relationships education because of disruptions in their schooling or not receiving enough information in foster and residential care. Peer pressure and introduction to sexual activity – often alongside drug and alcohol use – in residential care were also influencing factors (Knight and Chase, forthcoming).

## Becoming a parent

Despite the fact that the vast majority of young people had not planned their pregnancies, most young people interviewed felt that becoming a parent had been a positive experience. A number had mixed feelings about being a parent and felt that if they had their time again they would have delayed having a child. Relatively few felt that the experience overall had been a negative one, either because they were too young to deal with it, or because the complications in their lives had made parenting difficult.

Positive experiences centred primarily on the love and enjoyment they felt they received from their children. For some young people, parenting signified a sense of achievement or proof of their ability to cope. Many talked about becoming a parent as a step towards maturity, one that had promoted a positive change in them. For some, being a mum or dad meant that they enjoyed a new-found status or level of respect. Others described experiencing a replaced love that they had never received themselves:

> 'He is such a happy baby . . . even when he hurts himself he just looks at you and laughs . . . there is nothing I don't enjoy.'
>
> > (Young woman, age 16, parent at 16 years, one child)

> 'Giving birth was one of the best things ever. I'm really proud of my son and of myself for the way I've brought him up and the fact I've done it myself.'
>
> > (Young woman, age 18, parent at 15 years, one child)

> 'It is just the experience . . . fantastic to have that experience . . . words can't describe how fantastic he is.'
>
> > (Young woman, age 15, parent at 15, one child)

> 'My baby is my pride and joy at the moment, he is the love that I never had, the things I never had as a child.'
>
> > (Young woman, age 18, parent at 18, one child)

Several young people made reference to the 'calming' or 'settling' effect that becoming, or the prospect of becoming, a parent had had on them. Descriptions of how they had 'changed' as a result were often in stark contrast to how they had perceived themselves before having the child:

> 'I think I would have been in gaol if I hadn't of had him, as I was close to going to gaol. It was social services who told the judge that I was starting to sort my life out and was pregnant and that I was going to "anger management" [classes].'
>
> > (Young woman, age 18, parent at 15, one child)

> 'Having a child has calmed me down. I used to take drugs all the time like smoking dope until I found out I was pregnant, I used to get locked up all the time but I don't anymore. I stopped drinking as well, as I was a right little alchy, but I still smoked cigarettes. He [the baby] never asked to be there but he was there so I had to stop all those things.'
>
> > (Young woman age 17, parent at 16, one child)

'It changed me . . . it changed everything about me . . . it made me realise I am going to bring a life into the world, I need to grow up and stop acting like this, like a spoilt teenager.'

(Young woman, age 20, parent at 18, two children)

'If I didn't have X [baby], I would still be trying to kill myself on drugs. . . . If I didn't have X [baby], I would still be childish; if I didn't have X [baby], I would probably be dead.'

(Young woman, age 19, parent at 17, one child)

'I didn't give a fuck, I didn't need to get a job, get housing, because everything I am doing just affected me, no one else . . . I think the baby is a way to better myself. Now I am thinking, in three years' time I need to have a steady job, I need to have this, I need to have that . . . and the only reason is because of this baby.'

(Young woman, age 17, pregnant with first child)

While young men and women interviewed shared very similar views about the meaning and experience of becoming parents, collectively the relationship of young fathers with their children was more complex. Some were directly involved in bringing up their child or children, others reported being involved with some of their children but estranged from others, and some had no part in their child's life at all. Yet all of those who were not involved talked about wanting to be involved on some level or another, and about the barriers that existed to being an active parent.

The meanings that young men gave to becoming a parent were very similar to those of the young women interviewed. Particularly strong was the wish to replace their own family in some way, alongside wanting to be a better parent, especially a father, to their own children. Many also talked about the stabilising effect that becoming a father had on their lives. Being able to provide well for the mother and child materially was a major issue, and 'Wanting them to have things that they never had' – whether a wide screen television or the 'best trainers' – was really important:

'I love it, it's the best thing that can happen to a bloke really . . . I've always got money, she's always provided for, I don't do drugs around her, or drink. I only smoke a bit of pot now and again.'

(Young man, age 24, parent at 16, three children)

'I've got responsibilities now, I have to stop going out there robbing people – that's what I used to do. You are talking about a person out of foster care. When I was little, I never had my Dad about . . . I'm there a bit more, I am there for the little one and I will always be there until he is older. . . . My Dad only took up with me when I was 13. [Now] I see my Dad as a friend, but I don't want my son to see me as a friend – I want him to see me as a Dad.'

(Young man, age 20, father at 19, one child)

'When I am with him [son], there is no other feeling like it. It's great.'
(Young man, age 22, parent at 18, one child)

'I am pleased the way things are going. A lot of people are happy about it and I know the baby is wanted.'
(Young man, age 17, partner pregnant with first child)

For many of the young people interviewed, parenting was seen as a chance to do things differently and to give their own children a better experience than they themselves had had:

'I just like being able to teach him things, bring him up the way I want him brought up instead of all these different families bringing him up like I was.'
(Young woman, age 19, parent at age 18, one child)

'Nothing will ever happen like that to X [baby]. I will always be there for her . . . it's a good thing that I've been through what I have. You know what I mean? 'Cos she's going to have the best in life definitely. . . . She's never going to go through what I've been through. . . . It hurts to even think about it.'
(Young woman, parent at age 17, one child)

The more negative perceptions of becoming a parent described by a minority of young people related to a range of factors including loss of independence and freedom; loss of friendships and social opportunities, and subsequent isolation; or a sense of being overwhelmed by the responsibility and the new demands placed on them:

'In a way, I'll say now I am still not ready to be a father, I'm still too young, if she'd have gotten rid of it I'd have been happier. I wouldn't be tied down so early. I would still prefer to go out and party. Now, I just get on with it and deal with it.'
(Young man, parent at age 19, one child)

'If I knew then what I know now I would get rid of it. People can promise a lot when you are first pregnant but not be so willing to help when you have the baby. I would tell other young girls it's not as easy as you think it is going to be.'
(Young woman, age 18, parent at 17, one child)

## Factors influencing how well young people cope as parents

It is important to recognise that many of the young people interviewed were content with their lives as parents, received ongoing support and help, and reported positive experiences of the transition to independence and parenthood. For others, however, the process was more difficult and, at times, painful.

What clearly emerged was a continuum of support needs for young parents in and leaving care. An ability to cope was felt by professionals to be linked to personal characteristics and not necessarily to a disrupted childhood. It was also linked to the type of support the young person was receiving. The importance of a trusted confidant or just someone 'to be there' emerged as key to how well supported young people felt from when they became pregnant to becoming a parent. The young people who described positive experiences of service access and use most usually attributed this to the presence of key individuals who had helped them. What was important was having a single person there for them on a range of levels, someone who could be relied upon for support over a period of time, who could assist them in accessing a range of support and services and, most importantly, someone whom they could trust. Instability created by changes in staffing or frequent moves was therefore a major barrier:

> 'Who you trust is about finding the right person to talk to about personal things. When a professional talks with you just to fill in paperwork it puts you off, it feels like it is just work to them and not that they are interested in who you are. You want someone you can relax with, talk with and enjoy a joke with too . . . it's more about the attitude of the worker or adviser than their age or professional background.'
>
> (Young man, age 22, father at 15, four children)

Many young people were open about the extra support they wanted, or wished for. Those who had never experienced parenting before and were without family backing were most in need of practical support:

> 'I feel I need more help with how to deal with the practical things with the baby and how to cope to understand life.'
>
> (Young woman, age 16, pregnant with first child)

## Different sources of support

The young people interviewed were in a range of settings including foster care, supported housing units or living independently. None, at the time of interview, were in residential care. They were asked who or what had helped them from the point at which they discovered that they were pregnant until the time of the interview.

### Support from partners

Of the young women in this study, twenty-four (51 per cent) reported being with a partner at the time of the interview. Where relationships were working well, the support of a partner was seen as invaluable, and many professionals identified the presence of a supportive partner as a key factor in enabling young people to cope.

Importantly, support could also be derived from a new partner, after the father of the child had left:

> 'After my "ex" left, I met my current boyfriend. He treats the baby as if it is his own and the baby loves him.'
>
> (Young woman, age 18, parent at 17, one child)

One young person talked about the difference it made having a supportive partner with her third child compared with having no one there for her other two children, who were now in foster care. She felt that her partner's presence at the birth was why she has more of a bond with her third child.

### Support from family

Many professionals saw both historical and current influences of family as key factors in contributing to how well a young person later coped as a parent. Positive family relationships generally, either their own or their partner's, were identified as central in providing young people with a wide range of emotional, financial and practical support. Both young men and women described receiving assistance from parents of partners who had strong family ties and had not experienced being in care.

When young people had encountered at least some positive parenting in the past, this was felt to have a beneficial impact on their ability to cope, and it was more likely that a line of communication with their birth families would be maintained. In some cases, young people described how having a baby enabled bridges to be built between themselves and their own families, especially their mothers:

> 'Me and my Granny [main carer] get on better. We used to be at each other's throats all the time, but now she's my best mate because she wants to help the baby and she just loves him. I didn't think she thought I was responsible or anything before.'
>
> (Young woman, age 17, parent at 16, one child)

> 'It has helped build a better relationship with Mum and Dad again.'
>
> (Young woman, age 17, pregnant with first child)

> 'She [Mum] opened her door with open arms which surprised me because I hadn't talked to her for two years.'
>
> (Young woman, age 20, parent at 18, two children)

However, this experience was by no means universal and was dependent on the nature of the young person's previous relationship with family members. A number of young parents described highly volatile relationships with family, and improved relationships immediately following the birth of the baby often dissolved later. Some professionals commented that many of these young people entered care as a result of the breakdown of relationships at home. Here, part of the work, they felt, was to help rebuild family support structures. Family mediation and efforts to promote the involvement of the extended family in supporting young parents was seen as helpful in this respect.

### Foster care

Foster care placements for young mothers and babies for the most part were highly valued, although in one or two instances foster carers were said to have blocked access to the baby's father. However, where they worked well they were seen as providing the opportunity for continuity of support at an emotional as well as a practical level. As one young woman explained:

> 'They [foster carers] gave me space to think about things and also gave advice. They treated me like one of their own children. My foster Mum came with me to the scans and was at the birth like a mother. They offered to let me stay with them when I had the baby but I wanted my independence.'
>
> (Young woman, parent at 17, one child)

Yet, despite the obvious benefits of this type of placement, there remained some confusion both for the mother and the carer over their roles and responsibilities. Foster carers were uncertain as to when and to what extent they should intervene, what their duties were with respect to the young person and the baby, their statutory duties to Social Services, and the extent to which they carried the function of 'assessing' the mother's skills. Young mothers described complex interactions and mixed messages from carers and social workers. As one foster care manager said:

> 'Is the foster carer there to assess the parenting skills of the young person, is she there to look after the baby or not? How do you define roles? It's very hard being a foster carer because you want to give young people a normal experience, and yet there are lots of rules and boundaries. Some carers don't want to "grass them up" to the social workers because they know that they will see it as a significant thing that they didn't come home last night, and it will affect this young person's chance of keeping the baby . . . and that it can be as whimsical [sic] as the allocated social worker. If it was a different team and a different social worker then you might have a different response, the foster carer knows that.'

And a young mother said:

> 'She [social worker] says I should not let him [baby] go to foster care so much . . . but he hasn't got nobody else . . . so she says to her [foster carer] try not to help her so much . . . try not to be around [baby] so much . . . that is so annoying. She [social worker] claims she [foster carer] helps me so much they

want to move me to a mother and baby unit to monitor me. I say if I'm there who's going to help me? When she had her children she had her family around helping . . . I haven't got the family so my foster carer is helping me . . . they are annoying . . . there won't be no one there [mother and baby unit] to help . . . then if I crack they are going to take him.'

(Young woman, age 16, parent at 15, one child)

### Social Services

Relationships between young people and Social Services departments varied enormously. Most young people had had a series of different social workers. A number talked about really positive relationships where the worker had offered support when needed but had not interfered excessively or broken trust. Other relationships were more complex, and becoming a parent often added a different dimension to the perceived role of the social worker. For young people less trusting of this service, social workers' actions were seen as largely consisting of scrutiny and assessment.

Child protection assessment procedures, both pre-birth and ongoing, were a central theme in the perspectives of young parents and many felt they were under closer scrutiny than their peers who had not been in care. Once again, trust emerged as a crucial element within the child protection process. There was an evident 'them and us' culture, whereby the Social Services system in particular, and any other services seen to collude with Social Services (such as health visitors and family support workers), were viewed very negatively by young people who believed that they were being judged and 'set up to fail'. While some young parents 'survived' the assessment process and felt a sense of achievement once they were deemed competent parents, there was clear evidence from what other young people said that fears about how they would be judged and assessed prevented them from asking for the support they needed. While the importance of the assessment process in itself is not at question here, more could be done to ensure greater transparency and create a more supportive and trusting approach to child protection. The following anecdote, recounted by the coordinator of a voluntary sector young parents' project, illustrates these points:

'A young Mum who was in care and the child was in care because she hurt him – was then moved into foster care with the child. Then from there she went to a family centre. And part of the programme was that she had to attend here [the teenage parenting programme]. She has now attended for 18 months, her child is off the child protection register and she has her own accommodation. She now enjoys being a parent. Here she felt there was trust. We didn't do anything without talking to her first. We supported her and attended all her case conferences. She saw all the reports before we read them at the case conference. She actually said that she didn't feel "false" here, whereas she had to continually put on a front when she was at the family centre because she felt she was being watched. They see [the teenage parenting programme] as very different from Social Services; we don't make any decisions for them . . . they have to make decisions for themselves. If there is a child protection issue then we would encourage a young person to phone Social Services themselves, and if they don't then we would invite Social Services in.'

### Leaving care services

Access to either statutory or voluntary sector leaving care support varied enormously and reflected the different developmental stages of leaving care services at that time (2002 and the early part of 2003). One of the research sites with a well-established statutory leaving care service provided several tiers of support, tailored to the specific individual needs of the young person. Young parents described having access to a leaving care social worker, a leaving care worker (not necessarily a qualified social worker, but there to offer practical help, advice and support) and a mentor who would visit for weekly support, mainly to do with parenting. Support was provided on a daily basis when necessary with the young person deciding jointly with the worker when and how it would be reduced. A strong emphasis was placed on linking young people into other services such as Sure Start Plus, general health services and educational support.

In another site, some young people had access to leaving care services through the voluntary sector. In the two other sites leaving care services were less well established but were expanding in accordance with the Children (Leaving Care) Act 2000. Consequently not all young people we spoke to had an allocated leaving care worker. Where young parents did have access to a leaving care worker they repeatedly described the holistic nature of the support they derived from them, their accessibility, and the fact that they were 'there for them' on many different levels:

> 'She [leaving care worker] takes me shopping every week and helps with the decorating and with the child. A good worker is someone you can relate to and talk to, and they don't act like they know better (respect).'
>
> (Young woman, age 19, parent at 17, one child)

> 'My leaving care worker came every morning for a few hours during the first few months after the baby was born, she would do the bottles, watch the baby while she was in the bath and used to do my shopping for me. . . . Now they is going to help us with a nanny during the day, just so I can have some time with me friends as well, because I am really lonely, 'cos I never see my friends.'
>
> (Young woman, age 17, parent at 17 years, one child)

> 'He [leaving care voluntary sector worker] came with me to all my antenatal classes. . . . He used to stay with me for two to four hours at the hospital while they were doing my scans or whatever. . . . They [voluntary organisation] gave

the most support. If it weren't for them, I wouldn't have been able to keep X [baby]. Social Services would have come and taken her off me.'

(Young woman, age 18, parent at 17, one child)

Importantly, where the leaving care service was well established, young people were able to develop trust in their leaving care worker, despite previous negative experiences of social services:

'She [leaving care worker] is honest, unlike other social workers. She is always on the end of a phone and on my down days rings me, and talks me through it. She's different, you can trust her.'

(Young woman, age 16, pregnant with first child)

'Social Services haven't really done nothing – but the After Care Team have helped a lot, we have talks, they help us with debt and stuff, anything I need help with.'

(Young woman, age 18, parent at 17, one child)

'X [social worker at the leaving care team] . . . he's a godsend. He's really nice to me. He's the best. I've had three other social workers and I don't like them. He really likes children, I can't believe he's a social worker.'

(Young woman, age 17, parent at 17, one child)

'Everyone needs someone to talk to and it helps if someone is open with you too. I like people who make time for you and take time to explain things to you. It's important that someone asks you how you are feeling and if you are OK about what is going on both "in care" and out of care services.'

(Young woman, age 17, pregnant with first child)

A number of professionals described how additional resources could enable the provision of a much more intensive level of support and at the same time offer young people concrete things in terms of housing and benefits that they would not have received before. One social services manager said:

'The structure of the service is such that it allows more support to young people, particularly where there are complex issues. Here, we can jointly allocate a case between a social worker and a personal adviser [PA] . . . so the PA is able to do a lot more support work with the young person . . . I have great hopes and expectations of the role of the PA.'

A key difference was that, unlike other services, leaving care services are very much 'young people-led', in that within them care leavers are more actively involved in making decisions about what they want and need through consultative and jointly agreed pathway plans.

### Primary care services

Although many young people spoke about feeling 'judged' and unsupported by some health professionals, the support of those who related well to young people was highly valued. This was especially true of specialist midwives and support services, such as those provided through Sure Start Plus initiatives (which existed in three of the research sites), or other specialist teenage parenting midwifery services:

> 'I had a good midwife . . . a really good midwife . . . she was really nice . . . I started seeing her when I was fourteen weeks pregnant and she supports me even now . . . I drop in to see her.'
>
> (Young woman, age 16, parent at 16, one child)

Of a Sure Start midwife, one young person commented:

> 'She is very good and makes contact with the social workers, and gives me home visits when I haven't got the energy to get up.'
>
> (Young woman, age 16, pregnant with first child)

> 'My midwife was fantastic . . . She discharged me two weeks ago, so she kept me on longer than she should have done really. . . . But we got on really well, we were like friends . . . she gave me her home phone number.'
>
> (Young woman, age 15, parent at 15, one child)

Another young parent talked positively about a local specialist young parent project with an associated befriending scheme:

> 'When I was pregnant I got a friend, X, I am really close with her now. She's my daughter's godmother. She doesn't work with them no more, but we're still friends. She was there when I was having the baby and everything.'
>
> (Young woman, age 18, parent at 16, one child)

One young person described the support she had received from a midwife as well as a Sure Start adviser in relation to the stress she was experiencing at school. Together, they had helped her explore alternative forms of educational provision through the local young mothers centre. Another young woman talked of the benefits of having a specialist drugs liaison midwife who knew how to deal with the situation and understood the issues:

> 'She didn't just tell you to stop. She was able to look at your psychological well-being as well.'
>
> (Young woman, age 22, parent at 18, two children)

The team leader of a specialist teenage midwifery service in London described how, because of their expertise, they could provide a different quality of service to young parents. This included being at case conferences, an observation confirmed by a young parent:

> 'My midwife was excellent, she came with me to every case conference.'
>
> (Young woman, age 16, parent at 15, one child)

As with social workers, young people held differing perceptions of health visitors. Once again, the key to success appeared to lie in there being opportunities to build positive relationships:

> '[Of a health visitor] She was lovely! She didn't judge me at all. I only saw her three times. I had to move, so changed health visitor.'
>
> (Young woman, age 17, parent at 16, one child)

> 'I didn't like her at first because I thought she was a bit of a snobby person, but once I got to know her more I think she is lovely. . . . She sits and listens to us, even if it's not about the baby, but I need to talk.'
>
> (Young woman, age 17, parent at 17 years, one child)

### Housing

Adequate, appropriate and affordable housing, or indeed the lack of it, was a recurrent theme in young people's accounts. Many of them described enormous difficulties in securing suitable housing for themselves and their child and the high degree of vulnerability that came with this. Some were placed in unsafe environments where drug use was prolific, others faced a series of damp and impractical rooms in bed and breakfast accommodation. Several experienced violent incidents and at least two young women were raped. Young fathers, especially when estranged from the mothers of their children, described the lack of suitable accommodation in which to spend time with their children.

Some young women had been placed in supported housing units or specialist mother and baby units with trained support staff. On the whole, they viewed this type of accommodation positively. Hostel staff were described as being generally supportive in housing tribunals and helped with teaching to cook. Young people also described how hostel workers often accompanied them to look at more permanent accommodation, and acted as advocates if they were being pressurised into accepting substandard housing placements. One young woman still in a housing association mother and baby unit said:

> 'Since I've been here I've felt more confident with doing things. They do help. No matter what they are doing, unless they are already helping someone else they will just drop it. Even if it is really important paperwork, they will just drop it and help you. I think it's brilliant. They really make you feel at home.'
>
> (Young woman, age 19, parent at 18, one child)

Another young person, looking back on her experiences of a unit run by another housing association, said:

> 'The unit was great. It was safe and they showed you how to do things. Like I didn't know how to manage my money properly [before], but within a month of being there I could do it. I was there less than a year and moved out a month before her first birthday.'
>
> (Young woman, age 21, parent at 17, one child)

And a specialist midwife said:

> 'I think a good thing for young parents leaving care are the mother and baby units. They seem to be a positive thing, they need a balance in between, rather than stepping out on their own. They need someone who is there but not standing over you. Most of them seem to welcome that.'

### Education, employment and training

Encouraging young parents back into education, training and employment in order to avoid long-term effects of social exclusion is central to the success of the government's teenage pregnancy strategy. Many young people in the study talked about having been 'disengaged' from education at a very young age, and therefore having few or no qualifications. Despite their previous disaffection with education, a large majority of the young parents interviewed had aspirations to return to education, training or employment at some point in the future.

In one research site, considerable emphasis was placed on educational support for young parents. Alternative and non-formal educational opportunities provided valued opportunities for flexible learning. An educational support project with an on-site crèche, sharing Sure Start Plus facilities, enabled young parents to receive extensive support at a range of levels. The service was reportedly well used by young parents who were care leavers.

## Conclusions

We opened this chapter with a question: Is early parenthood such a bad thing? This study cannot pretend to provide any straightforward answers, although it has highlighted some of the many, often complex, support needs of young people in and leaving care. It has also begun to unpack some of the broad assumptions that underpin policy and practice, that all young people start with the same opportunities and life chances which are curtailed by early parenthood.

There is no question of the need to redress the many imbalances in terms of access to support, care, education and career prospects that young people in and leaving care have faced in the past. There may, however, be an argument that for some, as was frequently testified by the research participants in this study, parenthood provides new opportunities: opportunities for reflection and for emotional healing, providing stability and enabling them to move forward. Surely in the long term what we hope for is a more equal starting point where parenthood is a life choice for all young people that can be weighed up against other options available to them. But in the meantime the reality for many young people in and leaving care is that parenthood may be the best choice available, even if that choice is not always a conscious one.

If we accept this, then the key to what makes the difference between being able to cope as a young parent and losing the unequal struggle is consistent emotional and practical support. Yet the need does not begin with the onset of parent-hood. Many of the young people interviewed discussed situations in which they had needed support, irrespective of becoming pregnant or a parent. Dealing with violence, homelessness, drugs, alcohol and mental and emotional health problems were some of the difficulties mentioned. There is therefore a clear need to provide young people in care with someone whom they can trust and confide in from an early age. Such a person could offer guidance and support at a number of levels, but could also act as an interface between the young person and mainstream services.

Young parents do clearly have support needs over and above those of other young people leaving care. The non-judgemental nature of this support is vital, particularly given the range of concerns about being under scrutiny and their abilities as parents constantly being monitored. As a result they often felt that their own needs were overlooked or dismissed, with the sole focus being on their child. Feeling that they themselves are valued as individuals is crucial to their ability to access and accept appropriate support.

The research revealed the potential and already evident success of some leaving care services that within a short space of time have gained respect and appreciation from young people. The holistic and consistent nature of the help provided was often in stark contrast to previous experiences of sporadic support from overloaded and inaccessible mainstream Social Services departments. There appeared to be at least anecdotal evidence from the research that an appropriate level of support to young parents could reduce the probability of their children being placed on the child protection register or taken into care. Clearly this whole issue requires further exploration, but it does raise important questions about how resources are made available to support services, which determines how much they are able to invest in order to have this level of impact. The reality expressed by a number of professionals was that the best care packages were simply not affordable. Yet they may be the only way to avoid the often cyclical outcome of children being removed and subsequent pregnancies.

A number of young people in the study also expressed greater trust in services aligned to the voluntary and/or non-statutory sector or that were perceived to be somehow distanced from statutory provision. Young people and professionals repeatedly mentioned new services such as Sure Start Plus, specialist midwifery teams and some voluntary sector services as providing essential and well-received kinds of support.

What this research has shown is that with appropriate, consistent and continuing support it is possible for young people with a care background to be good parents and to derive great satisfaction from their new role. Many of those interviewed were clear that becoming responsible for a child had been a turning point in their life which had set them on a much more positive trajectory than had seemed likely before. We cannot say if this picture is overly optimistic because to date there is virtually no research on the longer-term outcomes for young people in and leaving care who have children in their teenage years. Such research is urgently needed given the tide change over recent years in attitudes and practice and the emerging evidence from studies like this one of the potential benefits in becoming a parent to some young people. We may find that early parenthood is not always such a bad thing after all.

## Acknowledgements

Our thanks go to all members of the research team including Ian Warwick, Maria Zuurmond, Kim Divers, Lisa Ruxton, Stuart Watson, Sarah Heathcote, Claire Maxwell, Ekyua Yankah and Antonia Simon; to all the staff at TCRU who supported the project including Charlie Owen, Penny Mellor, Steff Hazlehurst; and to Peter Aggleton, the Project Director.

# 7 Looking back

## Experiences of private fostering

*Charlie Owen, Edwina Peart and
Sofka Barreau*

Among the Baatombou in Northern Benin, West Africa, at least in rural
situations, fosterage is not the exception but the norm. People think that
biological parents are less able than foster parents to provide a good education
for their children. The Baatombou therefore find it very reasonable to give
their children to other persons to be fostered, without any negative conno-
tations. To the contrary, people trying to prevent their biological children
being taken by others are seen as bad. . . . Even in this West African context,
where fostering is a very common phenomenon, Baatombou norms and
behaviour appear extreme.

(Alber, 2004: 33–34)

In Britain, it has not been uncommon for children to be brought up away
from home by strangers. An obvious example is children at boarding-school. But
there are other examples, one of the most outstanding being the evacuations of
the Second World War when millions of children were moved from cities to the
country or abroad for their safety (Inglis, 1989). Similarly, children of military
and diplomatic families are routinely educated in Britain while their parents
are stationed abroad. Rudyard Kipling, for instance, was sent at the age of six to
be looked after by strangers in England while his father was stationed in Bombay.
Kipling wrote about the experience on several occasions, of which the best known
is the semi-autobiographical short story *Baa Baa, Black Sheep*, published in 1888
(Kipling, 1999).

The tragic death of Victoria Climbié, at the hands of her great aunt and her
aunt's boyfriend, brought to wider public attention the fact that some children
from West Africa are sent to Britain for their education (Laming, 2003: 3.5).
While some end up living with relatives or people known to the family, many
come to live with strangers, an arrangement that is categorised in Britain as
private fostering. While regulation of private fostering-type arrangements in
Britain was first introduced in the Infant Life Protection Act 1872 (Pinchbeck
and Hewitt, 1973), the term 'private fostering' does not appear to have been used
until the Children Act 1948, which introduced registration for foster carers
(Mumford and Selwood, 1976).

As well as children coming to Britain without their parents, it is also common practice for Nigerians living in Britain, often as students, to have their young children privately fostered by a British family. The writer Buchi Emecheta came to London from Nigeria in 1962 as a young mother with her student husband. She has written about her experience in her autobiographical novel *Second Class Citizen*:

> after all, the children would not stay with their parents. . . . They would have to be fostered. Nigerians with children sent their children away to foster-parents. No sane couple would dream of keeping their children with them. . . . As soon as a Nigerian housewife in England realised that she was expecting a child, instead of shopping for prams, knitting little bootees, she would advertise for a foster-mother.
>
> (Emecheta, 1974: 44)

However, Emecheta refused to have her children fostered:

> Everybody expected Adah [Emecheta] to do the same. It came as a big surprise, therefore, when they realised she was not making any attempt to look for a foster-mother.
>
> (Emecheta, 1974: 45)

To illustrate the strength of the expectation, she quotes her husband as saying:

> 'Everybody laughs at us in this place. No African child lives with his parents. It is not convenient; it is not possible. There is no accommodation for it. Moreover they won't learn good English. They are much, much better off with an English woman.'
>
> (Emecheta, 1974: 45)

This chapter will look retrospectively at the experiences of adults who were privately fostered as children. With the exception of the work of Bob Holman who has researched the subject over a long period (Holman, 1973, 2002), very little has been written about private fostering. Although there are some similarities between private fostering and local authority fostering, especially kinship care or placement with relatives (Broad et al., 2001), there are some important differences. In particular, privately fostered children have not been deemed at risk of harm or neglect and have not been taken into public care for that reason. On the contrary, they are voluntarily placed with foster carers by their own parents. The voluntary nature of the arrangement inevitably affects the way in which children experience this type of fostering.

## Private fostering

The Children Act 1989 defines private fostering as occurring when a child is cared for and provided with accommodation by someone other than a parent or relative (Children Act 1989, section 105 (1)), for a period of twenty-eight days or longer. Regulations specify that both parents and carers have a duty to notify the local authority of these arrangements. Although the local authority is not obliged to approve or register private foster carers, it does have a responsibility to look after the general welfare of the child, which includes visiting the foster home. The extent to which local authorities act upon this duty varies (Clarke, 2002). Some provide designated workers for this group of children and actively seek out such placements, while others are unaware of the arrangements that exist in their locality and make no attempt to find out about them. As a result, at the time of writing there is little available information on private fostering placements and no national statistics on the numbers of children or carers involved.

The private nature of the procedure, and the fact that the majority of known placements are not notified or monitored (Social Services Inspectorate, 1994), was noted by Sir William Utting. In his report of the review of the safeguards for children living away from home he identified privately fostered children as a particularly vulnerable group and made a number of recommendations concerning private fostering arrangements (Utting, 1997). However, a subsequent review of progress in all care arrangements for children since the publication of the report noted that few improvements had been made in this area and that few, if any, safety checks were in place (Stuart and Baines, 2004). The Children Act 2004, however, now includes measures to strengthen the current notification system and establish national minimum standards for private fostering which will be enforced through inspection.

This chapter presents some of the material gathered from a research project, funded by the Department of Health and Department for Education and Skills, on the experience and motivations of those involved in private fostering, either as parents, carers or as children. The focus here is on the experiences of twelve adults (three male and nine female), interviewed as part of the project, who were privately fostered as children. It was decided not to interview young people being fostered at the time of the research because of the ethical difficulties this might involve. In addition, twenty-nine private foster carers and five parents who had children privately fostered were interviewed, and their views are included where appropriate.

Adults who have been privately fostered as children are difficult to contact and consequently the sample was gathered from a range of sources. The British Association for Adoption and Fostering (BAAF) Private Fostering Interest Group provided one contact. Another came through personal contacts of a member of the research team. The rest of the interviewees came from responses to advertisements and articles placed in magazines and newspapers in the Black press. Participants were thus a self-selected group. The majority were of West African origin, one was from Southern Africa and one from the Caribbean. All were in the 30 to 45 age range, and all had post A-level qualifications and professional jobs. The interviews were semi-structured, face-to-face and mostly conducted in people's own homes, on average lasting one and a half hours.

### Reasons for fostering

The interviewees were asked why they believed their parents had had them privately fostered. Collectively, respondents saw the move by their parents very much as a childcare issue and gave two main reasons why they thought they had been fostered. First, a combination of work and study had made it impossible for their parents to care for the children themselves since the parents' schedules did not fit into regular patterns that could be met by nurseries or childminders, even if the fees had not been prohibitively expensive. Second, difficult personal circumstances, such as an unexpected pregnancy or marital discord, which tended to be present along with the need to work, again made day care impossible. One interviewee, speaking of her mother's decision, stated:

> 'The pregnancy was very unexpected. They hadn't been together long and I think they probably split up quite soon after. There was options what to do: my father wanted my Mum to have an abortion, my mum's family back home wanted my mum to send me over to them, neither of which was really suitable at the time and my mum wanted to obviously carry on her nursing training, I think she'd only been doing a year of it, and I think her original aim had been to be a midwife, a psychiatric nurse, a general nurse and a midwife, and so the only option really she said . . . she recalls being really, really depressed in a sort of bed-sit, pregnant basically with most of her friends dropping her, so the option was really for somebody else to look after me at that time.'

These main motivating categories were also heavily influenced by cultural factors. Many of those who were cared for were aware that their parents came from a very different cultural environment, where childcare responsibilities are shared amongst the whole community and do not rest exclusively with the birth parents. These cultural norms are somewhat distorted in a British context and further complicated by the impact of racism (Rashid, 2000). Many of our interviewees spoke of the difficulties their parents experienced settling into British society. One said:

> 'I think, you know, my Mum was a bit of an African princess and . . . she just couldn't cope by herself. You know, in Ghana you have house helps, you've got your Mum and Dad there, your brothers and sisters all that extended family network and I think, it was just, I don't know what she was doing 'cos I know she wasn't working full time, but I think looking back, she just couldn't cope. . . . And basically I think she went to bed for thirty years, with depression, but at the time I didn't understand it as that.'

The fact that racism operates through the creation and application of stereotypical images, of both Black and White people, can mean that those coming from colonial backgrounds are raised viewing White society in a more progressive, favourable light than their own community (Prevatt Goldstein, 2000). One interviewee felt that in the 1950s and 1960s finding White families to care for their children was a fashionable thing to do and conferred some status on the family involved. Emecheta made the same point:

> No one cared whether a mother was suitable or not, no one wanted to know whether the house was clean or not; all they wanted to be sure of was that the foster-mother was white. The concept of 'whiteness' could cover a multitude of sins.
>
> (Emecheta, 1974: 45)

None of the interviewees suggested any other motivations for using private fostering than work and study combinations and difficult personal circumstances. There was, however, variation in how acceptable these motivations were considered to be. This point was reinforced by private foster carers we interviewed. Carers confirmed that most of the parents they had contact with struggled to balance their need to survive, their drive for education and their desire to provide for their children long term. They also acknowledged some of the difficulties these parents faced without the support of their extended families: many considered that they themselves took on part of this role, which was reflected in the use of the terms *Nanny* or *Mum*. A few of them mentioned the fact that the parents preferred a White English family as carers.

Recent anthropological studies in West Africa have suggested that shared childcare is a normal cultural practice (e.g. Goody, 1982; Page, 1989; Notermans, 2004). In their study of West African couples in London, Goody and Groothues (1979) showed how local traditions as well as the parents' personal circumstances affected the child care options open to them and the decisions they reached. Since nine of our twelve privately fostered interviewees were of Nigerian or Ghanaian parentage, this may have contributed to their parents' choices for them. Goody and Groothues (1979) also suggest that parenting can be divided into distinct responsibilities. Physical care is only one element; providing for a child financially is another, and these can be separated. This point is echoed and elaborated by Barrow (1996) speaking of the Caribbean. She suggests that financial responsibility, known as minding a child, has higher status and is seen as the more important task.

These traditions of communal childcare and separating parenting into distinct tasks are concepts that are not currently popular within British society. Instead, the emphasis is on attachment theory, bonding and exclusive parental responsibility for raising children. This raises ambivalent feelings in those who are cared for. Of our sample, the majority (seven) expressed some understanding and appreciation of their parents' motives, although, at times, this understanding had been reached after a struggle:

'I feel in this day and age you know it shouldn't be necessary I mean, there are so many other options available though I don't understand what the imperatives are particularly if they are living here. Obviously if people come from abroad and . . . rather than live abroad then they have to perhaps consider it as an option, because they don't have the networks they can place their children in so under those circumstances I see it as being a legitimate way, having your child looked after.'

About a quarter (three) were unhappy about the decision their parents made and felt that, faced with the same difficulties today, there would be alternatives to private fostering.

'I don't really see, I'm not – er – how can I say this without criticising Mum? I'm not – I – I – I'm not very supportive of people privately fostering their children in the present times unless, I mean I'm sure there's extenuating circumstances and everything but in the majority of cases I don't feel they need to . . . I mean in today's world there are . . . options other than private fostering you know so . . . I mean there is always something you know out there that when private fostering was really a big thing they didn't have those options like that.'

Two interviewees expressed complete satisfaction and stated that this form of childcare had worked well for them:

'I've got a very positive experience about it . . . it was one of the best things that happened to me in my life you know . . . for me as a person you know I wouldn't change anything because I really do think that . . . part of why I turned out to be who I am today is due to the influence that I drew from that woman . . . she was the person helping me, she didn't have to, you know . . . but she helped me financially, she helped me morally, pretty much she was always there for me, you know.'

### Age and duration

Ten of the twelve interviewees were privately fostered as babies. The earliest placement began when the child was 10 days old, two began at six weeks, one at four months and two at six months. Four placements began after the child was a year old. In some cases interviewees in this group could not be specific about the age they were fostered since they were too young to have clear memories and are unable or reluctant to raise these issues with their parents. One placement started when the child was between the ages of four and five and another when they were 15 years old.

The shortest placement within our sample was eighteen months and the longest was changed into an adoption after ten years of private fostering. In this instance, the interviewee continued to live with his adoptive parents into adulthood.

Between these two extremes one placement was for two years, one lasted three years, two were for four years, three lasted between six and seven years, one was for eight years, one for eleven years and one for twelve and a half years. No consistent relationship emerged between the age a placement started and its duration, nor could any particular arrangement be considered typical.

In our interviews with private foster carers, the youngest age they reported a child being placed was three days old and the longest placement duration was 18.5 years. They reported that the majority of children were placed between the ages of six months and a year old. The most common ages for leaving their carers were around five, seven and 11 years. This seems to correspond with educational transition points: starting school, moving to junior school or going on to secondary school.

There was a range of opinion within our sample of privately fostered interviewees concerning the early start and the length of placements. One-third (four) considered this a neglect of parental duty and an act that potentially, if not actually, put them at risk. Some of these interviewees expressed anger that their parents, particularly their mothers, delegated this most intensive period of child-rearing to another person. The other two-thirds (eight) can be divided into two roughly equal groups. The first consists of those who were either happy with the private fostering arrangement in itself, or had reached some resolution in later life that allowed them to feel that their parents had done the best they could in the circumstances. Those in the second group either did not really disclose how they felt about this issue or were not fostered at an early age.

### Contact and relationship with parents

No connection was found between the amount of contact maintained with the birth family during the placement and the relationship with the family generally. We separated respondents into three groups in terms of their relationships with their birth parents and families; those who described their relationships with family as poor; those who described improving relationships; and those who felt the relationship was good.

Poor relationships were ones in which the respondents described continuing resentment and difficulty relating to their parents in ways they considered appropriate for families.

One interviewee, who was fostered from six months to 13 years of age, said:

> 'They're not your parents anymore, you know: they're your biological parents. There wasn't an attachment, and even when I lived at home, well in my mum and dad's house for five years, we never ever really formed an attachment because I just think I was too old by then. If it had been the other way round it would have been different, but I just think that your formative years are when you make your attachments, and I was 13 you know almost independent so it was just too late. . . . I just hated it there . . . it wasn't like how my friends are with their parents: it just wasn't like that. It was just weird.'

LIVERPOOL JOHN MOORES UNIVERSITY
LEARNING SERVICES

Improving relationships were ones in which, despite difficulties in the past, there was some commitment by those who had been fostered to resolving these difficulties. They reported doing so either through asking questions and raising issues with parents, or recounted reasons for being grateful to a parent, recognising the difficulties they were faced with and not blaming them for their shortcomings:

> 'Yeah, I couldn't understand. I was angry for a bit, but now I'm not because there's nothing I can do about it. I can live. If I'd have known about it my life could have been a lot different and some things couldn't have happened, wouldn't have happened or whatever and I'd be a different person than I am today. But I don't really mind the person I am today either, so there's pros and cons to everything. My philosophy now is there's no point in me being angry about things that have happened in the past that I have no control over anyway.'

Good relationships were ones in which respondents felt their parents had made a good choice of carer, and private fostering was seen positively as another form of child care:

> 'I'm more sympathetic because I don't think I could have handled looking after both me and my sister. Like I was saying, in Nigeria you had a lot of help, and she didn't have to do very much really because everyone was around her and because she was pregnant with me. It was like, everyone was kind of like, oh she's pregnant you know we'll look after the older sister, and let her rest. And then when she came here, it was a lot harder because she had to start working immediately and er, personally I think that, my foster parents we still talk to, they were really good so she made a good decision and put us to the right people. And – er – [I] don't really regret her doing it really, because I enjoyed time with them and I still do when I go back and see them.'

Improving and good relationships combined made up half of the sample (six) and poor relationships a quarter (three). The other quarter comprised three respondents for whom there was less data, although none that suggested either regular contact or a positive relationship with their birth families, probably an indication that these relationships were poor.

The respondents with good family relationships had regular direct or telephone contact with their parents. In these cases, all interviewees also felt they had positive relationships with their carers and up until the point of interview had maintained contact with them. In the improving family relationship group the picture was more mixed. Two of the four respondents had relatively short placements of four years and regular contact with their parents during the placement. The other two had experienced placements of eight years and a complete childhood respectively, during which time they had irregular and very limited contact with their parents. However, they seemed to have come to terms with their childhood experiences, having resumed contact in a manner that enabled them to appreciate and empathise with the difficulties their mothers had experienced at the time when they were fostered.

Those with poor family relationships either had long placements of seven years or more, or did not know their parents well prior to being fostered, since they had been cared for by other relatives in their country of origin. Three respondents from this group suffered abuse in their carers' homes, but this was also true of two respondents in the improving family relationship group.

Overall, it is difficult to establish which factors facilitate or impede the development of a good relationship with the birth family. Most of the cared-for described having to work at their family relationships to varying degrees and not being able to take them for granted.

The foster carers interviewed mostly described poor relationships between the children in their care and their birth parents. Some carers were supportive of parents, and this seemed to help towards building a positive relationship between the parent and child. Others were more critical of the parents, sometimes even to the children:

> 'I don't think they always portrayed my Mum in a very positive light either. I do remember once she came to visit me and she'd given me some money for ice cream and I remember the foster mother actually saying when my Mum had left, 'cos they always acted very nice and pleasant when my Mum was there, over the top you know – but I remember when my Mum left she said to me, "Oh you can't even buy yourself an ice cream with that money".'

Many foster carers seemed to be torn between on the one hand feeling that they were the real parents themselves, and wanting this confirmed through the allegiance of the child, and on the other, recognising the child's need to be loved by and to give love to the birth parents. Opportunities for the children to have regular contact with their parents seemed to help clarify these relationships and the expectations surrounding them.

### Mistreatment

A major concern over private fostering in the past and one that still remains is that, due to the lack of monitoring of placements, children within these arrangements are especially vulnerable. The Utting report described private fostering as a honey-pot for abusers (Utting, 1997). The private nature of the arrangement can mean that there is no one protecting the child's interests and that there is little redress if mistreatment occurs. Interviewees in the study were asked whether they had ever been mistreated while living with their foster carers. Four respondents revealed incidents of abuse, all perpetrated either by the carer or by a member of the carer's immediate family. There was one report of physical abuse, one of sexual abuse, one of mental and physical abuse, and one of sexual and mental abuse. In all cases, the child was under the age of 12 at the time.

In both of the cases involving sexual abuse, interviewees recounted blocking out these traumatic memories. One stated:

> 'I only came to terms with it when I was about 28, or 26, I saw a programme on sexual abuse on the television and I suddenly realised, oh hold on, because the rest of the time I just kind of blanked it out of my mind, and I realised that that was what happened to me and I became very tearful and I cried. And I began to acknowledge it for the first time. It was affecting me and stuff like that and over the years I've worked through it and I'm able to talk about it now whereas before I would never, ever have said anything about it.'

The other explained:

> 'I think probably, you know, one of the reasons why I'm so vague, there is a lot about my childhood that I just don't remember. I just do not have any memory of it at all. Yeah, yeah definitely, especially, you know, the sexual abuse, you know, you do feel ashamed of it. I know what happened, you know, and I know it happened more than once but I can't remember the detail of it. You do feel ashamed, you always feel ashamed.'

In one case of physical abuse, the child was approximately a year old. Her injuries resulted in facial disfigurement requiring plastic surgery. She recounted her mother's story, detailing the carer's refusal to allow her mother to see her when she visited. Forced to return the following week, her mother still had to insist that she see her child. She said:

> 'Mum said, no: I want to see her, I don't care if she wakes. She said when she saw me she just started screaming, what have you done to my child and she took me away. . . . I think the mentality of the visiting African wasn't what it is today where they feel they can cry foul. It was just something that happened and okay it won't happen again.'

These data support the view that children within private fostering are particularly vulnerable. Of the four respondents in this study who recounted such incidents, in only one instance was the physical abuse acknowledged by their parents. In this case it was so obvious that it could not be ignored. One of the two who suffered sexual abuse disclosed this to her parent when she was back in her care, but her mother did not believe her. The other respondent did not recall the incident until adulthood and made no mention of whether it had ever been raised with her parents.

The respondent who suffered mental and physical abuse, speaking of her parents, stated:

> 'No, I've never really told them how bad it was. When I left my carer I didn't want to go. I was like, I don't know my parents, I don't want to go and live

with them. I lost all of my friends. I still called my carer Mum and I used to ring her because my friend was still there. So they sort of thought that I really obviously loved her and I did in a funny sort of way.'

### Race and culture

An aspect of private fostering that has received a lot of attention is the trans-racial nature of most of the placements (Holman, 1973, 2002). Eleven of the twelve privately fostered interviewees, all of whom were Black, had been fostered in White British households. This issue is part of a larger debate in social care (Prevatt Goldstein, 2000). One major strand of criticism argues that children so placed will be ill-equipped to deal with the racism they will face in their lives and that their image of themselves in particular and of Black people generally will be based on the attitude of their White caretakers. Their lack of personal knowledge will mean that their carer's opinion cannot be easily refuted (Gill and Jackson, 1983; Maxime, 1986). Our interviews included several questions relating to issues of race and culture. It was often difficult to separate the data on these two, since respondents saw the issues as interchangeable.

Nine of the eleven transracially fostered interviewees described varying levels of discomfort with their own culture and community, or recounted a time when this was the case. This included feeling different from their biological siblings and others in their ethnic group and occupying an outsider position. Some felt that this difference could be identified by others and that they suffered discrimination within their own ethnic community. It is interesting that the remaining two interviewees who did not describe such discomfort had both spent time in their parents' countries of origin. However, this factor alone does not account for their lack of cultural unease, since two other respondents also had this experience.

Only one respondent stated that her friends were predominantly White. The others described times in their lives when this had been the case, but they had either made conscious choices to be in a community with other Black people, or their personal circumstances changed and their opportunities for meeting other Black people increased. A few maintained mixed groups of friends and were happy with this.

None described receiving support for their birth culture from their carers. Some spoke of subtle messages that made it uncomfortable for them to raise cultural issues. Five of them spoke of the culture shock they experienced and the adjustment they had to make on returning to their parents' home. This was often in relation to parental expectations about chores and discipline.

The perceived lack of support for their culture identified by those who had been fostered was in direct contradiction to the perceptions of the carers interviewed, most of whom thought they had made efforts to support the children's culture. However, this cultural support mostly took the practical form of hair and skin care. Despite their positive statements it was clear that often this support was minimal and sometimes ambivalent. Some carers felt that adequate cultural input could be obtained from regular visits home. Most carers had negative views of aspects of West African or Black culture (Peart *et al.*, 2005). They were keen to point out that the children they cared for are largely born in Britain and need to know British culture. Some felt they offered the best of both worlds.

All interviewees were asked questions about race, including whether they had experienced racism and how this was dealt with by their carers. Only one could not recall any racist incidents. The experiences of racism can be divided into various strands. Most spoke of their experiences of 'sticking out' as a child. Often this is because there were only a few Black children in their localities. They described attracting a lot of attention and wanting to withdraw from this. While they were often unaware of the concept of racism at the time, they nevertheless felt that many people were not nice to them. One said:

> 'I had a lot of attention focused on me because I was the only Black face in the crowd. I wasn't really comfortable with that but I learned, you sort of learn to deal with it.'

The largest category of racism was that experienced at school. This was also acknowledged by the carers, though they tended to minimise its impact and to regard it as an expression of children's changing allegiances. Only one person felt that her carer dealt with racism effectively. The majority described feelings of being misunderstood and seen as part of the problem.

They also identified racism from their carers and their carers' families. One respondent spoke of the fact that within her carers' household, Black people were referred to as 'darkies'. She said:

> 'It was only when I went back as I was older and they were talking and part of me was thinking, well don't you realise that I am sitting in the room and don't you realise that's offensive? Is that how you talked about me and my family? But you think, oh God, don't go there, don't even think about it. I just don't think I could sit there and challenge that. I thought, well they've grown up in such a different culture at that time, a very working-class English culture and to actually go into that sort of racism when you know they'd given me so much.'

Most of the group described a point of coming to the realisation that they were Black and making a conscious effort to acquire information on their specific ethnic identities and family history. They also detailed what they considered to be helpful factors that had increased their resilience, such as boxing and having a rebellious character. All described a journey of self-appreciation involving rejecting societal stereotypes.

Few carers recognised that their Black privately fostered children had experienced racist incidents. It was evident that the carers found it difficult to acknowledge or deal with the feelings of violation and hurt that their charges must have experienced. As one carer put it:

'You could say at times that you think it's racism, but then you talk to your English friends and their kids are going through the same at school. So it isn't necessarily because they're Black, it's just kids being kids, which is horrible at times isn't it?'

Song (2003) has suggested that Black and White ethnicities are qualitatively different, in that discrimination makes ethnicity a more conscious identity for Black people. She terms White ethnicity as a passive rather than an active ethnicity. Therefore, it seems obvious that the White carers specifically have to extend themselves in order to understand the impact of racism and the importance of a strong ethnic identity. Consequently, it is not surprising that the carers failed to recognise the reality of racism as experienced by those they fostered, and were unable to help them understand and deal with it.

## Conclusion

At the beginning of this chapter, we pointed out that long-term out-of-home care is not unknown in Britain. It has a long history, usually based on the argument that it is best for the children – for example, for their safety or their education. It is worth reiterating here that private fostering is essentially a childcare rather than a cultural issue. This is confirmed by the experience of interviewees in this study, who mostly accounted for their fostering in terms of their parents' circumstances and their need for childcare. However, private fostering's cultural slant means it is easy to racialise the practice. It is also worth pointing out that African children are not the only ones to be covered by private fostering regulations. In particular, there would seem to be a growing body of young teenagers (mostly White) who either leave home or are thrown out by their parents and who end up staying at the home of a friend, a relative, a neighbour or even a complete stranger (Holman, 2002; Barreau, 2004).

The people interviewed in this study who had been privately fostered detailed a number of negative experiences in their placements, yet still retained in many instances great affection for their carers. They also talked of the benefits they felt they had received. While there was a lot of ill feeling and resentment directed towards birth parents for placing them in foster care, there was also evidence of understanding and empathy towards parents and a will to work towards reconciliation.

Some interviewees gave examples of mistreatment or abuse of a sexual, emotional and physical nature, and this raises particular concerns. None of the perpetrators had reportedly been held to account for their actions, and only one of the victims had been offered any professional help and support. The potential for this degree of abuse, affecting one-third of this small sample of respondents, coupled with the lack of adequate protection or subsequent support, must be a major criticism of private fostering practice.

In terms of culture and racialised identities, the evidence suggests that many of the Black children and young people cared for within White British households experienced a degree of identity conflict. Such conflict cannot be assigned solely to their care encounter, since the discomfort identified may be present more widely in the Black population, given the pervasive influence of racism. However, it was obvious from the interviews that the care experience did not provide an environment where these issues could be explored or resolved. In addition, participants reported that they often felt conspicuous in their foster families. Many respondents in this study spoke of feeling like an outsider within their own ethnic group.

We return to the contention that transracial fostering ill-equips the cared-for to deal with racism. There is no evidence from this study that this is true; privately fostered interviewees have faced racism intimately and developed strategies for dealing with it. They have, however, done this on their own. The fact that many recognised that there were limits and restrictions in their friendships and relationships with White people implies that they actively constructed a safety zone that may be taken for granted by others.

The Utting Report recommended registration of private foster carers (Utting, 1997), which would take us back to the position of the Children Act 1948. However, this recommendation was explicitly rejected by the government (Department for Education and Skills, 1998). The need to consider the regulation of private fostering was reiterated by the Laming Inquiry into Victoria Climbié's death (Laming, 2003: 17.97), but once again registration was rejected by the government (Department for Education and Skills *et al.*, 2003). The Children Act 2004 includes the option of a registration system should its regulatory guidelines prove to be insufficient.

Registration might reduce some of the problems described by interviewees, but it is clearly no panacea. Some of the people spoken to through the course of this research have suggested that private fostering is changing, and increasingly being carried out within the birth parent's community, thus making it less likely that children will be cared for in White British households. If this is true, however, it is probable that carers and parents will be even less likely to notify the local authority of private fostering arrangements. Clearly there is a need for a better understanding to evolve of the dynamics and complexities surrounding private fostering arrangements and how these are changing over time. Only then will it be possible to consider how such arrangements can best be regulated to ensure that they promote and sustain the well-being of children whose care is provided through such arrangements.

## Acknowledgements

We should like to acknowledge the help and support of the BAAF Private Fostering Interest Group in conducting this private fostering study. More especially, we should like to thank all those who gave us their time to take part in our interviews.

# 8 Residential care

## Lessons from Europe

*Pat Petrie and Antonia Simon*

Although many children who come into public care in England spend some time in residential care, this is rarely part of their long-term placement plan and the majority stay for only a short time (Department of Health, 1998a). The opposite is true for most European countries where young people who come into care are likely to spend much longer periods living in residential homes. Despite this difference, it is probable that residential institutions will continue to play a part in provision for children in care in England for the foreseeable future. Understanding how young people live in residential care within other European countries may provide some important lessons about how better to provide for young people in residential care in England, a system which so far has proved extremely resistant to improvement (Berridge, 2002).

This chapter is about living and working with young people in residential homes, and in particular considers how well young people are prepared for life after leaving care. It draws on findings from two studies, both funded jointly by the Department for Education and Skills and the Department of Health, to be reported at length in a forthcoming book (Petrie *et al.*, 2006). The aim of the studies was to identify possible lessons for English social policy, at a time when there is serious concern about the standards to be found in residential care and about the consequences of poor practice for children in care. A major aim of the studies was to illuminate what is known as social pedagogy or the 'pedagogic' approach to looking after children and young people in group homes.

What follows is a short account of the two studies, followed by an overview of the concept and practice of social pedagogy, a recognised profession, in five countries in continental Europe. Many of the differences between the countries discussed in this chapter may be attributed to differences in policy towards out-of-home care and residential care in these countries. Two aspects of policy are seen as important: issues relating to the reasons for placing young people in residential care as opposed to foster care, and those relating to staff training and education. The Danish and, to a somewhat lesser extent, German, residential homes are staffed by members of the social pedagogy profession, while in the UK staff training and education is conducted at a much lower level than in either of the other countries.

## The studies

The first study used a qualitative approach to explore residential care policy and the part played by social pedagogy in five European countries: Denmark, France, Germany, the Netherlands and Belgium (Flanders). This study offers a theoretical understanding of 'pedagogy' as a background to the empirical work described in the rest of this chapter. A case study design, with purposive sampling, was adopted to explore in detail pedagogic policies, training and practice. Countries were selected for variations in population size and administrative structure, and because they provide particularly interesting illustrations of the pedagogic approach. For each country, a national expert wrote an overview of residential child care, occupational standards and pedagogic training. Research team members interviewed staff and students in pedagogic training centres, staff and residents in children's residential establishments, and national and regional policy-makers with responsibility for residential care and workers' training.

The second study permitted a detailed account of the experiences of young people and of residential care staff in England, Germany and Denmark, and adopted a more quantitative methodology. It evaluated the contribution of policy and practice to the well-being of children and young people in England, Denmark and Germany, and in particular the role of the pedagogic approach. The study focused on children's residential establishments: twelve in Germany, twelve in Denmark and twenty-three in England. The discrepancy in numbers of establishments arises because it was not possible to identify a sufficient number of children for the study from the rather small numbers living in each of the English homes. Interviews with heads of establishments, staff and children were conducted in the local language and, for Denmark and Germany, translated. In the European countries, in each establishment, staff with social pedagogic qualifications were interviewed: forty-nine in Germany and thirty-eight in Denmark. In England, fifty-two staff qualified in the fields of either social care or social work (Petrie *et al.*, 2005) were interviewed. Interviews focused on their practice in areas that are important for children's immediate and long-term well-being.

## Social pedagogy

In England, we do not often use the term 'pedagogy' except in formal educational contexts. Our European neighbours often apply it to a much broader set of services, covering, for example, child care and early years settings, youth work, family support services, secure units for young offenders, residential care and play work. A consideration of pedagogic policy and practice in continental Europe could help to clarify the challenges and opportunities inherent in the developing English context.

Although there is some literature on residential and foster care in different countries written in English (Gottesman, 1991; Colton and Hellinckx, 1993), comparative work has generally considered broader child protection issues (e.g. Harder and Pringle, 1997; Hetherington *et al.*, 1997; Pringle, 1998). Other literature on social pedagogy, available in English, often comes from academics with an interest in social work and social work training (Cannan *et al.*, 1992; Davies Jones, 1994; Lorenz, 1994; Crimmens, 1998; Higham, 2001) and tends to explore the extent to which the social pedagogy approach is preferable to that of social work. The work reported here focused particularly on the concept of social pedagogy and its application.

As used in continental Europe, the word 'pedagogy' relates to overall support for children's development. In pedagogy, care and education meet. To put it another way, pedagogy is about bringing up children and encompasses 'education' in the broadest sense of that word. Indeed, in French and other languages with a Latin base (such as Italian and Spanish) words like '*éducation*' convey this broader sense, and are interchangeable with notions of pedagogy as used in Germanic and Nordic countries.

Although parents are sometimes referred to as the first pedagogues, pedagogy is also a foundational concept that informs many sorts of services and provides a distinctive approach to practice, training and policy. In continental Europe, the use of the terms '*éducation*' and 'pedagogy' imply work with the *whole* child: body, mind, feelings, spirit and creativity. Crucially, the child is seen as a social being, connected to others and at the same time with his or her own distinctive experiences and knowledge.

Social pedagogy is sometimes used to mean pedagogy conducted on behalf of society, rather than the more private pedagogy performed by parents, but the term can also denote work with more vulnerable groups in society. Different countries have different emphases and use slightly different terms. In many countries there seems to be an organic pedagogic system (e.g. Petrie, 2001; Petrie *et al.*, 2002, 2006, forthcoming). The system's components consist of policy and practice, theory and research, alongside the training and education of the workforce. Thus each component of the pedagogic system feeds into, and draws from, the others. Our research identifies a number of key principles of pedagogic practice.

In the first place, pedagogy focuses on the child as a whole person. Its function is to provide support for the child's overall development. Pedagogy builds on an understanding of children's rights that is not limited to procedural matters or legislative requirements. The practitioner sees him or herself as a person in relationship with the child, not simply as a professional worker:

'Pedagogic theory is specially about relationships, child-rearing relationships.'
(Dutch academic)

'When you are holding a person in your hand, you are holding a bit of his life in your hand.'
(Principal, Danish training college)

Second, pedagogues are encouraged to reflect constantly on their practice, and to apply both theoretical understandings and self-knowledge to their work and the sometimes challenging demands with which they are confronted:

'It is a job where every day you must ask questions about yourself and your practice right to the end of your professional life.'

(French pedagogue working in a residential home)

Children and staff are seen as inhabiting the same life space, not as existing in separate hierarchical domains. Therefore, pedagogues are also practical, and their training primes them to share in many aspects of children's daily lives, such as preparing meals and snacks, or making music and building kites. Another important principle is that in group settings, children's associative life is an important resource. Workers should foster and make use of the group. There is also an emphasis on team work and on valuing the contributions of others in the task of 'bringing up' children that extends to other professionals, members of the local community and, especially, parents.

Whatever the setting – education, health, youth services, social services or nurseries – pedagogues usually work alongside other professionals and share the general aims of the establishment, while bringing their own distinctive principles, understandings and skills to bear. The work of the pedagogue is essentially personal. Students and staff interviewed often spoke of the work of the pedagogue in terms of the human person: head, hands and heart – all three being essential for the work of pedagogy. The personal, relational approach is emphasised in students' training and education, where fostering sound pedagogic values and attitudes is seen as at least as important as the acquisition of knowledge and skills. The head of a residential establishment in Flanders spelt this out in practical terms when describing how each worker in the establishment had two or three children for whom they assumed a special responsibility. He defined this not in administrative terms, but as:

'Being very interested in the child's wants, feelings, interests, thinking, fears and pleasures. On at least a weekly basis they have an individual talk with the child. It is a more intimate relationship – because otherwise the child doesn't have any relationships, or deep contacts, they just have food and care. And that is institutionalising. You could say that staff have to be able to build close relationships with children. It is not trying to replace parental relationships – you have to pay close attention and respect that.'

Pedagogic principles derive from a highly developed professional training and education, and relate to social policy that is conceived in terms of pedagogy. For example, pedagogic principles may be applied in cases where there is a particular concern for certain children such as in France, where there is a special qualification for pedagogues (*éducateurs*) working with young people in the youth justice system.

Professional pedagogic training involves the following:

- Theoretical subjects in the behavioural and social sciences.
- Skills training such as group work, working with conflict and challenging behaviour, and team work.

- Creative and practical subjects, such as art, drama, woodwork, music or gardening – media through which they can relate to children. Arts and practical subjects are also valued for their general therapeutic effect; they can help children to enjoy life and feel good about themselves.
- Optional study modules and practice placements for specific settings, such as work with disabled children or in residential care.
- Specialist options, and qualification, for work with adults (for example, in mental health settings) are available in some countries.

## Residential care in England, Denmark and Germany

We now report some of the findings from the second study, which evaluated policy and practice, including the contribution of the professional approach of the social pedagogue, to the well-being of children and young people in England, Denmark and Germany. A comparison is first made of how social policy towards residential care, as opposed to foster care, differs between countries. This is then followed by accounts of young people's own experiences of residential care, including the stability of their placement, group life, the support they received from staff and their own appraisal of living in a residential home.

### The position of residential care in social policy

As mentioned above, residential care in many European countries is often the placement of choice rather than a last resort as it tends to be in England. In both Germany and Denmark, there are more children in residential settings than in foster care, while in England, residential care is for a minority of young people, predominantly teenagers. As we discuss below, however, British social policy has always favoured fostering over residential institutions even though the supply of foster homes is frequently inadequate and an appropriate foster placement may not always be available. Furthermore, some young people are believed to be more difficult to place in foster homes than others, including older children, sibling groups, children who are members of minority ethnic groups and children presenting with particularly difficult behaviour (Utting, 1991; Waterhouse, 1997).

Table 8.1 shows the different proportions of children in residential care, compared with foster care, in the three countries. Importantly, only 12 per cent of English and Scottish children are in residential care, whereas the proportion in the other two countries is 54 to 59 per cent.

There are several reasons for this difference. First, for example, in Germany, many young people continue to use residential services –living accommodation with support from pedagogues – until well into their twenties, and, as will be discussed later on in the chapter, these young adults show up in statistics. Second, among the countries studied, residential care appeared to be used less predominantly for reasons of child protection than it was in England. Instead, it was more likely to be used to offer a positive upbringing for children who do not receive this at home; or, in the case of short-term and weekday provision (where children go

*Table 8.1* Proportions of children in residential placements in Scotland and England, Denmark and Germany

|  | National population (millions) | Young people in social care, looked after in institutions | % of all children in care |
|---|---|---|---|
| UK | 59.8 | 10,371 | 14 |
| Denmark | 5.3 | 5,907 | 54 |
| Germany | 82.2 | 82,000 | 59 |

Source: Combined figures for England, Wales, Scotland and Northern Ireland; children looked after by local authorities, year ended 31 March 2001: Regional Trends 37, National Statistics 2001 (see http://www.statistics.gov.uk/STATBASE/ssdataset.asp?vink=5950)

home at weekends), to supplement the care provided by parents. Where children are seen as not being 'brought up properly', or where they present with emotional and behavioural difficulties (including those leading to child protection orders), the relationship between the child and the staff is seen as central to upholding the main principle of the residential setting, that of providing a 'good' upbringing.

By contrast, the provision of care for looked-after children in England stems from a deliberate and sustained policy dating back to 1948 (see Chapter 2) of regarding fostering as preferable to residential care. This preference is also justified in the light of research findings. Sinclair and Gibbs (1998) found that only one-third of the homes they studied could be classified as 'good' by their criteria: two-thirds of the residents reported being miserable or unhappy in the month prior to interview and nearly two-fifths had contemplated suicide. The educational record of residential care in England is particularly poor, with three independent studies reporting that fewer than half of the residents attended mainstream schools and only a handful gained any qualifications (Berridge and Brodie, 1998; Bullock et al., 1998; Sinclair and Gibbs, 1998).

Young people looked after in residential settings in England are almost always those for whom other forms of placement have not succeeded, and as such they represent a particularly vulnerable and disadvantaged group. For example, in this study senior managers of homes in England reported much higher rates of both early pregnancy and criminal offences among young people in their care than in the other two countries (Table 8.2).

*Table 8.2* England, Germany and Denmark: the average percentage of resident young people in 2001 aged 19 or under to have been pregnant and/or to have committed offences, as a proportion of the total number of residents in 2001

|  | Average rate of pregnancies | Average number of juvenile offences per resident |
|---|---|---|
| England | 11.6% | 1.73% |
| Denmark | 3.1% | 0.16% |
| Germany | 4.6% | 0.09% |

## Staff qualifications

The higher reliance on residential care in the European countries studied also relates to staff being professionally qualified to meet the needs of the young people in their care, not just to look after their everyday care. The role of the pedagogue comes into play here.

In Germany, universities offer a diploma in social pedagogy, over at least four and a half years, leading to careers in research, teaching or management as well as work in residential establishments. The preferred qualification for employment in residential care and many other children's services is a diploma in social pedagogy, taken at colleges of higher education (*Fachhochschule*), over four and a half years. Others qualify in social pedagogy, at a lower level in specialised colleges (*Fachscule*) over the course of three years. Those who leave school with a less academic qualification study to become an *Erzieher* (or 'upbringer'). This is a lower level pedagogic training obtained over a three-year full-time course. Most staff working in residential settings are qualified either as social pedagogues or as *Erziehen*.

In Denmark, the usual qualification for working directly with children, on a daily basis, is that of the pedagogue and almost all staff working in residential care are thus qualified. Training takes three and a half years of work in a range of settings that cater for people across the life course. These include early years' services, out-of-school clubs, youth clubs and residential services. They are also prepared to work with people of all ages with disabilities, those with drug and alcohol problems, or those with criminal backgrounds. Furthermore, many foster-parents have also trained as pedagogues. Unqualified pedagogues are often young people who are working to gain experience before commencing their training.

In England, the recognised qualification for work in children's residential establishments is Level Three of the National Vocational Qualification (NVQ) in Caring for Children and Young People. This requires no prior qualification, although candidates may already have an NVQ at a lower level and some may have acquired A levels, GCSEs or degrees. NVQs are obtained on the basis of workplace-based units and/or supporting courses (often part-time). Candidates are required to demonstrate competence in critical areas related to their occupation, and judged against a national standard. Acquiring an NVQ can take up to eighteen months. New minimum standards specify that by 2005, at least 80 per cent of care staff should have NVQ 3, but despite vast investment in NVQ 3, completion rates look unlikely to meet the government target (Mainey, 2003). It is worth noting, too, that 'training' at this level has not been found to result in better practice or better outcomes for children (Whittaker et al.,1998).

Our findings accorded with these policy differences. We categorised the qualifications of all 1,007 pedagogic or care staff working in the forty-seven homes studied as high (university degree), medium (NVQ 3 or the German *Erziehet* level – although this requires longer training than the NVQ and has a higher entry point) or low, where staff had little or no formal training. England had the highest proportion of workers with no qualifications, the lowest level of educational qualifications and the most diverse range of qualifications. The main qualifications among staff were:

- English workers: 26 per cent held the NVQ Level 3.
- Danish workers: 76 per cent held a pedagogy qualification (degree level, obtained over three years).
- German workers: 57 per cent of workers held the *Erzieher* qualification (obtained over three years post-compulsory schooling), 26 per cent had obtained a pedagogy qualification, obtained over three years at degree level, in a *Fachhochschule* (higher education institution) and 6 per cent held a university diploma degree in social pedagogy at around the level of a Masters degree.

Paradoxically, it appears that although English staff work with a more dis-advantaged and therefore, perhaps, more challenging group of young people, their qualifications are lower than those of their Danish and German counterparts.

### Stability in residential care

In England, while stability for looked-after children is a government aim it is not yet realised in practice. A substantial literature refers to the short time that children spend in any care setting in England (Triseliotis *et al.*, 1995; Berridge and Brodie, 1998; Jackson and Thomas, 2000). Indeed, the overall picture of out-of-home care is one of extreme instability which is markedly worse in residential than in foster care (Jackson, 2002). Brown *et al.* (1998) reported one home where there were seventeen arrivals or departures within a single month.

The research illustrated some important differences in placement stability between the countries studied. Young people interviewed had, on average, lived in their current placement for just over eleven months in England, nearly twenty-five months in Denmark and nearly thirty-one months in Germany.

Having stable, long-term relationships is important because it is only over time that young people can gain enough information about another person (to 'learn' them, as it were), so as to know whether or not they are worthy of trust. A long-term relationship allows those concerned enough knowledge to be able to predict, to some extent, the other's likely response in a variety of circumstances.

Young people appreciate positive long-term relationships with staff and are often fully aware of what promotes these types of relationships. As a Danish young man, aged 17, remarked about staff:

'They are good. One has to come to know them, learn their language, learn to understand things. . . . You get quite a good life [here], you come to understand your life.'

A Danish 15-year-old, asked what she would tell a new resident about staff, casts some light on how staff changes can be unsettling:

'I think I would describe [them] as nice. Before . . . they were nice and helpful, now it is a strange relationship. The old ones if they were here then I would be so happy. They were genius, now the new ones are here they have a strange way of working.'

It is also evident from what the staff themselves said. A Danish staff member, answering a question about whether they had responsibility to advise young people, said:

'I think they [the young people] are very open, and often they come themselves and ask for help; especially the ones who have been here for a longer time and who feel secure and have confidence in us.'

(Denmark)

Another commented:

'They came to visit us when they knew that I and T [other member of staff] were still here. It means a lot that the old staff, with a history are (still) here.'

(Denmark)

What has emerged is a picture of English homes with fewer residents, but residents with more severe problems and a less stable placement history than their Danish and German peers. Although young people in the English establishments appear to require more qualified and stable staff than in the other two countries, in practice staff are less qualified and there are reportedly greater difficulties in recruiting suitably qualified staff and managing high staff turnover than in the other two countries.

### Living with other people

Compared to Germany and Denmark, there were, as noted above, far fewer young people in the English residential homes and at the same time a higher proportion of staff to young people. We found that the number of residents in the establishments studied ranged in England between two and twenty (mean 7.41), in Germany from four to 216 (mean 37.94) and in Denmark from fifteen to forty-six (mean 27.17).

The numbers relate to the young people living on the same site, within the same organisation, with the larger establishments dividing children into smaller separate groups. It also appears that the fewer young people accommodated, the greater the number of staff required. In England the staff/resident ratio was on average 2.09 per child (ranging from 0.78 to 4); in Germany, 0.82 (ranging from 0.40 to 1.77); and in Denmark 1.30 (ranging from 0.76 to 2).

The number of children resident who share their everyday lives has implications for the children's social life. Importantly, the pedagogic approach works with a group of children as a resource, and positive relationships between the young people are encouraged. The extent to which children feel they can trust other people, including their peers, is important for their well-being.

Young people were asked: 'If you had something on your mind or had a problem, whom would you choose to talk to about it. . . . Is there anyone else you would talk to?' It is perhaps encouraging that more than three-quarters of children in all three countries would speak to a member of staff about any problems. The English children, however, reported a more restricted circle of people in whom they could confide than the others. There are also differences in the extent to which their peer group was seen as appropriate for their confidences. Fourteen per cent of young people in England, 91 per cent in Germany and 32 per cent in Denmark said they would confide in a friend (either resident or non-resident). The finding speaks of the greater social isolation of the English young people. For example, an English girl, asked what she would tell a newly arrived child about staff, replied instead in terms of her feelings about her peers, expressing extreme mistrust of the other residents.

> 'I would say all the kids are gone in the head. I don't like them, I don't talk to kids in care, I don't trust them, I keep the door locked. Kids wouldn't come near me they wouldn't dare, they know I don't like them.'
>
> (England)

The mix of young people who find themselves in residential establishments in England creates persistent problems. Sinclair and Gibbs (1998) reported that the majority of unhappy experiences recounted by children were attributed to hostile relationships with other residents, bullying, abuse, or being drawn into self-harming or antisocial behaviour.

### Contact with families

Young people in Germany and Denmark were also more likely to confide in a family member (41 per cent and 54 per cent respectively) than those in England (27 per cent). There may be many reasons behind this difference. First, there are the differences between the populations studied and it may be that the more extreme circumstances of the English children mean that they are less willing to confide in family members. We should also consider the higher proportion of Danish pedagogues who saw themselves as responsible for liaison with families: 71 per cent compared with 51 per cent of German and 31 per cent of English staff. The importance of working with the children's parents is emphasised in the training of pedagogues and in practice. Fewer English children than others were in weekly contact with a member of their family involving at least a weekly phone call.

In England, 64 per cent of heads of homes said that families did not visit regularly (compared with 44 per cent of German heads and 17 per cent of Danish heads). In England, there seems to have been little improvement in this respect since the study by Sinclair and Gibbs (1998), which reported that the great majority of children in residential care wanted to be in frequent touch with their families (though not to live with them), but that this was achieved only for a minority.

### Education

A further sign of their greater social isolation and disadvantage was the fact that English young people were more likely to be outside of any sort of education than were their German or Danish counterparts. As well as its more formal function, education is itself a source of social relationships with adults and with peers. Sixteen per cent of English, 10 per cent of German and 1 per cent of Danish young people were not receiving any education and this was in spite of the English children being, on average, somewhat younger than the other two samples, with fewer residents aged 16 or over. Thirty-eight percent of the English children were in mainstream school compared with 29 per cent of Danes and 55 per cent of Germans. Others were educated in special units – in some case for only a few hours per week – or had visiting tutors; on-site schools were rare in England.

Not surprisingly, given that these were children with difficult histories, the majority of heads of establishment interviewed in all countries said they had some difficulties regarding the children's schooling or their progress at school (91 per cent of English heads, 83 per cent of German heads and 100 per cent Danish heads). Many heads spoke in terms of the child's disadvantaged or troubled background and their history of broken schooling. For example, all the Danish heads explained problems in these terms, while also mentioning other difficulties. This universal response seems to reflect the pedagogic practice of reflecting on all the circumstances that contribute to a young person's situation. English heads were more likely to perceive the main problem as residing in the child, often reporting that they were 'disaffected' from school (46 per cent, compared to 20 per cent of Germans and 25 per cent of Danes).

Supporting children's education is a key responsibility for pedagogues, but fewer than half of the young people in England (45 per cent) said they had spoken with a member of staff about their school attendance, compared with 60 per cent of the Germans and 74 per cent of Danish young people. Of these, the majority of Danish young people said their conversation had been very helpful (62 per cent), compared with German young people (48 per cent) and English young people (35 per cent). The differences between the three groups here, as elsewhere, correspond to the longer and more sophisticated training of the Danish pedagogues, with the English workers having the least thorough preparation for their work and the German staff falling between the two. Gallagher *et al.* (2004) draw attention to the importance of a qualified and properly supported workforce, in English residential homes, for favourable educational outcomes.

English and German heads were more likely to speak of problems with the school being unsupportive, or of systemic difficulties in the education system. For example, an English head spoke of the stigma of being a looked-after child living in a residential home, the failure of the school to draw up Personal Education Plans (PEPs) for children in care and of the low expectations that schools had for looked-after children. A German head spoke of the difficulties met in trying to find an appropriate new school for a young person, on the grounds that not all schools worked on a class teacher system while 'Kids need a relationship with a teacher.' A Danish head said that schools were not geared up for young people with behavioural and other problems.

### Health, housing and employment

In three other important areas, health, housing and employment, the English young people fared worse that those in Germany and Denmark. For example, none of the Danish heads reported any difficulties regarding the children's use of health services, compared with 78 per cent of English heads and 58 per cent of German heads who identified difficulties.

When it comes to leaving care, and preparation for independent life, young people have to be able to find housing and employment. Care leavers not in education, training or employment are at high risk of social exclusion (Jackson et al., 2002). All the heads interviewed in Germany and Denmark reported that they had policies regarding young people finding employment, compared to 75 per cent of English heads of establishment. The young people in the age group 15 to 18 were asked to say in what ways the staff had helped them with advice or practical assistance regarding employment, either in the past or for work in the future. Only 18 per cent of the English sample said they had received such help, compared to 40 per cent of the Germans and 40 per cent of the Danes. Again, this reflects the pedagogic tradition of addressing the whole person, including their future needs as well as more immediate concerns.

The heads of establishment were asked if they had any policies about supporting young people in finding independent accommodation when they turn 18 years of age. All the German and Danish heads had such policies, compared with just over half of English heads. We should also note that the Danish and German heads were more likely to be able to offer supported accommodation, sometimes linked to their establishment.

So with regard to schooling, use of health services, housing and employment, the English young people were less supported than in the other two countries. In part this related to their relationship with staff and to staff practice, and in part it related to other marginalising aspects of society. This reflects a general weakness in the English after-care system, which is beginning to be addressed by the establishment of leaving care teams within local authorities and the implementation of the Children (Leaving Care) Act 2000.

### Children's contact with the local community

Since resources are not exclusively derived from formal institutions of society, the research also considered the extent to which young people were accessing less formal community resources. The heads of establishment were asked if they considered it usual or unusual for children in their homes to take part in events and activities organised locally (these local events might include visits to local municipal leisure services, visits to religious groups, such as churches or mosques, and visits to other local residential units). The majority of heads in Germany (73 per cent) said it was usual but the majority of heads in England and Denmark considered this to be unusual (52 per cent and 67 per cent respectively). In England and Germany, the majority of the heads (74 per cent and 67 per cent) said that this was because of various difficulties with children's participation in local community events. However, the majority of Danish heads (70 per cent) did not mention any difficulties, and seemed satisfied with the level at which their children participated in the local community. This was in keeping with the finding that 36 per cent of Danish establishments had no explicit policies – or very weak ones – regarding young people's participation in the local community, compared with 32 per cent and 18 per cent respectively of those in England and Germany. At the same time, just over half of the Danish heads were in contact with local organisations, compared with 37 per cent of English and 75 per cent of German heads. So perhaps this contact was seen in Denmark as routine, rather than as a special policy. The English heads were also more likely to say that their policy was to blend in with the local community, or to keep a low profile, than heads in the other two countries (42 per cent, compared with 8 per cent in Germany and 18 per cent in Denmark – Table 8.3). This may relate to the greater stigma attached to residential care in England than in the other two countries, but it may also be related to the smaller size of the homes.

However, in answer to an open question about difficulties regarding young people's participation in local events, no heads in Denmark reported difficulties. In Germany, 29 per cent reported difficulties, and in England, 50 per cent of the heads felt either that children did not want to participate or that they felt excluded

*Table 8.3* Policies regarding contact with the community, as reported by heads of establishment

|  | England (%) | Germany (%) | Denmark (%) |
|---|---|---|---|
| No policy/weak policy | 32 | 18 | 36 |
| Staff liaison policy | 5 | 50 | 27 |
| Policy of regular communication with community organisations | 37 | 75 | 54 |
| Policy to try to blend in | 42 | 8 | 18 |
| Other policy | 11 | 17 | 0 |
| Policy to encourage children to participate in community events | 11 | 17 | 25 |
| Total number of cases | 19 | 12 | 12 |
| Missing cases | 5 | 0 | 0 |

from local community events (speaking sometimes of children's low self-esteem and lack of social skills). In England, a quarter of all heads believed that local people and organisations were unwelcoming – but no Danish or German head reported this.

That children did not take part in community events did not mean that establishments were out of touch with key agencies in the local community. Heads were asked with which agencies they were in regular contact, including the police. In England, all heads were in regular contact with the police, compared with 75 per cent of German heads and 42 per cent of Danish heads. Perhaps this speaks of the greater degree of marginalisation experienced by English children in care with respect to mainstream society.

A further illustration of this disadvantage is obtained by a consideration of children's holiday patterns. Young people were asked if they had been on holiday with anyone in the past year. As Table 8.4 shows, as many as 92 per cent of the Danish children had been on holiday with their establishment, while only 42 per cent of English and 54 per cent of German children had done so. In fact, for every category of person with whom they might have holidayed, the Danes scored higher than the other two groups while the English children consistently reported fewer opportunities for holidays with people in all the categories. A large minority of English young people (35 per cent) said they had not been on holiday at all over the past year. Note also that only 7 per cent had been away with their parents, compared with twice as many German and more than three times as many Danish young people.

The high proportion of Danish children responding that they had been on holiday with other people from their establishment speaks of the value that the Danes place on young people's collective life – although, as Table 8.4 shows, many of the Danish children had other holiday opportunities as well.

*Table 8.4* Holidays taken by young people in the past year

| Young people on holiday with | England (%) | Germany (%) | Denmark (%) |
| --- | --- | --- | --- |
| Establishment | 42 | 54 | 92 |
| Parents | 7 | 14 | 23 |
| School | 4 | 6 | 17 |
| Non-resident friends | 2 | 7 | 9 |
| Other relatives | 4 | 6 | 12 |
| Other | 9 | 29 | 20 |
| Not known | 0 | 3 | 1 |
| Not been on holiday | 35 | 14 | 0 |
| Total number of cases | 96 | 114 | 84 |

## Friends

The young people were asked about friendships with others, both within and outside the care home. Rather similar proportions of young people in each country said that they had socialised with friends outside the establishment, during the day and evening over the previous four weeks. More striking differences are to be found in the extent to which young people from outside had visited their friends in the establishment during the same period. While the three countries may have had very similar policies towards young people socialising with non-residents *outside* the establishment, when it comes to socialising with non-residents *inside* the establishment, the Danish establishments (and to some extent the Germans also) had a much more tolerant attitude than did the English establishments.

Thirty-seven per cent of young people in England, 53 per cent of young people in Germany and 59 per cent of young people in Denmark said a non-resident friend had visited them in their establishment during the day over the past four weeks. Thirty-two per cent of young people in England, 22 per cent in Germany and 48 per cent in Denmark said a non-resident friend had visited them in their establishment during the evening over the past four weeks, and 1 per cent in England, compared with 18 per cent in Germany and 29 per cent in Denmark, said a non-resident friend had stayed overnight with them in the establishment over the previous four weeks.

Staying with a friend overnight speaks of a closeness of relationship and mutual liking, and can also be a means of promoting such relationships. An invitation to stay overnight is less casually made, and may be seen as a greater indication of friendship than an invitation to visit during the day or evening. Staff policy about residents entertaining friends was not pursued in interview, but there was anecdotal evidence that the English homes, at least, viewed this as a risky procedure. In part, the finding may both relate and contribute to the relative isolation of the English children, itself connected to their greater instability of placement.

### Pedagogy and staff relationships with young people looked after

Next we turn to relationships between staff and children. Staff were asked to reflect on the last time they had provided emotional support to a young person and how they had done so.

In Table 8.5 we document the ways in which workers reported that they helped young people with their problems. This and other data illustrate a greater richness of response from the Danish compared to other staff. The table shows that 'listening' was an almost universal response for Danish pedagogues (97 per cent), closely followed by 'putting words to their feelings' (89 per cent). These are both key features of the pedagogic approach. In England, staff were less likely to conceptualise their responses to children in these terms. The most commonly reported strategy for English staff was 'discussed/talked with' the young person (74 per cent), with few English staff saying they had provided physical comfort through cuddling the young person (8 per cent) compared to 20 per cent in Germany and 32

*Table 8.5* Staff report of what they did the last time they helped a young person with problems

|  | England (%) | Germany (%) | Denmark (%) |
|---|---|---|---|
| Listened | 39 | 56 | 97 |
| Put words to their feelings | 2 | 18 | 89 |
| Discussed/talked with them | 74 | 66 | 53 |
| Cuddled them | 8 | 20 | 32 |
| Companionship (e.g. spent time with them) | 24 | 22 | 60 |
| Talked them round to do what staff thought was best | 6 | 4 | 5 |
| Gave strategies for dealing with situation | 31 | 20 | 47 |
| Made reference to rules or procedures | 8 | 0 | 5 |
| Referral to external agency | 14 | 0 | 13 |
| Other | 26 | 34 | 21 |
| Not known | 0 | 0 | 0 |
| Total number of cases | 49 | 50 | 38 |

per cent in Denmark. More Danish staff (60 per cent) answered the question in terms of spending time with the young person than did English (24 per cent) or German (22 per cent) staff. Likewise more Danish staff (47 per cent) said they gave the young person strategies for dealing with the situation, compared with nearly one-third (31 per cent) of English staff who said they had adopted this practical approach, with the German staff being still less likely to respond in this way.

These typical ways of working are borne out in other findings; for example, when asked about their responsibilities in relation to their 'key' child and what they were trying to achieve, three quarters of all respondents identified an approach that could broadly be called supportive of the child's development, including providing emotional support. Twice as many Danish as English respondents adopted this approach. In England, the most commonly reported approach for a key worker related to carrying out procedures required by law or by the local authority (60 per cent), with a somewhat lower response rate for providing emotional support (40 per cent). Twenty-five per cent of the English staff referred to short-term behaviour management as part of their role compared to 2 per cent of German and 8 per cent of Danish workers. In addition, only 23 per cent of the English sample made reference to long-term aims in relation to the child, compared to 71 per cent of Danes and 32 per cent of the Germans (see Table 8.6).

In summary, the English approach to working with children in residential care is more short term and seems less concerned with the whole child than approaches in other countries which have adopted pedagogic principles as integral to the provision of care to children living away from home.

*Table* 8.6 Staff answers to the question 'What are your responsibilities in relation to the child whom you know best/for whom you are a key worker'? *Probe for details and record verbatim.* What is your role in working with him/her? What are you trying to achieve?

| Responsibilities | England (%) | Germany (%) | Denmark (%) | All countries (%) |
|---|---|---|---|---|
| Supportive | 40 | 94 | 97 | 75 |
| Short-term behaviour management | 25 | 2 | 8 | 12 |
| Procedural approach | 60 | 4 | 5 | 25 |
| Reference to long-term aims | 23 | 32 | 71 | 40 |
| Other type of approach | 19 | 11 | 29 | 19 |
| Approach or role not known | 0 | 2 | 0 | 1 |
| | | | | |
| Total number of cases | 48 | 47 | 38 | 133 |
| Missing cases | 3 | 3 | 0 | 4 |

The differences between Germany and Denmark may reflect the more highly qualified Danish workforce. Much of the qualitative data reveal that staff in Germany and Denmark had greater professional confidence in dealing with young people. This emerges, for example, from a qualitative analysis of staff responses to the question whether they had a responsibility to give advice as to how young people lived their lives. While most staff considered it part of their work to advise young people (94 per cent English staff, 90 per cent German staff and 100 per cent Danish staff), interesting differences were found as to how they did this. For Danish and for English staff a detailed account of their reply was recorded. Some staff, around the same proportion for each country, objected to the terms in which the question had been couched, problematising the term 'advice', but the ways in which they did so were different. Some of the English staff seemed to take a more relativistic viewpoint: 'Can advise [them] if they ask, but we're not qualified to say what they should be doing' and: 'Not strictly, no. There is what's socially acceptable and what's not, but you can't live anyone's life' (England). By and large, the English workers' responses were less informed by theory than were those of Danish staff, and they seemed to have less professional security than their Danish counterparts. The Danish pedagogues' replies revealed greater confidence in their own values, and in their own relationships with the young people: 'I advise them about how they have to be as a person, that to be honest is a value for me', as the following examples of Danish responses illustrate:

'For me the examples are not that important, but the process. It is important to follow up so that they feel remembered. We have talked about hash and [substance] abuse and about the physical consequences and the impact on school work. I have said to a young person. . . . [Is] your life worth so little that you are [should be] allowed to do it [take drugs]? It is about presence, respect, it is the process that is important also in their lives.'

'We can only move things [forward] together [i.e. with child], and we can only do so when they believe in us, they dare listen to us and only then is what we say useful for them.'

'Advice as such does not have a big effect. In dialogue, you make them think a little. It helps to be in dialogue. You tell what you think and they tell what they think. [It's important] that we give space for their understanding of reality. Advice in my opinion doesn't have a big effect, whereas to be in dialogue [about something] does.'

### What the young people thought

The young people were asked whether they considered the staff had made a difference to their lives in any way. The majority of the young people said the staff had made a positive difference to their lives although this was reported by fewer English (53 per cent) than German (64 per cent) or Danish interviewees (67 per cent). The English young people were more likely to say the staff had made no difference or to offer mixed views about the impact of the staff on their personal lives than the young people in Germany or Denmark.

Several features of their responses require comment. First, the largest group of all answered in terms of their improved behaviour. Twenty-three per cent of the whole sample thought that staff had made a positive difference in this respect, with more of the English group (45 per cent) doing so than the others (Denmark 33 per cent and Germany 34 per cent). At one level this is an encouraging finding. But at another level, that improvement in behaviour should have pride of place speaks of the problematic lives of the young people concerned and something of what they see as salient in their relationship with staff.

The next largest group thought that staff had made a difference in the matter of schooling and education. Again, this tended to be lower for the English young people than for the others.

### Young people's general appraisal of staff

The interview ended with a series of questions designed to obtain the young people's appraisal of staff. Did they think staff were fun?; did they consider them reliable?; and would they confide in them? These items were grouped together for analysis. Three average scores were obtained for each country for positive, negative and mixed responses. The differences between young people from the three countries were small: for example on the positive rating, the average for England was 6.5, for Germany 6.7 and for Denmark 6.9 – with the highest possible score being 12. Perhaps the relative homogeneity of findings says something about the extent to which looked-after children are willing to speak openly, whether to praise or to be critical, about those on whom they may be most dependent.

The young people were also asked what they would tell a newcomer about the workers in their residential establishment. A selection of comments – positive, negative and mixed for each country – tells us something of how they got on with staff.

Examples of what the English young people said included statements such as:

'[They are] lovely, I love them all to bits, I think they're brilliant and trustworthy.'

(Female, age 16)

'They're generally all right but they take too long to do things, just sit out back having a fag when they could be helping us out and wonder why we get pissed off.'

(Male, age 15)

'One is nice, some act like they just come to get the money and go home, act like they care but don't.'

(Female, age 14)

Examples of what the German young people said included:

'That these understand everything, that they have already been through it, they are very sympathetic in any case.'

(Female, age not specified but approximately 12–14)

'Most of them are bastards and some not.'

(Male, age 13)

'How they can be and that they suck in some cases, e.g. if you go to bed later than it's prescribed, if you have done some rubbish [behaved badly], if they're in a bad mood.'

(Male, age 13)

Examples of what the Danish young people said included:

'They are very helpful. They cannot always help but then they refer to somebody else or ask you to wait to the following day. They are people who have surplus energy for you – which [I] have not always experienced at home.'

(Female, age 15)

'I think that they are nice sometimes. Sometimes they can be strict . . . when you do not listen to them – but it is . . . okay, because we have to listen to what they say.'

(Male, age 13)

'To sit in the living room, to be cuddled, that is also nice.'

(Male, age 12)

The content of what the English young people had to say often differed from that of the other young people. For example, the reference by a Danish young person to being cuddled has no counterpart in the answers of the English young people. Almost one-third of the Danes reported that they would cuddle a child (as one response among many), compared with 8 per cent of English staff. This is discussed at length elsewhere (Cameron, 2004) and may be related to the preoccupation in Britain with the risk of sexual abuse, or the risk of abuse allegations (Farmer and Pollock, 1998; Rickford, 2004).

Some of the quotations given above, as well as other evidence not reported here, suggest a more considered approach on the part of the Danish and, perhaps to a lesser extent, on the part of the German young people. It is as though they have in some way come to understand what pedagogy is about, and frame their answers in a more reflective mode than do the English young people. This greater deliberation may stem from many causes. We may be seeing differences in national cultures and differences arising from the greater disadvantage of the English population. But a level of difference may also result from the pedagogic approach of staff, one of whose aims is to provide role models for young people, including to encourage young people to be reflective about their lives. To be capable of standing back and thinking about one's present circumstances is a powerful resource to take into adult life.

## Conclusions

In undertaking studies of residential care in Europe, our intention was to identify lessons for English policy and practice. The aim was especially to examine the contribution of social pedagogy as the basis for staff training and practice. The findings show some of the ways in which different national policies have an impact on young people's lives and can either promote successful transitions to adult life or further undermine young people.

The English children were disadvantaged in many ways, compared to the others: there were more problems in maintaining contact with their families; staff seemed to have a less tolerant attitude towards overnight visits from their friends, and fewer of them went on holiday than their peers in other countries. They also received less support from their care-givers for schooling, for their future employment and for obtaining independent accommodation. Notably, it was more likely for bridging accommodation to be provided for the Danish and German young people, and for German and Danish young people to stay with, or remain attached to, their care establishment into adult life. By contrast the English young people, though usually less competent to live independently, often left at around age 16, making their transition to adult life far earlier and more abrupt.

A young person's developing independence and fulfilment of his or her potential are central to pedagogic work in European residential care. In England, they are core principles of the National Minimum Standards for Children's Homes, under the terms of the UK Children's Act (1989). A key outcome target within the Care Standards Act (2000) is that 'Children receive care which helps prepare them for and support them into adulthood'. Standards specifically require provision of individually appropriate personal, health, social and sex education for young residents and services aimed at developing individual identity. Arguably, the breadth of pedagogic training is uniquely placed to ensure that residential care staff are qualified to meet these objectives and the study findings support this viewpoint. Fewer of the English staff were qualified at all, and those who were qualified had for the most part received less training and education than had either German or Danish staff. In fact the Danish staff had the highest level of qualification of all three countries. These differences are often reflected in the findings, with the more highly qualified Danish workforce reporting professional behaviour and attitudes that seemed to be most supportive of children's development. The English staff often did least well, taking a more short-term approach, while the Germans, by and large, fell somewhere between these two extremes (Petrie *et al.* (2005) report more fully on this and on many other aspects of the study).

However, the findings depend not only on length and level of staff training: there is also the matter of the specific approach of the social pedagogue. There was evidence of the greater professional confidence of the social pedagogue, of their being more reflective in their approach, and of their taking a more holistic view of the young person. To take but one aspect of staff practice: whether or not they reported that they would respond to a child's problems by physically comforting them. The lack of direct human physical contact may be a great deprivation for children and young people. The willingness of the pedagogue to provide physical contact and cuddles speaks both of the professional confidence of staff themselves and of the confidence that their employers have in them. It also relates to pedagogic principles of seeing the child as a whole person, rather than the more procedural approach that was typical of English responses.

When considering the lives and prospects of young people in care in England, the broad policy picture clearly needs re-examination. Foremost is how to bring the training and qualifications of English care staff up to the level of their counterparts in many European countries, but there are other important issues to be taken into account. Especially relevant is whether it is time to look again at fostering as the preferred option for looked-after children to such an extent that residential establishments play an extremely minor part in child care, often as a last resort for young people who have severe problems.

Some of our English respondents spoke in terms of a residential service that had been 'run down' locally, a 'Cinderella' service, while at the same time being very expensive. A question arising from the study is: What should be the relative proportions of residential and foster placements? Some might suggest that the ideal position would be for all children to be looked after in family settings, and none cared for in residential units. But the number of foster placements is insufficient and cannot, at least in their present form, meet the needs of all children. So, how can a policy be developed that avoids the concentration of children with severe problems within the residential system? This has been shown to be detrimental to themselves, other young people and staff, and carries a heightened risk of stigmatising people brought up in children's homes. There have been good reasons in the past to distrust residential care, but perhaps there are equally good reasons to question its position as a residual service for difficult-to-place young people. A better way forward may be to develop its potential strengths. By living collectively and alongside properly trained adults, children learn, not least, to get along with other people. The pedagogic model of viewing the children's group as itself a resource may point a way forward to a more hopeful future for residential care in Britain.

## Acknowledgements

The authors would like to thank our research colleagues in continental Europe: Professor Marie Bie and Filip Coussée at the University of Ghent; Professors J. Van der Ploeg and E. Scholte, University of Leiden; Professor Dr Herbert Colla, Dr Thomas Gabriel, Rouven Meier, Tim Tausendfreund, Michael Tetzer, at the University of Lüneburg; Professor Alain Bony, CNEFEI Suresnes; M. Guy Dréano, formerly of BUC Resources; Jytte Juul Jensen, Jydsk Paedagog Seminarium, Århus, and Inge Danielsen at the Copenhagen Paedagog Seminarium. Thanks also go to all members of the research team at the Thomas Coram Research Unit: Janet Boddy, Claire Cameron, Ellen Heptinstall, Susan McQuail and Valerie Wigfall. Not least, we wish to thank Sharon Lawson for her supportive role as Project Administrator.

# 9 Advocacy

## Giving young people a voice

*Christine Oliver*

Over the course of the past two decades, children's advocacy has moved from the periphery to centre stage in the field of children's social care. This development has been supported by changes in legislation including the 1989 Children Act and the 2002 Adoption and Children Act, and social policy (Department of Health, 1998e; Children and Young People's Unit, 2001; Department of Health, 2002) which, while establishing children's welfare as the central principle in decision-making, also opened a door to greater acceptance of the value and desirability of involving children and young people in decisions about their care. Within this changing political climate, advocacy has emerged as one of a number of means to assist children in voicing their opinions and needs to social care professionals and to make service providers more accountable to them (Oliver, 2003b). Thus, advocacy may be described as operating at the interface between children's services and young service users.

This chapter focuses on one particular theme: the extent to which advocacy functions as a touchstone for highlighting tensions in policy and practice between notions of 'children's welfare' and 'children's rights'. The usefulness of this theme as a means of understanding factors that have contributed to the development of advocacy services for children and young people, and the nature of some of the subsequent debates and dilemmas in advocacy practice, is also explored. It is argued that children's welfare and children's rights are not necessarily diametrically opposed concepts and that, indeed, advocacy may have a key role to play in fostering their integration, to the greater benefit of looked-after children and children in need.

The chapter begins with an exploration of the historical roots of advocacy, most notably in recent public investigations into the abuse of looked-after children, and changes in legislation and social policy concerning children's welfare and children's rights. This is followed by an investigation of common understandings of advocacy, including those of children and young people. Subsequently, key issues in advocacy practice are addressed, particularly in relation to debates concerning children's capacity to engage in decisions about their care, tensions between children's rights and parental rights, and children's rights to confidentiality. Next, the effectiveness of advocacy is explored, and factors that enhance or inhibit children's involvement in decision-making are identified. Finally, the future of advocacy for children and young people is discussed, and possible avenues for further progress identified.

## Background

Several authors (e.g. Franklin, 1995; Willow, 1996) have charted the rise of children's advocacy services. A key turning point has been identified as the appointment of the first children's rights officer for Leicestershire Council in 1987. Subsequently, Advice, Advocacy and Representation Services for Young People (ASC), which was established in 1992, and Independent Representation for Children in Need (IRCHIN) reflected a growing acknowledgement that young people needed independent representation in order to ensure their views were heard. The National Youth Advocacy Service (NYAS), a socio-legal agency that was set up in 1998, incorporated the former ASC and IRCHIN. During the 1990s, the number of advocacy services delivered by local authorities and national or local children's charities increased. This development was given particular impetus by the funding made available under the *Quality Protects* initiative (Department of Health, 1998e) which, while not mentioning advocacy specifically, sought to improve the 'life chances' of looked-after children and to enhance children's involvement in decisions about their care. By 2000, it was estimated that half (n=74) of all local authorities in England provided a children's advocacy service (Kemmis, 2000).

The majority of children's advocacy services are provided by the children's charities such as the Children's Society, Barnardos, NSPCC, NCH and National Youth Advocacy Service (NYAS), and a small number of local or regional charities. A minority of advocacy services are delivered directly by local authorities to young people in their care. While most advocacy services work specifically with looked-after children and young people, a smaller number aim to respond to the needs of children with disabilities, children involved in child protection processes, and young people in secure settings, including psychiatric and juvenile justice units.

## Welfare and rights in policy and legislation

While advocacy is commonly understood as one of a number of different approaches to fostering children's participation that is unequivocally children's rights-oriented, less attention has been given to the ways in which notions of children's rights *and* children's welfare have both contributed to the development of children's advocacy services. The 1989 Children Act, for example, enshrined the child's welfare as the central principle in decision-making but also established the rights of children to be consulted on their needs and wishes. In 1991, the UK government ratified the UN Declaration on the Rights of the Child. Article 12 of the Declaration is widely cited as providing support for children's rights to participation in decisions about matters that concern them. Other Articles in the Declaration highlight what may be termed children's 'welfare rights', such as their rights to safety, play, education and health care.

However, while children's rights may be understood as including legal and moral or universal rights, their enforcement has often proved difficult. For example, the duty placed on local authorities under the 1989 Children Act to initiate transparent complaints procedures should, in theory, provide means for looked-after children to have a disagreement with their corporate parent, to challenge decisions made about their care, and to make local authorities more accountable to them. In practice, however, complaints procedures have been widely criticised for being adult-oriented, inaccessible, lacking in confidentiality and difficult to negotiate without the support of an advocate (Utting, 1997; Aiers and Kettle, 1998). In this respect, Boylan and Boylan (1998) argue that advocacy represents an important means of turning children's theoretical rights to participation into a reality. The potential for advocacy to assist in this process has recently been enhanced by the Adoption and Children Act 2002 which, for the first time, placed a statutory duty on local authorities to provide advocacy for children wishing to make a complaint under the 1989 Children Act regulations.

Looked-after children's need for independent advocacy to protect their welfare and their rights was also acknowledged by Utting (1997), who drew a direct link between the stigmatising of looked-after children, the denial of their rights to participation and their vulnerability to abuse. He commented that 'looking after them [young people] would be easier and much more effective if we really heard and understood what they have to tell us' (Department of Health, 1998a: 102). Following the North Wales Tribunal, which investigated allegations of child abuse in children's homes, Taylor (2000) also concluded that looked-after children had a right to independent advocacy. Notions of children's welfare and their rights might therefore be interpreted as closely related, rather than separate and polarised concepts.

However, while advocacy may assist in enforcing children's rights, a further issue concerns the tension between children's right to participation, and their perceived capacity to exercise that right. Article 12 of the 1989 UN Declaration of the Rights of the Child, for example, implies that capacity is directly linked to age and maturity, and therefore leaves considerable scope for interpretation:

> States Parties shall assure to the child who is *capable* of forming his or her own views the right to express those views freely in all matters affecting the child, the views of the child being given due weight in accordance with the age and maturity of the child.
>
> (UN General Assembly 1989: Article 12; emphasis added)

A similar tension is reflected in the 1989 Children Act, which established a child's right to participation in decisions regarding their care as age-related; generally, more weight is given to the opinions of children aged over eight years. The 1995 Children (Scotland) Act considers children aged 12 years and above as competent to consider various options, and to form an opinion (Gallagher and Cleland, 1996).

A young person in public care may also encounter circumstances where his or her views and wishes differ from those of parents or carers. To some extent, the ambivalence that young people may feel in these circumstances is reflected in social policy, where the rights of children stand in an ambiguous relationship to the rights of parents. Piper (1998), for example, has drawn attention to the twin and contradictory trend in the greater acceptance of consulting children about their care, and a parallel emphasis on parental rights and authority. This tension is echoed in the recent launch of *Learning to Listen* (Children and Young People's Unit, 2001), which recommended that:

> The action departments take needs to reflect the age of the children, their maturity and understanding, and the extent to which their parents and carers will also be involved.
>
> (Children and Young People's Unit, 2001: 5)

Children's advocacy has therefore developed against a backdrop of competing discourses concerned, on the one hand, with children's rights to participation, and, on the other, with their welfare. In giving a voice to children and young people, advocacy may be interpreted as aiming to foster children's autonomy in relation to decision-making, particularly in relation to parental rights, including those of corporate parents.

## What is advocacy?

At its simplest, advocacy is most commonly defined in the literature as a process of enabling children and young people to 'have a voice' in matters of concern to them (Dalrymple and Hough, 1995). For looked-after young people, the kinds of decision-making in question might be broadly categorised as including 'life decisions' (concerning their living arrangements or choice of school, for example) and 'everyday' decisions (concerning their choice of friends, diet or clothes, for example).

While having a voice may at first glance appear to be an uncomplicated definition of advocacy, further exploration reveals its more profound implications. Speaking up or having a voice is described in the literature as of both literal and symbolic significance for those groups in society, including looked-after children and disabled children, that have been devalued and in other ways silenced (Gray and Jackson, 2002). According to Atkinson (1999), advocacy allows 'the person behind the label to be seen' and fosters a sense of social inclusion among those who may otherwise feel marginalised in society. This assertion may be expected to have particular resonance for children in public care, many of whom describe their experience of the care system as coinciding with a loss of individuality and respect.

Advocacy therefore draws within its orbit a complex web of themes and questions concerning power and powerlessness, the nature of adult–child relations, and the relationship between adult service providers and young users of care services. It is argued that advocacy is needed because children and young people, as social groups and as individuals, are silenced by adults in more powerful positions in society. Dalrymple and Hough, for example, state that children need advocacy because they form a relatively powerless group: 'Powerlessness and denial of rights are . . . crucial elements in identifying the need for advocacy' (1995: viii).

Advocacy may therefore be understood as a resolutely rights-oriented approach to participation that speaks to issues of social inequality and discrimination experienced by children as individuals, and as a social group. In this respect, the role of the advocate may be understood as one of balancing the scales towards a more just distribution of power between adults and children in decision-making arenas. Advocates aim to achieve this by acting firmly on the side of the service user (Herbert and Mould, 1992) and acting as far as possible as neutral conduits for voicing children's and young people's opinions (ASC, 1994). In theory – notwithstanding their adult status – advocates attempt to assist children to put forward their views, uncontaminated by adult interpretation.

This role may be described as distinctively different from that of other social care professionals, such as social workers, who may be expected to listen to the child in order to arrive at an interpretation of his or her 'best interests'. By contrast, advocacy is generally understood as resolutely eschewing involvement in deciding what might be in the 'best interests' of the child. Advice, Advocacy and Representation Services for Children (ASC), for example, describes the role of the independent advocate as:

> enabling and supporting young people to put forward their own views and opinions. . . . This means working from the young person's perspective, without the constraints of the concept of 'best interests', unlike social work practitioners or guardians *ad litem*.
> (quoted in Boylan and Boylan, 1998: 44)

However, it should not be assumed that in refusing to be involved in decisions about what might constitute the 'best interests' of the child, advocacy has no bearing on children's welfare. It is regrettable that less emphasis is given in the literature to the potential for advocacy to enable looked-after children to gain access to needed services, and thus to enhance their welfare. In this respect, Melton's (1987: 357–358) comprehensive definition of advocacy provides a useful corrective, combining both the 'rights' and 'welfare' aspects of advocacy:

> Child advocates endeavour to raise the status of children and increase the responsiveness and accountability of institutions affecting them. Advocacy consists of social action on behalf of children whether to increase their self-determination or to enhance the social, educational, and medical resources to which they are entitled.

## Children's perspectives

It is to be expected that, as a relatively new arrival on the scene of children's social care, many children and young people are likely to be confused about the exact meaning of advocacy until they come into contact with it. Consequently, their knowledge about advocacy may be described as largely experiential. Evidence shows that confusion about the meaning of advocacy among young people is common (South Glamorgan Advocacy Unit, 1994) and that some young people might initially confuse the role of advocate with that of social worker:

> 'My first thoughts of an advocate was that they were very similar to social workers, devil's spawn air heads.'
>
> (Voice for the Child in Care, 1998 : 74)

However, a review of young people's perceptions of advocacy highlighted a broadly consistent definition of advocacy among young people which included 'speaking up for someone, understanding, talking, making other people listen and consider their views. It was frequently described as helping, and the words "important" and "powerful" were used often' (Children's Commissioner for Wales, 2003). This confirms the findings of earlier research among looked-after young people who expressed the need for a 'powerful adult' to help them voice their frustration with their lack of involvement in care planning and decision-making, lack of information and dissatisfaction with the availability of after-care support (Boylan and Boylan, 1998). Some evidence suggests that, once young people have experienced advocacy, they have an instinctive grasp of its main purposes, namely to support them in putting their views across (Patel, 1995) and to understand their rights (Boylan and Wyllie, 1999). Of particular importance is the expectation that advocates will use young people's language to communicate their views (Wyllie, 1999; Noon, 2000).

## Advocacy in practice

As we have seen, legislation and social policy tend to reflect and reinforce a conceptualisation of childhood as a stage in the life cycle in which emotional and cognitive capacities are developing but immature and that, therefore, children's 'fitness' to be involved in decision-making is open to interpretation. The emphasis given to working in partnership with parents may also be expected to enhance the likelihood of conflicts of interest emerging between young people and their parents or carers, and disputes about how their welfare and their rights might be protected. Conceptualisations of the child in social policy and of their position within the family both contribute to the ambivalent status of children in debates concerning their right to confidentiality.

## Welfare/rights

Is it possible to secure children's welfare without respecting children's rights? Is welfare not a right? It would appear that, as a result of working with children of different ages, abilities and family circumstances, advocates are frequently engaged in ethical dilemmas that partly result from tensions between notions of children's welfare and children's rights.

Garner and Sandow (1995: 21) suggest that the tension between welfare and rights has its origins in differing notions of protection:

> The dilemma here is for parents, teachers and legislators: should we lower the age at which we begin to listen to children's views and allow them rights, even at the cost of exposing them to external dangers and the risk of failure, or raise it in order to protect them as long as possible?

Dalrymple (2001) argues that a needs-focused approach to children is unlikely to support them in claiming a right to advocacy. However, others have argued against such a polarity between rights and needs (Hill and Tisdall, 1997). Timms argues that determining the 'best interests' of the child relies to a large extent on subjective interpretations, and that such a model may actually produce a more punitive form of care than one based on a children's rights perspective. She claims that 'there are clear illustrations, not of the mutual exclusivity of rights and welfare but of how rights can regulate and inform welfare':

> This is based on the belief endorsed by the experience of the National Youth Advocacy Service that a clear working knowledge of the rights of children and young people can act as a necessary corrective to imprecise definitions of best interest. . . . Independent and effective representation is the mechanism through which a healthy synthesis of rights and welfare may be achieved.
>
> (Timms, 2001: 151)

## Rights and capacity

Some advocates have questioned the view that children's capacities are strictly age-related. Garner and Sandow (1995), for example, point out that young people are accorded different rights at different ages: they have the right to marry at 16 years, to join the armed forces at 17 years and to vote at 18 years. The Gillick Ruling in 1986 also established the right of young people under the age of 16 to seek medical advice without parental consent, provided they are of sufficient maturity to understand the advice given. The linking of age with capacity is not therefore without its contradictions.

The literature indicates that children's advocates are more likely to conceptualise barriers to children's participation as social and structural, rather than simply age-related. Gray and Jackson (2002) argue that a right to a voice throughout history has been 'bestowed according to the fluctuating perceptions of an individual's ability to benefit from that right' (p. 7). Given that there is a degree of arbitrariness involved in determining the age at which children are considered capable of engaging in decision-making, the question arises: Who decides on a child's capacities? To some extent this question is side-stepped by advocates who take the view that children have a right to express their views, whatever their age or disability:

> The significance of advocacy lies in the recognition that a person's own skills may not include the ability to speak for him or herself, for intellectual, social, emotional, developmental or physical reasons. The recognition of an individual's right to a hearing despite any or all of these difficulties places advocacy within the context of human rights.
>
> (Garner and Sandow, 1995: 1)

What are the implications of this stance for the practice of children's advocacy? It is argued that children may be enabled to participate if advocates and other professionals develop their own communication skills and attempt to make decision-making arenas and processes more child-friendly (Boylan and Wyllie, 1999). It is, perhaps, a result of a child-centred way of working that advocacy has become sensitised to different levels of maturity and capacity among a variety of individual children that cannot be simply attributed to the chronological age of the child. Good practice in advocacy is concerned with ensuring that the advocate takes into account the communication needs of the individual child by, for example, exploring a situation from the child's perspective, proceeding if and as he or she wishes to do so, by supporting the child in decision-making fora, and by maximising the child's capacity to communicate his or her wishes and feelings by considering the use of letters, tapes, drawings or any other medium selected by the child (Boylan and Wyllie, 1999).

For children with disabilities it is advertised that sufficient efforts should be made to determine their needs and wishes, for example, through interpreting non-verbal signs of what they want, before communicating them to other parties (Advocacy 2000, 2000). However, ASC (1994) warns that, while advocates should take steps to improve their communication skills and use a variety of different methods to communicate with disabled children, including techniques to facilitate non-verbal communication, they should be aware of their limitations, and not become involved in important decisions if they have not been able to ascertain the child's view.

Some pioneering work has already been achieved in enhancing the participation of disabled children in decision-making through advocacy (Greene, 1999), and via the use of innovative research methods to explore disabled children's views and perceptions about their care (Morris, 1998; Russell, 1998; Ward, 1998). These studies have shown that disabled children's participation in decision-making can be facilitated through a variety of methods, including the use of visual images, signs, interpreters, a variety of support aids and equipment, and by enlisting the support of a known and trusted person. In circumstances where children and adults have high support needs, sounds, facial expressions, body language and silences provide important clues to ascertaining their wishes (Foundation for People with Learning Disabilities, 2000). The literature on advocacy for adults with disabilities is also relevant in this regard. Scott and Larcher (2002), for example, advise that, in order to work effectively with people with communication difficulties, advocates need to know about different types and degrees of communication difficulty, and the effect this may have on the individual.

### Children's rights vs. parents' rights

In the history of the movement for women's equality, debates have often focused on the consequences of social and legal equality for women's traditional role in the family as wives and mothers. Similarly, debates about children's rights are often informed by their status in the family, in which children are not infrequently socially constructed as possessions of their parents (Eekelaar and Dingwall, 1990). In this context, it is hardly surprising that parents are assumed to be their child's best advocate. Indeed, it is argued that advocacy services have developed with an emphasis on the needs of looked-after children precisely because they have been separated from their parents, their 'natural' advocates (Herbert and Mould, 1992). How then might advocates intervene in family life to support children's rights to express their views and wishes, without undermining parents' rights?

In this context, a key issue for advocacy practice with looked-after children concerns the negotiation of potential conflicts of interest between young people, parents and carers. The literature tends to focus on children who have contact with children's services, but continue to live in the parental home, such as some disabled children, or children involved in child protection processes. With respect to advocacy for disabled children, Russell (1989) explored the impact on parents when a young disabled person is involved in self-advocacy and concluded that the transitional needs of parents should also be supported if self-advocacy with disabled children is to be effective. She also states that agencies must work together with young disabled people and their parents to agree common objectives and complementary roles rather than working solely in partnership with parents.

Pike (2002) argues that advocacy for children with learning difficulties and their families is the neglected dimension of family support. It is claimed that, given the plethora of uncoordinated services, it is understandable for parents of disabled children to perceive themselves as experts in their children's care, and as their child's best advocate, but that difficulties arise when the needs of parents and the needs of the child are not separated. Pike recommends that, before developing a separate children's advocacy scheme, a coherent system of parental support be in place.

In relation to child protection processes, the literature indicates that children may be expected to encounter differences of opinion concerning the weight given to their views and wishes, as compared with those of their parents. The evidence suggests that few children or young people involved in child protection processes have access to advocacy and, indeed, that there is a considerable degree of ambivalence on the part of health and social care professionals concerning its appropriateness. In particular, it has been noted that while considerable effort has been made in recent years to include parents in child protection procedures (Scutt and Hoyland, 1995; Lindley and Richards, 2002), greater ambivalence has been expressed about children's participation.

Boylan and Wyllie (1999) have argued that advocacy can represent a challenge to the child protection system, to assumptions about children's capacities and rights, and to assumptions concerning the rights and roles of parents. Nevertheless, they state that promoting partnerships between young people, advocates, parents and social workers can achieve positive outcomes for children. In order to achieve this, they argue that the child protection system must become more child-centred and less concerned with fitting children into adult-oriented structures and procedures. In their evaluation of one advocacy service for children involved in child protection processes, the authors found that advocates relied on social work staff for referrals, and that often social workers would contact parents, rather than children directly, to discuss the child's advocacy needs.

### Confidentiality

Children's right to confidentiality highlights the ethical dilemmas and debates involved in protecting children's rights *and* their welfare. It is common practice in social and health care that confidentiality should be maintained unless information is disclosed to indicate that the client or a third party is at risk of significant harm, or if the client agrees to disclosure. However, research indicates that children's fear of the consequences of talking to an adult and their mistrust of adults generally has been cited as a barrier to providing more effective support and enhancing their protection from abuse (Butler and Williamson, 1994). Young people in this same study complained that they mistrusted adults, particularly in the care system where breaches of confidentiality and lack of privacy were described as commonplace. Consequently, some advocates have expressed the view that they should be in a position to offer complete confidentiality. By contrast, many Social Services departments that fund external advocacy services might be expected to contest such a view.

A discussion of confidentiality between two directors of Social Services illustrates this dilemma (Douglas and Obang, 2001). Obang argues that 'the function of the advocate as a proxy for the voice of the child does not, however, negate a role shared by all other professionals – the ultimate protection of the child' (p. 44). Douglas, however, claims that: 'while young people will sometimes talk of abuse they have suffered, or offences they have committed, the key role for an advocate is to get alongside a young person and help them to make their own decisions'. He acknowledges that advocates play a supportive role, but that they also have a duty of care: 'overriding confidentiality may be justified only if either the young person or other vulnerable people would be placed at great risk by the advocate remaining silent' (p. 44).

*Young people's perspectives*

Knowledge about young people's opinions on these debates is growing apace. A recent consultation exercise with young people (not all of whom were looked after) concerning the relationship between advocacy and making complaints identified young people's perspectives on the 'rules' which advocates should abide by (National Care Standards Commission, 2003). These were summarised as an ability to advise children on their rights; to provide information; to listen to the child and not 'butt in'; to offer advice only when asked, and to let the child make his or her own decision. It was also felt that the advocate should keep everything confidential.

Young people identified an advocate as 'just someone to talk to who's not friend or family', 'quiet people who listen'; and someone who avoids offering 'false hope of action' (pp. 9–10). They also felt that young people should be involved in the selection of advocates because 'you have to trust the advocate' and 'have faith you will be treated seriously'. Young people also reported that advocates should be sufficiently well qualified to represent children, particularly in relation to legal proceedings: they should be 'hard tested' and tested repeatedly to ensure their skills and knowledge were kept up to date. It was also important that advocates adopted a neutral position (rather than bringing in their own concerns: they 'mustn't tell their own story or cry on the young person's shoulder' (National Care Standards Commission, 2003: 9–10). It would appear that the most recent investigations of advocacy for children and young people are beginning to explore young people's perspectives and that this may add a further dimension to the competing discourses on children's welfare and children's rights.

## Effectiveness of advocacy

How successful might children's advocacy be in helping to form a bridge between notions of children's welfare and children's rights? Two key sets of factors can function as barriers or facilitators to the integration of children's welfare and children's rights: the attitudinal and the economic.

*Professional resistance*

A strategy that focuses upon achieving a balance or synthesis between welfare and rights, by allowing children to 'have a voice', assumes the willingness of adults to listen and, even more importantly, to act. Indeed, given adult control of resources and decision-making procedures, the impact of advocacy must rely to some extent on adult benevolence:

> Advocacy can change the dynamics of a meeting, and can swing things in the child's favour. But it doesn't always work, and when it doesn't you end up sharing the child's powerlessness.
>
> (quoted in Atkinson, 1999: 36)

Boylan and Boylan (1998) claim that some care professionals welcome and encourage advocacy, but that others tend to perceive advocates as creating problems where none previously existed. They identify resistance to advocacy as a symptom of professional expectations of children's compliance and a lack of regard for children's rights. Indeed, some might perceive professional resistance as a sign that advocacy is in fact having an impact on the way children's services engage with looked-after children and young people. Atkinson (1999: 27), for example, views professional resistance as a natural corollary of advocacy's independence:

> Advocacy must be, and be seen to be, independent of services. Ironically, the more separate and independent it is, the most likely advocates are to encounter resistance from services, and to experience the reality of institutional barriers.

Other studies suggest that despite initial professional resistance to advocacy, over time, this can be reduced. A study of advocacy in Scotland (including advocacy for children and young people) found that professional resistance was common during the early stages, but that those involved in advocacy schemes eventually developed a more productive working partnership with staff and the managers of services (Lindsay, 1997). This suggests that positive partnerships between advocacy schemes and children's services are indeed achievable.

However, the same study concluded that, in a minority of cases, the provision of independent advocacy functioned as a cause of continuing tensions between care staff and advocates. In these circumstances, attitudes to participation varied according to the interest and commitment of unit managers and those of staff. Training programmes were identified as an effective way of persuading staff teams of the benefits of greater user involvement. This important finding suggests that, for advocacy to be effective, the goodwill of individuals at senior levels is important, but that attitudes to children's participation among staff teams are also significant. This may mean that there is a relationship between receptivity to advocacy and organisational cultures. Boylan *et al.* (2000) suggest involving looked-after children in the training of social care professionals as an important means of improving staff attitudes, and therefore care services.

### Market economy of care services

Regardless of the diversity of perspectives on children's welfare and their rights, evidence indicates that the market economy of care services can block progress in achieving either. Boylan *et al.* (2000) claim that because the role of social workers is now focused on assessing needs and devising packages of care, they are increasingly only able to offer what is available, rather than what is needed. Morris (2000) concluded that decisions concerning disabled children's care are often service-led and constrained by local authority budgets, regardless of the child's expressed needs and wishes. Indeed, evidence suggests that some social workers would like to be more responsive to children and young people, but that limited resources constrain their capacity to act. Some social workers in this position turn to advocacy services as a means of enlisting an independent agency to assist children in enforcing their rights and gaining access to needed services. Timms (2001), for example, notes that since the National Youth Advocacy Service (NYAS) was set up in 1998, over 3,000 cases of bad practice were referred, approximately one-third of which were referred by social workers who felt unable to advocate on their client's behalf.

## Empowering children and young people

In light of the limited research undertaken on advocacy, it is perhaps not surprising that advocacy outcomes have not been documented in a systematic way. Nevertheless, there are encouraging signs that advocacy can have a positive impact on the welfare and rights of children and young people. Advocacy's focus on the individual child and his or her circumstances could therefore have an important ameliorating effect on the widespread tendency to view children in public care as a homogenous group. One advocate reported that:

> Advocacy has a significant role, and one that has status, especially in review meetings. . . . The advocate can support the child's wishes and help them take a stand and can see their point of view instead of labelling them or blaming them, as even social workers are wont to do.
>
> (Quoted in Atkinson, 1999: 36)

It has been claimed that, to be effective, advocacy needs to operate at two levels: the emotional and the instrumental (Lee-Foster and Moorhead, 1996). Willow (1996) has argued that participation in decision-making can contribute to enhanced coping and decision-making skills, and lower levels of psychological problems among looked-after children. As far as 'hard' outcomes are concerned, advocacy may be expected to have an impact on placement choice, or access to education services for care leavers, for example:

> Having an advocate can be incredibly important to a young person. Your presence can help a lot in reviews. Sometimes social workers change their mind before a review if they know that an advocate is going to be there.
>
> (Quoted in Atkinson, 1999: 36)

Research also suggests that advocacy can have a positive impact, even if desired outcomes are not achieved. A study by Simons (1995), for example, found that of twenty-three people who had used advocacy schemes (age unspecified), all were positive about the experience, even though they did not always achieve the outcome they wanted. Moreover, none of those benefiting from the support of an advocate abandoned their complaint before the end of the procedure. It may therefore be the process, as much as the outcome of advocacy, that empowers young people:

'I think advocacy is really important. I had no one, no family, nowhere to run to. I came here as a refugee, with just my brother and sister. Every child should know about advocacy. It's really important to have someone to talk to, someone who is independent, outside of social services, someone who is there for you. I also know what it's about: having a choice, having a say in moving or staying put, and having someone to talk to.'

(Voice for the Child in Care, quoted in Atkinson, 1999: 38)

There is also evidence to suggest that advocacy can play an important, if not the only, part in changing organisational cultures. The Chailey Heritage Centre, for example, has adopted a multi-modal approach to giving young people a voice. The centre has introduced a children's charter, good practice guidelines, a young person's group and an independent advocacy scheme (Marchant, 1998). These different components might be expected to mutually reinforce and encourage a culture of listening to children and young people. However, less is known about the extent to which advocacy services have a positive impact on organisational cultures in larger systems, such as local authorities. Early indications suggest that many advocates are frustrated that more local authorities do not use advocacy as a form of performance audit on the quality of their services for looked-after children and children in need.

## Conclusions and signposts for the future

The history of the care of children and young people who, for whatever reason, could not be cared for by their birth parents offers a cautionary tale of the damage that can be done in the name of welfare. As shown in Chapter 2, in each period in history, care provided by the state and charitable organisations has been founded on notions of what is most commonly considered beneficial or appropriate for a child or young person of a particular age or social background. In retrospect, such notions, which may appear to be based on common sense, have been shown to represent historically and socially distinctive constructions of children, and of childhood. To take a critical view of contemporary developments in the care of looked-after children is therefore important, and yet difficult to achieve. Contemporary providers of care, and commentators on it, form part of the social and cultural value system which influences how children and young people are cared for in the present, and it is not always easy to identify and then to reflect critically upon the norms that underpin such care systems. It may be that the recent emergence of advocacy signifies an urgent need to re-examine contemporary notions of children's 'welfare' and children's 'rights', and that advocacy affords a means of creating a bridge between these two concepts.

Despite the lack of rigorous or extensive research on advocacy for children and young people in public care, there are early indications that advocacy can have a positive impact on enabling young people to participate in decisions about their care. More generally, advocacy serves to underline the importance of listening to children and young people about their views and wishes as of right, but also as a means of achieving both stability and quality of care for looked-after children and children in need. However, in terms of its own development, advocacy would appear to be at a turning point. The 2002 Adoption and Children Act legally recognises advocacy for children and young people and therefore may raise its status and profile. On the other hand, the Act may lead to the narrowing of the focus of advocacy towards complaints procedures at the expense of more common but no less important concerns raised by looked-after children and young people. Such a development would be regrettable, since there are strong indications that, by standing by young people, advocates can encourage social care professionals to look again at their decisions, to take young people's views more seriously and to reflect more closely on the relationship between children's welfare and children's rights.

## Acknowledgements

I would like to thank the Department of Health for funding the original review of advocacy services. I would also like to express my thanks for the helpful comments and suggestions made by colleagues Peter Aggleton and June Statham. The advice and support offered by the editors and other contributors to this book were also appreciated.

# 10 Promoting young people's participation in research

*Valerie Wigfall and Claire Cameron*

## Introduction

Conducting research with children and young people in and after care raises a number of methodological problems. The population is relatively small, and is dispersed, stigmatised and excluded in many ways. This chapter starts from the premise that existing studies may offer only partial evidence and insights about this group of young people. The reasons for this stem from the practical challenges in conducting research in this field, not least the complexities of gaining access to children and young people who are eligible to participate. These factors ultimately can have implications for the kinds of research conducted, the size of the sample of young people included and the extent to which their lives and experiences are typical or representative of children and young people within or leaving the care system.

On the other hand, policy-makers rely increasingly upon the evidence drawn from such research, despite its limitations, to support both policy and practice decisions. Since the introduction of the modernisation agenda for the public sector in the UK, social work services are required to base practice on 'the best evidence of what works' (Department of Health 1998b: 93). While the need to strengthen evidence-based research with children in and leaving care has contributed to the drive for 'hard' quantitative information in the form of statistics and monitoring data, there has also been a parallel push for more qualitative research. This is coupled with a growing recognition that children and young people have a right to be consulted, and their voices should be listened to and acted upon. For research to be relevant to public care practitioners and policy-makers, therefore, it is important to ensure that studies use a variety of methods to encompass the breadth of experiences of young people both while they are in care, and afterwards when they move on in life.

The chapter starts with an examination of evidence-based practice relevant to children's social care, and the extent to which the existing research information base for children and young people in and leaving care is able to provide such evidence. It goes on to consider some of the distinct methodological challenges of conducting research with this particular group of young people and suggests various ways in which researchers might respond to these. The chapter then presents as a case study an account of a recent research project examining services for young people leaving care. At the time of writing, this project was still in the fieldwork stage. However, a description of the processes involved in setting it up, developing a sample of young people and ultimately conducting the research, illustrates some of the methodological problems confronted along the way and how researchers at least in part resolved them. Material is also drawn from other studies referred to earlier in the book in order to demonstrate that researchers focusing on groups of young people in care and care leavers are often faced with similar dilemmas.

## Evidence-based practice

### *Recent trends*

The importance of high-quality research for policy development and delivery has increased with the growing emphasis on 'evidence-based practice'. This approach has characterised the UK government's agenda since 1997. The White Paper on *Modernising Government* stated:

> This government expects more of policy makers. More ideas, more willing-ness to question inherited ways of doing things, better use of evidence and research in policy making and better focus on policies that will deliver long term goals.
>
> (Cabinet Office 1999: 16)

Many of the initiatives introduced by government have generated a need for new knowledge in the form of evidence to justify proposals. Research has of necessity become more utilitarian, linked with social and economic development. Drawing on experience in the field of health, social care programmes and interventions have come to rely more upon validation by 'before' and 'after' measurements, or comparison groups. Evaluation has increasingly become a requirement in new initiatives, and is included as a routine part of many programme designs (e.g. Sure Start, New Deal, Neighbourhood Renewal, Children's Fund). At the same time, the need for evidence has been linked to a new managerialist approach, rooted in monitoring, performance targets, procedures, outcome measurements, cost-effectiveness and value for money when resources are limited (Clarke and Newman 1997).

In the social care field, while the value of improving the knowledge base has not in itself been challenged, questions have been raised about the reliance placed on certain approaches to producing the evidence. It has been suggested, for example, that an over-emphasis on certain types of evidence-based practice might lead to changes being viewed as simple cause-and-effect processes, rather than understanding how the context and progression of social care can bring about intended and unanticipated outcomes (Sheldon 2001; Webb 2001). Nevertheless, with the drive for greater accountability in relation to funding allocations, the government has introduced new requirements, putting pressure on local authorities to produce statistics on needs, outputs and outcomes, a move that has been described as both anti-ideological and pragmatic (Solesbury 2002). This urgency to produce figures that can justify relevant expenditure, coupled with a lack of time and resources to check the reliability of the information, mean that the research is not always as thorough as it might be. Often, with large-scale baseline data, information is generated at different moments in time, under different conditions and relating to different geographic areas, making meaningful comparisons all the more difficult, as indicated in Chapter 3.

## Absence of research on young people in and leaving care

The problems of establishing a sound evidence base are particularly relevant to research with children and young people looked after by local authorities, or those who are leaving care. Much research published over recent years on the health and well-being of young people in and leaving care has acknowledged the lack of any substantial earlier research base to underpin the study in progress. For example, when researchers were invited by Barnardo's to undertake a review of the evidence of what works in creating stability for looked-after children, they were confronted with a lack of any reliable baseline data, and very little research evidence of what creates stability, despite compelling evidence that instability and changes of placement are extremely damaging to children (Jackson and Thomas 2000). Similarly, Broad (1999b) described how he was reliant on data derived from a survey of leaving care projects in England and Wales in 1996, together with data previously gathered in 1992/1993, to establish a national dataset for young people leaving care. Broad's work highlighted the need for more leaving care research across distinct geographical areas, groups and at different points in time, in order to generate findings that were representative and which could provide the required level of detailed evidence to inform policy and practice.

### Involving practitioners

In the field of social services practitioners have increasingly been urged by government to question 'what works' in an endeavour to improve practice – 'Excellent councils will ensure that knowledge based practice informed by research evidence is supported and applied in everyday practice' (Department of Health 2000a: 29). Yet traditionally, the relationship between research and practice has not been an easy one (Atherton 2002). Local authority Social Services departments have generally not been research-led and have tended to rely on experience rather than research evidence (Sheldon and Chilvers 1995). Some of the barriers to change mirror those found in the health care field (Newman *et al.* 1998; NHS Centre for Reviews and Dissemination 1999), and include lack of individual motivation, lack of clarity about roles and unsympathetic organisational cultures. When central government has tried to promote research within local government, this has tended to come in the guise of 'Best Value' or 'Performance Management', suggesting a managerialist rather than a research agenda.

In an effort to reduce some of these barriers, a number of consortia have been set up to promote partnerships between researchers and practitioners. Linking researchers and practitioners, they include *Making Research Count*, a collaborative venture between ten English universities and local authority Social Services departments; *Research in Practice*, a partnership between the Dartington Hall Trust, the Association of Directors of Social Services, the University of Sheffield and over seventy-five English local authorities, voluntary child care organisations, and Local Strategic Partnerships and Primary Care Trusts; and *the Centre for Evidenced-based Social Services*, a partnership between the Department of Health and a consortium of Social Services departments in South West England, based at the University of Exeter. The Social Care Institute for Excellence's (2004) review of research and social care further highlights the commitment to and belief in the importance of research for improving social care practice, examining the use of its findings by social care staff and how it can be promoted in social care practice.

Sharing similar objectives, these initiatives have attempted to broaden interpretation of what counts as evidence-based practice in relation to health and social care. For example, *Making Research Count* prefers to use the term 'knowledge-based' in common with the Social Care Institute for Excellence. Similarly, *Research in Practice* identifies a tripartite relationship between practitioner wisdom and user perspectives, along with research. It defines an evidence-based approach as one that is 'informed by the best available evidence of what is effective, the practice expertise of professionals and the experience and views of service users' (Barratt and Cooke 2001: 2).

Certainly, there is room for improvement in the way that research is disseminated, implemented and adopted, and current failings undermine the adoption of evidence-based practice in the field of child and family social work (Barratt 2003). Indeed, if evidence-based practice is to be promoted, developed and sustained, it will require much stronger collaboration between all the relevant stakeholders.

## Research with children and young people: problems and challenges

There is a strong argument for more participatory approaches to research which can both counter the over-emphasis on performance management or cost-effectiveness (Humphreys *et al.* 2003) and, even more importantly, provide opportunities for the views and perspectives of the intended beneficiaries of policy and practice, particularly those at the margins of society, to be heard and taken account of. There are signs of movement in this direction. Just as the emphasis on evidence-based practice has grown, so too has the importance of involving children and young people in the policy process gained credence over the past decade. Article 12 of the United Nations Convention on the Rights of the Child

(UNCRC) asserted a child's 'right to express an opinion, and to have that opinion taken into account, in any matter or procedure affecting the child, in accordance with his or her age and maturity' (Newell 1993). The 1989 Children Act in England and Wales, the 1995 Children (Scotland) Act, and the 1995 Children (Northern Ireland) Order were all influenced by the government's ratification of the UN Convention, and in particular adoption of Article 12. In the fields of health, education and social work, the importance of hearing children's views and incorporating them in legal decision-making is now widely recognised. Increasingly, children are seen as competent social actors (Qvortrup 1994; James *et al.* 1998; Prout 2002) capable of offering their views on their own experiences within a social world.

Alongside the acknowledgement of promoting the active participation of children and young people in decisions affecting their lives, there is a considerable literature outlining the ethics and practice of research with children (e.g. Christensen and James 2000; Lewis and Lindsay 2000; Harker 2002; Alderson and Morrow 2004; Sinclair 2004). Such ethical considerations of informed consent, power, confidentiality and child protection, which lie at the heart of ethical guidelines for good research practice, directly affect the ways in which researchers work with children and young people, and at times pose important ethical dilemmas.

Published studies rarely directly address the practical difficulties encountered in the research process of working with children. Cree *et al.* (2002) advocate the need for reflexive research with children in the light of potential gaps that might occur between principles of good practice and practical realities. A few studies (Butler and Williamson 1994; Thomas and O'Kane 1998; Heptinstall 2000; Gilbertson and Barber 2002), refer to particular methodological issues of working with children in care, and Broad (1999b) has unusually acknowledged some of the specific challenges of conducting research with young care leavers, notably their high mobility and lack of stability. More often, such difficulties are not mentioned. Indeed, Curtis and colleagues (2004) when confronted with the realities of researching 'hard to reach' children and teenagers, question if they are the only researchers to have experienced problems, given the disinclination of other researchers to report on these.

Certainly, in virtually all of the research studies concerning young people in or leaving care described in this book, researchers have encountered practical difficulties of one kind or another, either in setting up the studies, identifying samples, or simply conducting the research. From our collective experience, methodological challenges in conducting a high-quality enquiry among this particular subgroup of children and young people would seem to be very much the norm rather than the exception.

## Negotiating access

When working with children and young people generally, researchers can rarely approach them directly to invite them to participate. Because of child protection regulations and the need to ensure that environments are safe, initial contact generally comes through parents or professionals (Harker 2002). With looked-after children, contact is most often made through local authority Social Services departments. Negotiating access can present a major challenge for researchers and can have a significant impact on the timing of the research.

In the first instance, particularly when working within the statutory sector, there may be a hierarchical process to follow in order to negotiate access to children and young people through directors of Social Services departments. If working across a number of departments, this is likely to be secured through approval for the research from the Association of Directors of Social Services (ADSS), which recommends a standardised application procedure to be followed when working with several Social Services departments. Although approval takes time to obtain, this route should, in theory, facilitate the subsequent progress of the research. Social Services departments are more likely to be cooperative if they are confident that research procedures have been formally assessed and approved. For studies in one particular locality, an alternative is to secure approval from the individual directors, whose support will be dependent upon the aims and methods of the research and how the programme impacts upon current organisational structures. Within the voluntary sector access is most likely to be agreed through senior representatives of voluntary organisations who are in a position to inform frontline workers about the nature of the research.

Once the research has been approved at senior management level, researchers need to navigate direct access to children and young people through front-line workers. The success of this will depend on issues as diverse as how well the research objectives have been communicated from senior management level to practitioners, to how frontline workers feel about their current workloads and demands. Unless attention is given to these factors, some practitioners may not only be resistant to accommodating the research in their everyday practice but may actually inhibit its progress either by withholding support, or by failing to cooperate with a research programme.

All too often, the goodwill of the practitioners is vital to the success of a project, particularly when practitioners operate as the gatekeepers to research participants. This applies across the whole spectrum of research but is perhaps most critical in research with children and young people for whom consent must be obtained before they can even be approached. In a recent US study, researchers reported having to negotiate with judges, agency administrators, social workers, lawyers and carers for permission before they could begin to interview children about their experiences in foster care (Berrick *et al.* 2000). The authors of this study suggested that because of these access problems, it was not surprising that the research literature so often fails to include the views and perspectives of children.

### Sample bias and sample attrition

The complications in negotiating access to research participants are inextricably linked to difficulties in ensuring that the research sample is representative or typical of those within the study group. In practice, the selected sample of children or young people will often depend on the extent to which gatekeepers, whether managers or frontline workers, facilitate or block, intentionally or otherwise, access to the potential sample. In an English study which sought a sample of children in foster care, Heptinstall (2000) observed that despite gaining management approval at the outset, the subsequent responses from the two local authorities participating in the research were very different. In one case, the sample was selected by management, once social workers had agreed to cooperate and had taken steps to secure the consent of birth parents. Researchers had no way of knowing how many children were eligible to take part in the research, for what reason they were excluded, or whether social workers had even conferred with birth parents or with the children themselves, making it impossible to assess the representativeness of the sample. By contrast, within the second authority, the names of all eligible children were passed to the researchers, who then liaised directly with social workers, birth parents, foster carers and children to gain consent for participation in the research. Overall, the researchers estimated that the study lost more than half (59 per cent) of potential participants in the research, due to a combination of exclusion by social workers, refusal by birth parents, or refusal by the children to participate. Furthermore, the process took so long that the researchers were forced to change the original research plan in order to meet the programme requirements.

The problem of sample attrition is not uncommon in studies of children in care, as McDonald *et al.* (1996) noted when comparing studies assessing the long-term outcomes of foster care. The authors observed that none of the studies reviewed considered the possibility of sample bias, as a result of such loss, in their analysis and write-up. The consequences of having a small, and possibly unrepresentative, sample may seriously weaken the external validity of research findings.

The interaction of factors affecting access and their consequent impact on the sampling process may give rise to bias in the research findings. For example, research findings may be overly positive if participants with the most severe problems are either screened out by gatekeepers, or decide themselves to opt out. Alternatively, they may be overly negative if researchers rely on particular agencies as the source of research participants, with the risk of excluding those who are coping independently, without recourse to professional help. As researchers, it is important to ask whether it is possible to produce the strong evidence base required by government under these circumstances. At the very least, we should be aware of the potential problems, and be extra rigorous in reviewing sampling strategies in order to explore ways in which they might be improved.

## Illustrative case study – young people and access to services

Having broadly outlined some of the problems inherent in conducting research with children and young people in and leaving care, the following case study provides a descriptive account of many of the difficulties discussed above, particularly during the early planning and initial fieldwork stages. The case study draws primarily on a Department of Health/Department of Education and Skills funded study which set out to examine how vulnerable young people, particularly those who have left care, access and engage with services affecting their health and well-being. Access to a range of services was explored including general and specialist health and social services; counselling; careers and advisory services; employment; housing; and education. In instances where the challenges faced in this project were shared with other research projects within the Thomas Coram Research Unit, these are included to provide further illustrative examples.

### The research plan

In common with some of the other research reported in this volume (Chapters 5, 6 and 7), the research into young people's access to services aimed to engage with a slightly older age group (17 to 24 years). Permission from social workers or parents to interview the young people was not generally a prerequisite to interviewing them, once initial contact had been made. Nor were gatekeepers directly deciding whether or not the research was in the young person's best interest and actively blocking participation, as has happened with other studies (e.g. Heptinstall 2000).

A preliminary phase of work commenced at the end of 2001, following soon after the enactment of the Children (Leaving Care) Act 2000, which was introduced in October 2001. The aim at the outset was to identify local authorities of varying types and geographic locations from which might be derived an initial sample of around a hundred young people in the process of leaving care, who were willing to participate in the study. Researchers planned to sustain contact with the young people and their responsible authorities over the following two years, with a view to commencing an in-depth interview phase of the work in the autumn of 2003. The anticipated attrition rate of the sample in the intervening period was predicted to be around 40 per cent, leaving a projected target figure of sixty young care leavers at the commencement of the fieldwork. Simultaneously with the commencement of the in-depth interviewing phase with young care leavers, a parallel sample of sixty young people defined as vulnerable and facing multiple difficulties, though not care leavers, was to be recruited via routes described below.

Given the Leaving Care Act's statutory requirement for local authorities to stay in touch and to support every young person leaving their care until they reach the age of at least 21, local leaving care teams were the obvious starting point both for identifying the care leaver sample and thereafter maintaining contact with it. In order to select a variety of authorities in terms of geographical location, demographics and numbers of young people leaving their care, a review of secondary sources related to local authorities was conducted, followed by a telephone survey of leaving care managers. As a result, a list was drawn up of twelve contrasting authorities that both expressed a willingness to join the study and appeared to be making good progress with the implementation of the Leaving Care Act.

Approval from the Association of the Directors of Social Services was obtained, following which the directors of the relevant authorities were contacted by letter. All gave their approval for participation in the research. Subsequent telephone or postal contact was then with team managers. Information leaflets briefly outlining the research project, including a tear-off strip for young people to give their consent to take part in the research, along with assurances of confidentiality, were then sent to each participating authority. The expectation was that the leaving care workers would introduce the project to all of the young people they met with, and invite their participation. The leaving care worker would then return the signed slip on behalf of the young person, after which contact between the researchers and the young person would be direct. No further input was required of the leaving care team, except in cases where contact was lost with the young person, and current whereabouts needed to be checked with the worker. Careful consideration was given to ensuring that the research would not place any unnecessary additional burden on existing workloads. Leaflets were distributed to the twelve leaving care teams in January 2002, with the expectation that the provisional target of 100 young people would be reached within two months.

Researchers were acutely aware that in seeking volunteers, there was the risk of not involving young care leavers who were eligible for the research but might not be motivated to take part, thus to some extent skewing the sample. This is always a problem when research relies on the consent of participants, yet participation cannot be forced. There was the added complication of asking young people to commit their time to research, the benefits of which would accrue to future generations of care leavers rather than to themselves. This raised the important dilemma of whether or not to offer some reward for cooperation, given that in doing so, the 'incentive' can prove more persuasive than a genuine desire by participants to further the research. In this case, in order to encourage the participation of as broad a spectrum of care leavers as possible, it was decided to offer a £20 gift voucher as a 'thank you' for completing the eventual interview and this was communicated to young people through the research publicity.

### The emerging problems

In the event, it soon became apparent that the timing of the research was not ideal. Many of the local authorities were in reality struggling to recruit their full complement of staff for the leaving care teams before they could even begin to get services up and running. Despite management support, research tended to be low on the agenda of practitioners, if it featured at all. Of the original twelve authorities, two withdrew early on, for which replacements were found. Numbers of recruits for the sample were painfully slow to appear, added to which the performance of the different authorities varied enormously. Despite persistent and ongoing contact, a third authority withdrew. By June 2002, six months into the sampling phase, the sample totalled a mere thirteen young care leavers, referred by three of the twelve participating local authorities. The remaining nine authorities had failed to produce a single recruit.

Yet, through discussion and collaboration within the research unit, it soon became apparent that these difficulties were not unique to this particular study. The variability of success in recruiting participants and support from local authorities was shared with a recent study of pregnancy of young people in and leaving care (Chapter 6). Despite an initial target set of ninety-six, the study achieved a sample of only sixty-three young parents, determined more opportunistically than had originally been intended. Researchers reported varied levels of local support across the four authorities concerned, had occasional difficulties identifying young people who fitted the selection criteria, and encountered some negative feelings about the research within one or two authorities primarily in relation to research overload. In particular, access to young fathers proved problematic since service providers rarely knew whether the young men they were working with were fathers. The group sought was highly specific, namely young men who either were or had been in local authority care, and who were either fathers or had a partner who was pregnant. When young men could be identified meeting these criteria, they were often experiencing other difficulties in their lives that made them reluctant to take part. Although the intended balance of one-third young fathers in the overall sample of young parents was achieved, young men were drawn mainly from two of the four participating authorities, and not equally from across them all.

A further study on private fostering arrangements for young people (Chapter 7) struggled to achieve its intended sample of fifty carers, fifty parents, and twenty young people who had previously been cared for. (It was decided not to interview young people who were still being fostered because of the ethical difficulties this might involve.) Starting from the premise that participants could be sourced through snowballing from an initial group of carers contacted via social workers, researchers found that although private foster families are obliged to notify local Social Services of their status, few actually do so. Of those foster carers with whom contact was made, almost all responded positively to the research. Thus they readily agreed to put researchers in touch both with parents whose children they had cared for, and with the young people themselves. This was agreed on the basis that they had maintained good relationships with birth parents and young people alike. Despite repeated efforts on the part of the researchers to follow up these leads, not a single contact with a parent was identified through an interviewed foster carer. Researchers were forced to tap into other potential ways of increasing the sample size such as through consulting Social Services records, working through health visitor teams or through other research projects that might have identified young people living within private fostering arrangements. The final sample achieved comprised thirty-five carers, three parents and twelve people who had been cared for. The majority of young people interviewed came via advertisements in magazines and newspapers, and were a self-selected group who wanted to talk about their experiences. Researchers had to concede that the final sample, in all probability, did not fully represent the range of experiences of those either providing or living within private fostering arrangements.

A study of social pedagogy in residential care settings with younger children (Chapter 8) demonstrated how access becomes even more critical, with the requirement for permission to be granted by parents, foster carers and/or social workers before proceeding with any contact with the children and young people. In this study, residential workers were intermediaries in securing the required permission, and to a certain extent controlled the interview process by directing the availability of interviewees. Again, the degree of cooperation varied, from those who went out of their way to facilitate the research, to those who were openly obstructive. Furthermore, the nature of the residential care setting meant that the young people could have misconstrued the research interview as part of the ongoing review process associated with being in care, and consequently either felt pressured into taking part in the research, rather than choosing freely to do so, or simply opted out in protest.

### Seeking solutions

Clearly, some of the difficulties encountered throughout the practical application of the research methodology are to a large extent outside the control of the researchers. For example, echoing what was found in the study of young parents in and leaving care, some authorities in the access to services study suggested that with the introduction of the Leaving Care Act, attention on young care leavers had shifted from a virtual absence of research to an effective overload in endeavours to establish how well the act was working, and what impact it might have. This, they felt, deterred volunteers from coming forward and affected the way in which those working with young people presented the research to them. The importance of avoiding the selection of local authorities that have recently been inundated with similar research projects is paramount. Just as important is ensuring that senior managers, in agreeing to take part in research, have duly taken into account the views and perspectives of frontline workers who will ultimately experience the demands of the research process. Even with these considerations, however, researchers are still faced with needing to ensure a balance in the range of authorities selected in relation to their geographical location, their demographic and socio-economic composition and the range of practice that they illustrate.

Other obstacles are however more practical and may be more easily resolved. A factor raised by leaving care teams to explain the poor response in the access to services study was the lack of incentive for the young people. They maintained that a £20 voucher eighteen months into the future was too remote an incentive and would not sustain the support of the young people, or prompt them to stay in touch with the researchers. Some even indicated that they felt young people were being 'used', and not being shown sufficient respect for their cooperation. To address this criticism, the decision was made to send a brief questionnaire to the young person at the point of signing up for the research, with two further questionnaires sent at four- to six-monthly intervals. For each completed and returned questionnaire the young person would receive a £20 voucher, plus the £20 voucher for the final interview. Following the introduction of this strategy the response rate improved, and the numbers in the sample increased, albeit slowly. Despite the fact that several young people recruited through the voucher scheme commented during their interviews that they would have done the research without the vouchers, the research team remains sceptical that so many would have maintained their commitment throughout without these rewards. A number of young people also commented on how much they looked forward to receiving the questionnaires because they gave them an opportunity to reflect on their lives and they also knew they would receive the reward for completing and returning them.

As the sample size increased, however, a third difficulty presented itself in that there continued to be a wide variation in the rate at which local authorities produced recruits. As a result the sample began to be severely skewed, with a disproportionate number from the north, more girls than boys, and very few care leavers from ethnic minorities. To remedy this, in the autumn of 2002, when the sample was still less than half its target figure, two London boroughs, a voluntary sector leaving care team and a local authority in South east England were invited to join the study. With the new authorities, a different approach was tried. Rather than liaising remotely with the team manager, a researcher attended a team meeting to present the project in person, in the hope that fieldworkers might understand better what was required of them, and give the research greater priority. Yet again, despite positive indications of support, and despite the new strategy with the questionnaires, the results were disappointing with only a trickle of new recruits, although this approach did help to redress the imbalance in our sample. With the addition of two further local authorities with leaving care teams known to be actively supportive of research, the target of 100 young care leavers was finally reached in May 2004, more than two years after the commencement of the study.

### Flexible and responsive research strategies

Although not part of the original research plan, the periodic questionnaires designed primarily to sustain contact with the young people proved to be invaluable in a number of ways. In the first questionnaire, respondents were asked to identify a contact person who might know of their whereabouts should they move on and the researchers lose touch with them. This has proved a very helpful strategy in maintaining contact. Although the management of the periodic questionnaires proved extensively time-consuming, researchers were able to track the moves made by the young person while also maintaining contact with them. The questionnaires collected brief outline data about services used by the young person and their perceptions about what had been helpful or unhelpful. This meant that by the time of the face-to-face, in-depth interview with the young person, there was already a record of what had been going on in the young person's life, and useful indicators to draw on if points did not come out directly in the interview. The responses to the questionnaire also provided some valuable quantitative data for the analysis. In addition, the questionnaires called on the expertise of the young people, and sought their advice on how improvements might be made to services offered to care leavers. Many young people responded with useful and practical suggestions about service improvements, based on their own experience. In the last two questionnaires, respondents were invited to identify and give contact details of any care leaver friends interested in taking part in the study, a technique that generated several more recruits to the study.

But perhaps the most important, yet in some ways unforeseen, outcome from the contact questionnaires was that by the time the face-to-face interview was arranged, there was a rapport established between the young people and the researchers, and in most cases a sense of commitment on their part to continuing their participation in research. Despite the renowned mobility of the care leaver population and the fact that it is notoriously hard to maintain contact with them, less than 10 per cent of the sample failed to return the first questionnaire once they had committed themselves to participating in the research. At the time of writing, 79 per cent of the final sample had returned all three questionnaires and had either completed or were about to complete the face-to-face interview. There had been only two young people who failed to keep the interview appointment. Once they had received assurances about maintaining confidentiality and the use of the data, respondents appeared comfortable about discussing personal issues, and were remarkably frank and open throughout the interviews. This response is thought to be due, at least in part, to the contact that was built up over time prior to the interview. Most of the interviews were conducted in the young people's homes, suggesting a degree of trust on their part.

### Engaging practitioners

The explanation for variations in recruitment to the study between local authorities lies, at least in part, in the response of the frontline workers. At the time of writing, it is clear from the interviews completed that in two local authority areas high numbers of young people were accessed through individual leaving care workers who took on board the requirements of the research, and went out of their way to draw it to the attention of their young care leavers. In both cases, the research was presented positively as an opportunity for young people to express their views. It was included, along with the package on offer from the leaving care service, at the first meeting, and as requested, *all* of the young people in their caseload were invited to sign up at that time. According to these workers, very few young people declined to take part. Equally, among the local authorities that subsequently joined the project, the two known to have a strong commitment to research generated a significant number of recruits in a matter of weeks, where the others once again produced none. Clearly, the message put across by the local authority department is crucial to the recruitment process, and without this cooperation the researcher struggles both to gain access to young people and to engage with the research participants who may be resistant or mistrustful of the research if their frontline workers are not supportive of it.

## Working with non-care leavers

An interesting comparison may be made between the recruitment of the sample of care leavers in this study and that of the comparative sample of young people 'in difficulties'. For the latter, a number of potential difficulties were identified which included belonging to a minority ethnic group; being a parent; having been homeless; experience of drug or alcohol-related problems; unemployment; having a learning difficulty; having left school without qualifications; living apart from family; having a physical disability; or having offended. It was specified that young people who had experienced at least two of these difficulties were eligible for inclusion. Flyers similar to those used for the care leavers group but adapted for the new sample were prepared. These sought volunteers for interview about service use, with the offer of a £20 voucher to thank them for completing the interview. Settings likely to be frequented by these young people such as hostels for homeless young people, voluntary sector support services, such as Barnardo's, youth offending teams and Connexions services were targeted. In the case of Connexions, efforts were made to identify young people who were classified as having the highest support needs. Flyers were distributed to workers in these settings who were requested to recruit volunteers, or put up posters. The aim was to interview fifteen young people 'in difficulties' in each of the four main locations from which the majority of the care leavers' sample had been derived. At the time of writing there have been no problems encountered in securing this comparative sample, and in fact at times there have been too many participants for the research project to accommodate. So why was this group so much easier to recruit?

To start with, although young people were accessed through service providers, in this case they were not from Social Services departments. Consequently, negotiation took place directly with a range of agencies and proved more straight-forward and less time-consuming than working through at times hierarchical and bureaucratic Social Services departments. By and large, once contact had been made with frontline workers and the research explained, they were readily supportive and anxious to help. Given that the targeted age range was young people aged 17 to 24, these workers generally seemed to be relaxed about intro-ducing the research project and then allowing young people to make their own decisions as to whether or not they wanted to participate. In some cases, workers provided contact details of young people who had volunteered to take part. These interviewees were then contacted directly and a date and time for an interview was arranged. Alternatively, appointments were made on behalf of researchers and space was made available to conduct the interviews within the organisation's premises. Importantly, there were no situations where workers suggested that what was being asked of them was burdensome or that they might find it hard to gain the agreement of young people to take part.

As far as the young people themselves were concerned, at the point when they met the researcher they knew very little about the research other than what was contained in the flyer, and the fact that they would receive a voucher in return for completing the interview. Unlike the care leavers sample, this group of young people had no long-term connection with the researchers. It is probably true to say that the financial reward for this group provided a stronger incentive to take part in the research, and the vouchers were therefore more persuasive than they were with the care leavers group. As such, there was a risk that the comparative sample of young people 'in difficulties' was going through the motions of co-operating with the research, simply to receive the payment. They were given the same opportunity to stop the interview at any time if it became uncomfortable for them, without affecting receipt of the voucher, and one opted to do this. Certainly, their understanding of the research tended to be looser because they had no experience of being in care, or recognition that their contribution would help future generations of young people in care, which was the case made to the care leavers to justify their support. It is important to note, however, that the experiences of the young people 'in difficulties' were equally multi-dimensional and thus not so different from those of the care leavers. The main distinction was that they tended to have less financial support if they were living away from family, making the prospect of the voucher reward more attractive. In addition, in the absence of the support of the leaving care service, the researchers were able to give information about local services or signpost the young people to sources of help where appropriate.

## Conclusions

In seeking to establish what constitutes effective or best practice in terms of policy and practice for children and young people in and leaving care, clearly there are major challenges for researchers. This chapter has endeavoured to explore some of the special demands when conducting research with this particular group of young people. What is very apparent from the experience of the contributors to this book is that all have encountered similar difficulties.

The examples illustrating some of the research challenges clearly highlight the nature of the research process and how, while still meeting the original research objectives, these may steer researchers along a somewhat different path to that originally planned. Indeed, the research process, most notably the recruitment of research participants, often demands additional skills of researchers beyond those traditionally associated with competent research practitioners, namely resourcefulness, creativity and innovativeness.

Acknowledging the key role played by 'gatekeepers', professionals at all levels who control the access to children and young people, it is crucial that adequate attention is paid to ensuring that they understand the importance and value of research, and that they feel valued as key participants in the research process.

While many frontline workers have unmanageably high caseloads that may discourage them from fully committing themselves to supporting research projects, their motivation can be further diminished by the low value placed on the outputs of research. The ability of gatekeepers to present the research positively and in a meaningful way to young people, and for the young person to make an informed decision about participation, is critical to ensure that their rights are upheld and that they are given equal opportunity to express their views. The examples cited above highlight the importance of identifying those practitioners within local authorities who value research and who are willing to advocate positively for it at a local level.

Overall, greater emphasis in research needs to be placed on improving the interface between practitioners and researchers so that, at the very least, there is a heightened appreciation among practitioners of how research can ultimately influence policy and practice, even if the impact of this is not immediately apparent. More radically, this interface could be strengthened through exploring new conceptualisations such as that of researcher-practitioner, evident within early childhood practice in the world-famous nurseries in the Italian region of Reggio-Emilia (Rinaldi 2005). Here, the conventional division between 'research' and 'practice' as inhabiting separate spheres is questioned and the teacher does not just promote learning but is actively curious about the child's culture and knowledge, and as such is considered a researcher as well as a practitioner.

Awarding more importance to 'knowledge-based practice' rather than overly depending on 'evidence-based practice', as described above, might help to further bridge the gap. *Research in Practice*, for example, proposes a 'range of multifaceted interventions' in order to achieve an evidence-based culture in social care that is both inclusive and participative (Barratt 2003: 149). This approach draws together national and local data and involves the views and experiences of a wider range of stakeholders. Practitioners need to be more actively drawn into the research process and the value of their experience and knowledge more fully recognised as relevant to the research findings. Greater efforts by researchers to engage practitioners as early as possible in the planning stages of research are likely to generate a better understanding of both research objectives and the benefits of bringing evidence to bear on their practice. While there are clear implications for researchers to address these issues in planning specific research projects, there is also a case to raise the profile of the importance of research both in the initial training and continued professional development of practitioners within the field of social care.

For children and young people to feel comfortable and safe to take part in any research study, researchers must adhere to high ethical standards. The ten topics in ethical research drawn up by Alderson (1995) and recently updated (Alderson and Morrow 2004) endorse a strong rights-based approach, rooted in justice and respect for children and young people in social research. Researchers need to think critically about the approaches they adopt in seeking the participation of children and young people, and to consider whether they consistently adhere to sound ethical practice and always have the best interests of young people in mind.

At times this might mean questioning the decisions of gatekeepers who can sometimes, with the best interests of young people at heart, decide that the participation of young people in their care is not appropriate, thus preventing them from making their own choices and decisions. Ensuring that the research is faultless in terms of ethical scrutiny can do a great deal to persuade gatekeepers that children and young people will certainly come to no harm, and are in fact likely to greatly benefit from their participation in the research.

In the final analysis, it is not a question of either research having to change to meet the demands of practice, or practice changing to facilitate research. Researchers and practitioners share common goals of understanding and improving lives. It is vital, therefore, that they work together more effectively, acknowledging respective needs and making concessions where required. What the above examples have shown is that there is no blueprint for research and that each individual study needs to be fine-tuned to the circumstances in which it is being carried out. This is particularly true when conducting research with children and young people in or leaving care who are often hard to reach, have experiences of being marginalised, and may have low expectations of what they can expect from participating in research projects. All research has its limitations. The examples described in this chapter required both the extension of resources to provide the increased incentives to young people and also additional time for researchers to establish and maintain contact with them. These additional inputs have implications for the research programme and budget. There may come a time when researchers have to accept that they have done the best they can to secure the widest possible participation of the sample group. Above all, it is important for researchers to question and reflect throughout the research process, to think critically about how and what is being done, to be able to adapt to circumstance and be constantly aware of the implications of the strategies adopted.

## Acknowledgements

The authors gratefully acknowledge the contribution of all who have participated in this study, notably the other members of the Young People and Access to Health and Other Services research team, Kristina Bennert and Antonia Simon, the many service representatives, and, not least, the young people themselves, whose commitment to the research has been exceptional.

# 11 Moving forward

*Sonia Jackson, Antonia Simon
and Elaine Chase*

As we pointed out in the opening chapter, the first few years of the twenty-first century have been a time of unprecedented activity at government level on behalf of children. It is too soon to know what impact this surge of legislation, policy initiatives and economic measures will have on young people in and leaving care. Policies aimed at all children, such as the goal of reducing child poverty or improving health, may have more effect in the long term than those targeted at children in care. Moreover, being in care is not a fixed condition. There is a constant tension, as we showed in Chapter 2, between the need to protect children from harm and ensure that their basic needs are met and the principle of keeping them in their own families as far as possible. Almost twice as many children pass through the care system in the course of a year as are being looked after at any one time, and we should also be concerned about those children on the margins of care. On the other hand, there is a special responsibility for children and young people who are separated from their families, which has been the focus of this book.

At times we have had to struggle to maintain our 'positive perspective' as we contemplate the many failures of the past and the continuing problems of the present. Too often children have been removed from unsatisfactory homes only to be further abused or to have their most basic needs neglected. And for some young people, the fact that separation from birth parents is regarded as something to be avoided at all costs leads to a great deal of instability and uncertainty, sometimes resulting in their moving backwards and forwards repeatedly between home and different care placements.

Much of what is written about children in care has a profoundly pessimistic tone. It dwells on the fact that children in care have 'complex needs', 'challenging behaviour' and on the 'damage' that has been done to them by their past experiences. It ignores their potential for growth and recovery, if only they were given the opportunity. What we have tried to show in the preceding chapters, however, is that the picture is far more mixed than this view would suggest. It is also possible for local authority care to bring about positive changes in children's lives when they cannot live in their own homes. As a result of the provisions under the Children (Leaving Care) Act, local authorities can also offer comprehensive support to young people during their transition from care. However, these possibilities unfortunately are not yet universal realities for children and young people at this critical stage in their lives, and the evidence reported in this book shows that wide differences remain in local authority practice.

Chapter 10 described some of the difficulties for researchers in identifying and maintaining contact with young people as research participants and how this has contributed to the large gaps in our knowledge. We suggested in Chapter 3 that the gathering and publication of outcome data and using it to set targets for progress can be an important mechanism for improvement in young people's experience and life chances. But the pressure to meet targets can also detract attention from the broader and equally important aim of ensuring that children and young people have happy and enriching experiences within their care placements, something that it is hard for outcomes data to measure. Moreover, there are many areas where there is a serious lack of published information and evidence from research. This applies particularly to the transitional period between care and independence, where past evidence comes mainly from specialist support schemes for care leavers, which by definition are more likely to be used by those in difficulties. In fact we know very little about what happens to these young people, or those who appear to have fewer problems, once they are defined as 'independent'. There are no prospective studies following looked-after children for extended periods of time both while in care and through several years of their adult lives. As a result, although we know something about the incidence in disadvantaged populations of people who have been in care, such as homeless people or those with drug and alcohol problems, there is no reliable information from longitudinal studies to tell us what proportion of young people in care are drawn into the criminal justice system, or how many become teenage parents, or for that matter how many go on to get good jobs, start families at an appropriate age and lead relatively unproblematic lives.

Another important area on which there is far too little information concerns children in care from minority ethnic backgrounds. Some minority groups are over-represented in the care population and others rarely have children coming into care, but there is only anecdotal evidence and a few small-scale studies seeking to explain why or how this happens, or what the young people's experiences are of the care system.

The limited research evidence on Black children in this book comes from two widely different studies. Most of the privately fostered people interviewed for the study in Chapter 7 were West African, and a high proportion of the successful young people in the By Degrees study (Chapter 5) originated from minority ethnic families. Neither of these groups can be considered typical. It is encouraging, however, that all the respondents had done well despite some experiences of racism, and some clumsy and often unwanted attempts at ethnic matching.

There is an obvious risk of over-emphasising the positives and underestimating the many factors in the lives of children separated from their families that contribute to unhappiness and poor outcomes. However, although the contributors to this volume write from different professional and disciplinary positions, they do so within a common theoretical framework which we described in the opening chapter as the 'strengths perspective'. We believe that the different research studies reported in this book demonstrate a more hopeful approach by rejecting the negative labels that too often attach themselves to young people in care and emphasising instead their capacity to recover from painful experiences and move forward in their lives.

There are some very fundamental issues which underlie all these studies, some closer to the surface than others. It may be helpful to stand back a little and look at the overarching philosophical framework within which services are provided for children and young people separated from their families. This has been more often discussed in the sphere of early years provision and child care than in relation to full-time care for children away from home, but the principles apply equally well to the services we provide for children and young people looked after by local authorities.

The American writer, Ronald Lally, suggests that there are three basic conceptualisations of children's rights and societal responsibilities towards them that help to explain child care policies and practices in different countries (Lally, 2005). The first conceptualisation is 'economic rationalism' which argues that the quality and price of services should be determined by the market and public expenditure kept to a minimum. We can see that, despite all the rhetoric to the contrary, our child care system still contains some elements of the economic rationalist approach. The excellent intentions of the Children Act 1989 were undermined by the contradictory insistence of the government of the time that none of the changes it envisaged should involve any extra costs. The quality of foster and residential care is still determined largely by what local authorities are prepared to pay and the investment they are prepared to make (or not make) in the education and training of carers. Until the Children (Leaving Care) Act 2000 forced local authorities to think again, the duration of care was often determined by cost factors, not the needs of the young person, while the operation of the market ensured that they were discharged from care to live in the least desirable areas and most dilapidated housing. It seemed that the main preoccupation of some Social Services departments was to divest themselves of financial responsibility for young people in care at the earliest possible moment. There remain entrenched assumptions about the allocation of resources and the timing of the transition from care to independence which, even after official implementation of the Children (Leaving Care) Act 2000, it seems very hard to shift.

Since 1997 we can see that there has been a movement towards the second conceptualisation of social responsibility towards children, the instrumental view, which sees the child as an adult in the making rather than a person in his or her own right, or as Gunilla Hallden graphically expresses it, 'the child as project' as opposed to 'the child as being' (Hallden, 1991). In this view, care needs to be of sufficient quality to prevent people from becoming a burden on society when they grow up. The purpose of care, and education, is to ensure adequate functioning in the future, defined mainly in economic terms. The goals that stem from an instrumentalist perspective are legitimate and important, as we show in

Chapter 4, but limited. They fail to value the young person's life experience for its own sake. They are focused on solving or preventing problems and lead to services provided at a minimum rather than an optimum level.

The third conceptualisation regards services for children as an opportunity for educational and social enrichment, not preoccupied with remedying deficits but rather with providing children with rich opportunities for interesting and enjoyable experiences. This model of public generosity towards children, which is most commonly to be found in Nordic countries, is the antithesis of the economic rationalist philosophy (Cohen *et al.*, 2004). Lally concludes: 'To some extent, services for children in every society reflect the perspectives of economic rationalism, instrumentalism and generosity. Yet I have seen that the more a society leans toward social and educational enrichment as its conceptual base the better it serves its children' (Lally, 2005: 45).

In order to make the strengths perspective a reality in everyday practice, we need to move beyond the instrumentalist position and adopt the principle of generosity as the basis for our provision for young people in care. This would immediately help our thinking about two basic questions: (1) Is it possible for the state be a good parent? (2) Is it the job of the care system to act as an engine of social mobility and a mechanism for redressing inequalities in society? The first question was partly answered by Sir William Utting when he wrote in his report on residential care that there was no way that a public body could 'replace or replicate the selfless character of parental love' (Utting, 1991: 26). At the same time he pointed out that the manner in which a local authority should discharge its parental responsibility under Section 22 of the Children Act 1989 is specified in the Guidance (Department of Health, 1991a, 1991b) to a far greater extent than the parental responsibility of natural parents. So it is clear, and was made even more explicit by the *Quality Protects* programme, and the letter from the then Secretary of State, Frank Dobson, that accompanied its launch, that the local authority is at least expected to emulate the behaviour of a good parent, even if it cannot replicate it (Department of Health, 1998e).

But what model of corporate parenting is envisaged? Should it be based on what the child or young person might have expected if their family had been able to look after them at a minimum acceptable level? Or should the standard be that of some theoretical average family, from which the chance that a child will come into care is estimated to be one in 8,000 (Bebbington and Miles, 1989)? For much of the twentieth century the answer would have been determined by the social class of the child's family of origin but that will no longer do. For too long, the discourse of social exclusion, and raising aspirations and achievement, as discussed in Chapters 4 and 5, has ignored the importance of barriers created by social class and failed to recognise that social mobility is an inevitable and desirable con-sequence of providing high-quality corporate parenting. Yet it is evident that if the government were to succeed in raising the educational attainment of children in care substantially, that would result in many of them moving into a different class of society from that of their birth parents. Educational aspirations and social mobility are intimately connected.

Another source of discomfort in discussion of the relative quality of parenting provided by local authorities is the recognition that children looked after may have the advantage of material resources that are not available to other children living in the same communities whose families look after them well enough despite low incomes and multiple social disadvantages. There is a perceived unfairness about this which sometimes makes it hard for elected members to argue for more resources for young people in care or for those who look after them, although paradoxically, and as we have shown in Chapter 4, a great deal of money is spent by local authorities in ways that do not produce any benefits at all for looked-after children.

What do the different studies reported in this book tell us about how local authorities might better fulfil their role as corporate parents? The need for a more holistic approach to care and after care is a theme that emerges from several chapters, and most strongly from the account of the pedagogical approach in Chapter 8. In Denmark and Germany residential care is seen as a positive option, not as a last resort for the most difficult and unmanageable young people as it is in the UK. The young people generally appear to enjoy a close, trusting relationship with staff, but also to remain in regular contact with their families. Education is given great importance, and residential workers consider support for learning and liaison with schools as among their key functions, whereas little progress has been made towards ensuring that residential care provides a positive educational environment in the UK. Most significantly, in relation to the theme of this book, residential care staff in Denmark and Germany see their responsibilities towards young people extending far beyond the immediate period of residence, to include (though at a much later age) all the preparation for independence and practical help with employment and accommodation that in the UK would fall to after-care teams, if provided at all.

The view of residential care in continental countries as a satisfactory form of living away from home for young people may certainly be attributed to the existence of a specific profession with its own ideology and system of education. In contrast to the very low levels of education and training to be found among staff in children's homes in England, in Northern European countries the majority of staff have at least three years' tertiary education and sometimes five. It is unlikely that there will be any substantial improvement in UK residential care or that social workers and placement finders will begin to see it as a positive option, thus introducing a better mix of young people as residents, unless there is a fundamental change in the education, training, pay and conditions of residential care staff.

The benefits of the pedagogical approach may be seen not only in the quality of the young people's everyday lives but in the reflective ethos of pedagogy, which seems to be passed on by the staff to the young people they care for and must stand them in good stead as they move, at their own pace, into adult life. Another way of putting it is that residential workers and foster carers with a background in pedagogy make a conscious effort to develop emotional literacy in the young people they look after, or equally important perhaps for their adult relationships, emotional articulacy. Well-meaning attempts to involve young people in decision-making and to take account of their perspectives are apt to founder if they fail to nurture the ability to put their feelings and wishes into words. Perhaps this is where advocates come in, and, as Chapter 9 shows, advocacy can be a very effective means for young people to get their point of view acknowledged and acted on. But it may be that the growth of advocacy services is a measure of how far we have moved away from the idea of the social worker who has a personal relationship with a child and sees it as their job to promote the child's interests and well-being.

Living apart from one's family need not and should not mean losing contact with them. In fact this is one area where there has been a very marked improvement over recent years. However, contact on its own is not enough. It needs to be meaningful and purposeful contact, and for that to happen social workers need to work with birth families proactively, not simply arranging meetings but giving serious thought to how the meeting can be pleasurable for both parents and children and lead in some cases to reunification rather than driving them further apart. The negative attitudes to birth families that we noted in Chapter 2 may still linger in some areas of the care system, notably in residential care, where the findings reported in Chapter 8 suggest that maintaining contact and good relations with families takes low priority in the UK compared with other European countries. Regarding birth families as a potential resource rather than merely a problem is a good example of how the strengths perspective can point to radically different practice. Chapter 5 showed that, even when parents are far away or were not able to provide good enough daily care for their children, they can still be an important source of motivation and emotional support.

One theme that is highlighted by all the studies, despite the diversity of subject matter, is the need for such support, available as needed, if young people are to fulfil their potential, whether as university students or as young parents. The precise form that this support should take will differ according to circumstances, but all the studies show that to be effective it must have an emotional as well as a financial component. Young people who have not had the chance to form a secure attachment to one carer may find themselves alone in the world on leaving care unless they have a continuing relationship with a social worker or personal adviser. Even when the young person has had a successful long-term foster placement the local authority continues to play an important role as corporate parent in this respect. The introduction of leaving care personal advisers since 2001 has, as we have shown in Chapter 6, gone some way towards providing support to care leavers which has an emotional as well as a functional role, yet there is still none or very limited personalised support for children while in care, outside the immediate care setting. This has extremely damaging consequences for those in unsatisfactory foster placements, and still more in residential units with their typically high staff turnover and low level of personal engagement with residents.

The conclusion we draw from several of the studies reported on here is that most young people need continued support from a known and trusted person well into adulthood. The urge to push young people prematurely towards independence is highly detrimental to their well-being and tends to undermine their natural resilience. The practice of German and Danish children's homes, where young people can stay until they feel ready to leave, sometimes into their mid-twenties, contrasts with the practice in England of pushing them out at 16 or 17 to live in public housing, often of low quality and in undesirable areas. Foster care, too, should be funded to offer continuing support and in some cases accommodation for a much longer period, so that the transition from care to independence can happen in a way that is determined by the maturity and readiness of the individual young person rather than the dictates of bureaucracy. Even the academically successful young people whose experiences are described in Chapter 5 wanted to feel that their care authority, as represented by a named individual, still took an interest in them and was available to offer help and support if needed.

Throughout this book the authors have suggested ways in which their research findings may be used to improve the experience and life opportunities of looked-after children. Young people themselves, as we have tried to show, have clear ideas about what has enabled them to succeed and fulfil their aspirations and what needs to change. But how is this information to be conveyed to policy-makers, practitioners, carers and service users? There is a strong argument for a change in the pattern of research funding so that dissemination becomes an integral component of every project, and that sufficient resources are allocated from the beginning of a project to ensure that such dissemination takes place. Current research by the Social Research Association has found that few funding bodies have clear policies or guidelines on dissemination, and the implications of new media and forms of communication have not yet been taken on board.

The other big question is about resources to put what we know into practice. So often, when reporting our findings at conferences and workshops, we have been told that practitioners are well aware of the shortcomings highlighted by the research but lack the money or staff to do anything about it. In the end, this is a matter of political will and the value that we place on children in our society. When we see how, given the right conditions, young people in care can recover from extreme adversity and achieve success and fulfilment in their lives, how can we fail to provide the resources that they need? A truly successful care system that offers equal opportunities to young people who are looked after away from home can only be built on the principle of generosity. The foundations for such generosity have been laid, at least in words, by the formidable policy agenda designed to level the playing field of life chances for all children and young people. The challenge lies in translating these words into practice, and in ensuring that those who historically have had least access to emotional as well as financial resources somehow get a fairer share.

# Appendix
## Acts of Parliament and other national policies

**The Poor Law (1834)** was introduced as a measure to tackle poverty and remove homeless people from the streets. Poor people were accommodated in workhouses, clothed and fed, and children received some basic education. In return they would have to work for several hours each day.

**Infant Life Protection Act (1872)** made it law that any person who took in and looked after two or more children under one year of age for more than twenty-four hours for payment had to be registered by the local authority.

**Adoption of Children Act (1926)** introduced a legal framework for adoption and formalised adoption arrangements for the first time.

**Children and Young Persons Act (1933)** defined neglect and abuse with regard to children and young people, regulated children's employment and introduced the prosecution of children in England and Wales for homicide and other grave offences.

**Education Act (1944)** raised the school-leaving age to 15 and provided universal free schooling in three different types of schools: grammar, secondary modern and technical. Entry to these schools was based on the 11+ examination.

**Children's Act (1948)** established a children's committee and a children's officer in each local authority. It followed the creation of the Parliamentary Care of Children Committee in 1945 following the death of 13-year-old Dennis O'Neill at the hands of his foster-parents.

**National Assistance Act (1948)** abolished the old Poor Law and provided assistance to persons whose resources were insufficient to meet their needs. Distinctions between different groups of persons in need were replaced by a single system of national assistance administered by the National Assistance Board.

**Children and Young Persons Act (1963)** enabled local authorities in England and Wales for the first time to spend money on preventive measures to keep children with their families.

**Children and Young Persons Act (1969)** integrated services for children in need under local authority control in England and Wales. Its provisions were replaced by the Children Act 1989 which came into force in October 1991.

**Local Authority Social Services Act (1970)** established local authority social services departments in England and Wales. These combined the former children's, health and welfare departments.

**Children Act (1975)** was designed to make it easier for children to be freed for adoption without their parents' consent. It also introduced a new category of 'custodianship' intended to give greater security to foster-parents. However, its provisions were contingent on the availability of resources with the result that it was never fully implemented.

**Children Act (1989)** reformed the law relating to children and their families and adopted the rights of the child as a fundamental principle. It emphasised the child's welfare as paramount and enjoined courts not to impose a care order unless it was in the interests of the child to do so. Available online at: <http://www.hmso.gov.uk/acts/acts1989/Ukpga_19890041_en_1.htm> (accessed 4 April 2005).

**Care Standards Act (2000)** was introduced to ensure that the care of vulnerable people (including young people) in different types of supported housing was properly regulated, improve care standards and introduce consistency in the regulation of social care and independent health services. Available online at: <http://www.dh.gov.uk/assetRoot/04/01/22/84/04012284.pdf> (accessed 4 April 2005).

**Children (Scotland) Act (1995)** brought together different areas of law affecting children such as family, child care and adoption law. Its emphasis was on child-centred principles based on the United Nations Convention on the Rights of the Child. Available online at: <http://www.hmso.gov.uk/acts/acts1995/Ukpga_19950036en_1.htm> (accessed 4 April 2005).

**Children (Northern Ireland) Order (1995),** based on the 1989 Children Act (England), placed new responsibilities on local authorities to protect and promote children's welfare and to prepare children's services plans. Available online at: <http://www.northernireland-legislation.hmso.gov.uk/si/si1995/Uksi_19950755_en_1.htm> (accessed 4 April 2005).

**Quality Protects (1998)** was part of a wider strategy to address social exclusion, and in particular aimed to improve services for children in local authority care and those leaving care through local authority management action plans (MAPS). Available online at: <http://www.dfes.gov.uk/qualityprotects/> (accessed 4 April 2005).

**Children (Leaving Care) Act (2000)** ensured that children and young people accommodated by local authorities under the Children Act (1989) were provided with due care and support during their transition from care up until at least the age of 21 years or 24 if in full-time education.

**Adoption and Children Act (2002)** modernised the legal framework for domestic and inter-country adoption and introduced a new legal order, special guardianship, offering legal permanence for children for whom adoption is not suitable. Available online at: <http://www.hmso.gov.uk/acts/acts2002/20020038.htm> (accessed 4 April 2005).

**Choice Protects (2002)** was launched to improve outcomes for looked-after children by providing a greater degree of placement stability and giving children and young people and their families greater choice over care placements. Available online at: <http://www.dfes.gov.uk/choiceprotects/> (accessed 4 April 2005).

**Children Act (2004)** provides the legislative framework for improving children's lives and covers both universal services, accessed by all children, and targeted services, for those with additional needs. It aims to encourage the integrated planning, commissioning and delivery of health, social care and education services. Available online at: <http://www.hmso.gov.uk/acts/acts2004/20040031.htm> (accessed 4 April 2005).

# References

Action on Aftercare Consortium (1996) *Too Much Too Young; the failure of social policy in meeting the needs of care leavers*, Barkingside: Barnardo's.

Advocacy 2000 (2000) *Key Ideas on Independent Advocacy*, Edinburgh: Advocacy 2000.

Aiers, A. and Kettle, J. (1998) *When Things Go Wrong: young people's experiences of getting access to the complaints procedure*, London: NISW.

Alber, E. (2004) '"The real parents are the foster parents": social parenthood among the Baatambou in Northern Benin', in F. Bowie (ed.), *Cross-cultural Approaches to Adoption*, London: Routledge.

Alderson, P. and Morrow, V. (2004) *Ethics, Social Research and Consulting with Children and Young People*, London: Barnardo's.

Allen, I. and Bourke Dowling, S. (1998) *Teenage Mothers: decisions and outcomes*, London: Policy Studies Institute.

Arcelus, J., Bellerby, T. and Vostanis, P. (1999) 'A mental health service for young people in the care of the local authority', *Clinical Child Psychology and Psychiatry*, 4, 2: 233–245.

Archer, L., Hicks, L., Little, M. and Mount, K. (1998) *Caring for Children Away from Home: messages from research*, London: Department of Health/Wiley.

ASC (1994) 'The role of the children's advocate', *Childright*, 109: 19.

Atherton, C. (2002) 'Changing culture not structure: five years of research in practice in child care', *Managing Community Care*, 10, 1: 17–21.

Atkinson, D. (1999) *Advocacy: a review*, Brighton: Pavilion.

Aynsley-Green, A. (2004) *What are the implications of 'Change for Children' for R&D? Bridging the gap between politics, policy and practice*. Presentation available online at <http://www.ihs.man.ac.uk/ResearchNetworks/ProfAGreenslides> (accessed 22 February 2005).

Bald, J., Bean, J. and Meegan, F. (1995). *A Book of My Own*, London: Who Cares? Trust.

Barratt, P.M. and Cooke, J.C. (2001) *REAL Evidence Based Practice in Teams: action pack*, Sheffield: Sheffield University/Research in Practice.

Barratt, P.M. (2003) 'Organizational support for evidence-based practice within child and family social work: a collaborative study', *Child and Family Social Work*, 8: 143–150.

Barreau, S. (2004) 'On their own', *Community Care*, 38–39.

Barrow, C. (1996) *Family in the Caribbean: themes and perspectives*, Oxford: J. Currey.

Barth, R.C., Freundlich, M. and Brodzinsky, D. (2000) *Adoption and Prenatal Alcohol and Drug Exposure*, Washington, DC: CWLA.

Bean, P. and Melville, J. (1989) *Lost Children of the Empire*, London: Unwin Hyman.

Bebbington, A. and Miles, J. (1989) 'The background of children who enter local authority care', *British Journal of Social Work*, 19: 349–368.

Berrick, J.D., Frasch, K. and Fox, A. (2000) 'Assessing children's experiences of out-of-home care: methodological challenges and opportunities', *Social Work Research*, 2: 119–127.

Berridge, D. (2002) 'Residential care', in D. McNeish, T. Newman and H. Roberts (eds), *What Works for Children*, Buckingham: Open University Press.

Berridge, D. and Brodie, I. (1998) *Children's Homes Revisited*, London: Jessica Kingsley.

Berridge, D., Brodie, I., Pitts, J., Porteous, D. and Tarling, R. (2001) *The Independent Effects of Permanent Exclusion from School on the Offending Careers of Young People*, London: Home Office.

Biehal, N., Clayden, J., Stein, M. and Wade, J. (1992) *Prepared for Living? A survey of young people leaving the care of the local authorities*, London: National Children's Bureau.

—— (1995) *Moving On: young people and leaving care schemes*, London: HMSO.

Blackwell, L. and Bynner, J. (2002) *Learning, Family Formation and Dissolution*, Wider Benefits of Learning Research Report No. 4, London: WBL Centre, Institute of Education.

Blyth, E. and Milner, J. (1994) 'Exclusion from school and victim-blaming', *Oxford Review of Education*, 20, 3: 293–306.

Boddy, J., Cameron, C. and Moss, P. (eds) (forthcoming) *Care Work: present and future*, London: Routledge.

Boniwell, I. and Zimbardo, P. (2003) 'Time to find the right balance: positive psychology', *The Psychologist*, 16, 3: 127.

Borland, M., Pearson, C., Hill, M., Tisdall, K. and Bloomfield, I. (1998) *Education and Care Away From Home*, Edinburgh: Scottish Council for Research in Education.

Botting, B., Rosato, M. and Wood, R. (1998) 'Teenage mothers and the health of their children', *Population Trends* 93, London: The Stationery Office.

Boylan, J. and Boylan. P. (1998) 'Promoting young people's empowerment: advocacy in North Wales', *Representing Children*, 11, 1: 42–48.

Boylan, J. and Wyllie, J. (1999) 'Advocacy and child protection', in N. Parton and C. Wattam (eds), *Child Sexual Abuse: responding to the experiences of children*, Chichester: Wiley.

Boylan, J., Dalrymple, J. and Ing, P. (2000) 'Let's do it! Advocacy, young people and social work education', *Social Work Education*, 19, 6: 553–563.

Brill, K. (1991) 'The Curtis Experiment', Ph.D. dissertation, University of Birmingham, cited in R. Holman (1998) *Child Care Revisited*, London: Institute of Child Care and Social Education.

Broad, B. (1994) *Leaving Care in the 1990s: the results of a national survey*, London: The Aftercare Consortium/Royal Philanthropic Society.

—— (1998) *Young People Leaving Care: life after the Children Act 1989*, London: Jessica Kingsley.

—— (1999a) 'Improving the health of young people leaving care', *Adoption and Fostering*, 22: 40–48.

—— (1999b) 'Young people leaving care: moving towards "joined up" solutions?', *Children and Society*, 13: 81–93.

—— (2005) *Improving the Health and Well Being of Young People Leaving Care*, Lyme Regis: Russell House Publishing.

Broad, B., Hayes, R. and Rushforth, C. (2001) *Kith and Kin: kinship care for vulnerable young people*, London: National Children's Bureau and Joseph Rowntree Foundation.

Brodie, I. (2001) *Children's Homes and School Exclusion: redefining the problem*, London: Jessica Kingsley.

Brodie, I., Berridge, D. and Beckett, W. (1997) 'The health of children looked after by local authorities', *British Journal of Nursing*, 6, 7: 386–391.

Brown, E., Bullock, R., Hobson, C. and Little, M. (1998) *Making Residential Care Work: structure and culture in children's homes*, Aldershot: Gower.

Buchanan, A. (1999) 'Are care leavers significantly dissatisfied and depressed in adult life?', *Adoption and Fostering*, 23, 4: 35–40.

Bullock, R., Little, M. and Millham, S. (1998) *Secure Treatment Outcomes: the care careers of very difficult adolescents*, Aldershot: Gower.

Burghes, L., Clarke, L. and Cronin, N. (1997) *Fathers and Fatherhood in Britain*, London: Family Policy Studies Centre.

Butler, I. and Drakeford, M. (2003) *Social Policy, Social Welfare and Scandal: how British public policy is made*, Basingstoke: Palgrave Macmillan.

Butler, I. and Williamson, H. (1994) *Children Speak: children, trauma and social work*, London: Longman.

Bynner, J., Joshi, H. and Tsatsas, M. (2000) *Obstacles and Opportunities on the Route to Adulthood: evidence from rural and urban Britain*, London: The Smith Institute.

Cabinet Office (1999) *Modernising Government*, Cm 4310, 6, London: HMSO.

Cameron, C. (2004) 'Social pedagogy and care: Danish and German practice in young people's residential care', *Journal of Social Work*, 4, 2: 133–151.

Cannan, C., Berry, L. and Lyons, K. (1992) *Social Work and Europe*, Basingstoke: BASW/ Macmillan.

Centre for Research on the Wider Benefits of Learning (2005). Available online at <http://www.learningbenefits.net/> (accessed 5 April 2005).

Centrepoint (2004) *Youth Homelessness Statistics*, London: Centrepoint. Available online at <http://www.centrepoint.org.uk/main.asp?id=482_1952_19258> (accessed 1 February 2004).

Cheesbrough, S., Ingham, R. and Massey, D. (1999) *Summary Bulletin: reducing the rate of teenage conceptions. An international review of the evidence: USA, Canada, Australia and New Zealand*, London: Health Education Authority.

Cheung, S.Y. and Heath, A. (1994) 'After care: the education and occupation of adults who have been in care', *Oxford Review of Education*, 20: 361–374.

Children's Commissioner for Wales (2003) *Telling Concerns. A report of the Children's Commissioner for Wales' review of the operation of complaints and representations and whistleblowing procedures and arrangements for the provision of children's advocacy services*, Wales: Children's Commissioner for Wales Office.

Children and Young People's Unit (2001) *Learning to Listen: core principles for the involvement of children and young people*, London: CYPU.

Christensen, P.H. and James, A. (eds) (2000) *Research with Children: perspectives and practices*, London: Falmer Press.

Clarke, J. and Newman, J. (1997) *The Managerial State*, London: Sage.

Clarke, P. (2002) *By Private Arrangement: inspection of arrangements for supervising children in private foster care*, London: Department of Health.

Cleaver, H. and Freeman, P. (1995) *Parental Perspectives in Cases of Suspected Child Abuse*, London: HMSO.

Climbié Report (2003) *The Victoria Climbié Inquiry: report of an inquiry by Lord Laming*, Cm 5730, London: HMSO.

Clyde Report (1946) *Report of the Committee on Homeless Children*, cmd 6911, London: HMSO.

Cohen, B., Moss, P., Petrie, P. and Wallace, J. (2004) *A New Deal for Children? Re-forming education and care in England, Scotland and Sweden*, Bristol: Policy Press.

Cole, T., Sellman, E., Daniels, H. and Visser, J. (2002) *The Mental Health Needs of Young People with Emotional and Behavioural Difficulties*, London: The Mental Health Foundation.

Coleman, J. (2001) 'Focus: young fathers', *Young People's Health Network Newsletter*, 15, 1.

Colton, M. and Hellinckx, W. (1993) *Childcare in the EC: country-specific guide to foster and residential care*, Cambridge: Cambridge University Press.

Colton, M., Drury, C. and Williams, M. (1995) *Children in Need: family support under the Children Act 1989*, Aldershot: Arena.

Colton, M., Casas, F., Drakeford, M., Roberts, S., Scholte, E. and Williams, M. (1997) *Stigma and Social Welfare: an international comparative study*, Aldershot: Avebury.

Colwell Report (1974) *Report of the Committee of Inquiry into the Care and Supervision Provided in Relation to Maria Colwell*, London: HMSO.

Corlyon, J. and McGuire, C. (1997) *Young Parents in Public Care: pregnancy and parenthood among young people looked after by local authorities*, London: National Children's Bureau.

—— (1999) *Pregnancy and Parenthood: the views and experiences of young people in public care*, London: National Children's Bureau.

Courtney, M.E., Piliavin, I., Grogan-Kaylor, A. and Nesmith, A. (2001) 'Foster youth transitions to adulthood: a longitudinal view of youth leaving care', *Child Welfare*, 80: 685–717.

Cox, P. and Jackson, S. (eds) (2003) 'Researching social work', *Social Work Education*, 22, 1, February.

Cree, V., Kay, H. and Tisdall, K. (2002) 'Research with children: sharing the dilemmas', *Child and Family Social Work*, 7: 47–56.

Crimmens, D. (1998) 'Training for residential child care workers in Europe: comparing approaches in The Netherlands, Ireland and the United Kingdom', *Social Work Education*, 17, 3: 309–319.

Curtis Report (1946) *Report of the Care of Children Committee*, cmnd 6922, London: HMSO.

Curtis, K., Roberts, H., Copperman, J., Downie, A. and Liabo, K. (2004) '"How come I don't get asked no questions?" Researching "hard to reach" children and teenagers', *Child and Family Social Work*, 9: 167–175.

Dalrymple, J. (2001) 'Safeguarding young people through confidential advocacy services', *Child and Family Social Work*, 6: 149–160.

Dalrymple, J. and Hough, J. (eds) (1995) *Having a Voice: an exploration of children's rights and advocacy*, Birmingham: Venture Press/British Association of Social Workers.

Dartington Social Research Unit (1995) *Child Protection: messages from research studies in Child Protection*, London: HMSO.

Davies Jones, H. (1994) 'The profession at work in contemporary society', in M. Courtioux et al. (eds), *The Social Pedagogue in Europe – living with others as a profession*, Zurich: FICE.

Dearden, K.A., Hale, C.B. and Woolley, T. (1995) 'The antecedents of teen fatherhood: a retrospective case-control study of Great Britain youth', *American Journal of Public Health*, 85: 551–554.

Dennison, C. and Coleman, J. (2000) *Young People and Gender: a review of research*, London: Women's Unit/Cabinet Office.

Dennison, C. and Lyon, J. (2003) *Young Offenders, Fatherhood and the Impact of Parenting Training*, London: HM Prison Service.

Department for Education and Skills (DfES) (1998) *The Government's Response to the Children's Safeguards Review*, Cm 4105, London: The Stationery Office.

—— (2002) *The Children Act Report 2002*, Nottingham: DfES.

—— (2003a) *Autumn Performance Report 2003*, London: DfES. Available online at <http://www.dfes.gov.uk/cgi-bin/rsgateway.search.pl?cat=8&subcat=8_1&q1=search>.

—— (2003b) *Statistics of Education. Care Leavers, 2002–2003, England*, London: DfES.

—— (2004a) *Children Looked After by Local Authorities Year Ending 31 March 2003*, London: DfES. Available online at <http://www.dfes.gov.uk/rsgateway/DB/SBU/b000552/index.shtml>.

—— (2004b) *Statistics of Education. Outcome indicators for looked after children. Twelve months to 30 September 2003, England*, London: DfES.

Department for Education and Skills and Department of Health (2000) *Guidance on the Education of Children and Young People in Public Care*, London: DfES and DoH.

—— (2002) *Education Protects. Collecting and using data to improve educational outcomes for children in public care*, London: DfES and DoH.

Department for Education and Skills, Department of Health and Home Office (2003) *Keeping Children Safe: the government's response to the Victoria Climbié inquiry report and joint chief inspectors' report safeguarding children*, Cm 5861, London: HMSO.

Department of Health (1989) *Introduction to the Children Act 1989*, London: HMSO.

—— (1991a) *The Children Act 1989 Guidance and Regulations, Volume 3: Family placements*, London: HMSO.

—— (1991b) *The Children Act 1989 Guidance and Regulations, Volume 4: Residential care*, London: HMSO.

—— (1992) *Working Together under the Children Act 1989*, London: HMSO.

—— (1997) *Substance Misuse and Young People*, London: DoH.

—— (1998a) *Caring for Children Away from Home: messages from research*, Chichester: Wiley.

—— (1998b) *Modernising Social Services*, cmnd 4169, London: HMSO.

—— (1998c) *Modernising Social Services: promoting independence, improving protection, raising standards*, London: HMSO.

—— (1998d) *Quality Protects Circular LAC (1998) 28*, London: DoH.

—— (1998e) *Quality Protects: framework for action*, London: DoH. Available online at <http://www.dfes.gov.uk/qualityprotects/>.

—— (1998f) *Someone Else's Children: inspections of planning and decision making for children looked after and the safety of children looked after*, London: DoH.

—— (1999a) *A New Approach to Social Services Performance*, London: HMSO.

—— (1999b) *Me, Survive, Out There? New arrangements for young people living in and leaving care*, London: DoH.

—— (1999c) *Framework for the Assessment of Children in Need and their Families*, London: DoH, DfES, HMSO.

—— (2000a) *A Quality Strategy for Social Care*, London: HMSO. Available online at <http://www.doh.gov.uk/qualitystrategy/execsum.htm> (accessed 2 February 2005).

—— (2000b) *Assessment Framework for Children in Need and their Families*, London: DoH.

—— (2001) *Children (Leaving Care) Act 2000 Regulations and Guidance*, London: HMSO.

—— (2002) *National Standards for Agencies providing advocacy for children and young people in England*, London: DoH.

—— (2003) *Social Services Performance Assessment Framework Indicators 2002–2003*, London: DoH.

Department of Health, Social Services and Public Safety (2003) *Children Order Statistics. 1 April 2002–31 March 2003*, Belfast: Department of Health, Social Services and Public Safety. Available online at <http://www.dhsspsni.gov.uk/publications/2004/ Child02_03.pdf>.

Dixon, J. and Stein, M. (2002) *Still a Bairn: through care and aftercare Services in Scotland*, Edinburgh: Scottish Executive

Douglas, A. and Obang, D. (2001) 'A question of confidentiality', *Community Care*, 8 November. Available online at <http://www.communitycare.co.uk> (accessed 14 February 2005).

Dumaret, A-C. (1988) 'The SOS Children's Villages: school achievement of subjects reared in permanent foster care', *Early Child Development and Care*, 34: 217–226

Editorial (15 March 2003) 'Achieving health for children in public care. New Department of Health guidance emphasises a rounded approach', *British Medical Journal*, 326: 560–561.

Eekelaar, J. and Dingwall, R. (1990) *The Reform of Child Care Law*, London: Routledge.

Emecheta, B. (1974) *Second Class Citizen*, London: Allison and Busby.

Emler, N. (2001) *Self-esteem: the costs and causes of low self-worth*, York: Joseph Rowntree Foundation.

Essen, J., Lambert, L. and Head, J. (1976) 'School attainment of children who have been in care', *Child: Care, Health and Development*, 2: 339–351.

Evans, R. (2000) *The Educational Attainments and Progress of Children in Public Care*, Ph.D. thesis, Warwick, Coventry: Institute of Education.

Farmer, E. and Owen, M. (1995) *Child Protection Practice: private risks and public remedies*, London: HMSO.

Farmer, E. and Pollock, S. (1998) *Sexually Abused and Abusing Children in Substitute Care*, Chichester: Wiley.

Feuerstein, R. and Krasilowsky, D. (1967) 'The treatment group technique', in M. Wolins and M. Gottesman (eds), *Group Care: an Israeli approach*, New York: Gordon and Breach.

Firth, H. and Fletcher, B. (2001) 'Developing equal chances: a whole authority approach', in S. Jackson (ed.), *Nobody Ever Told us School Mattered: raising the educational attainment of children in care*, London: British Agencies for Adoption and Fostering.

Fletcher-Campbell, F. (1997) *The Education of Children Who Are Looked After*, Slough: National Foundation for Educational Research.

Fletcher-Campbell, F. and Hall, C. (1990) *Changing Schools, Changing People: the education of children in care*, Slough: National Foundation for Educational Research.

Foundation for People with Learning Disabilities (2000) *Everyday Lives, Everyday Choices*, London: Mental Health Foundation.

Fox Harding, L. (1997) *Perspectives in Child Care Policy* (2nd edn), London: Longman.

Francis, J. (2000) 'Investing in children's futures: enhancing the educational arrangements of "looked after" children and young people', *Child and Family Social Work*, 5: 23–33.

Franklin, R. (1995) *The Handbook of Children's Rights, Comparative Policy and Practice*, London: Routledge.

Gallagher, B., Brannen, C., Jones, R. and Westwood, S. (2004) 'Good practice in the education of children in residential care', *British Journal of Social Work*, 34: 1133–1160.

Gallagher, R. and Cleland, A. (1996) 'Legal Proceedings and the Children (Scotland) Act 1995: a children's rights perspective', *Representing Children*, 9, 4: 210–225.

Galloway, D., Armstrong, D. and Tomlinson, S. (1994) *The Assessment of Special Educational Needs – Whose Problem?*, London: Longman.

Garner, P. and Sandow, S. (1995) *Advocacy, Self-advocacy and Special Needs*, London: David Fulton.

Garnett, L. (1992) *Leaving Care and After*, London: National Children's Bureau.

Gibbons, J., Conroy, S. and Bell, C. (1995) *Operating the Child Protection System: a study of child protection practices in English local authorities*, London: HMSO.

Gilbertson, R. and Barber, J. (2002) 'Obstacles to involving children and young people in foster care research', *Child and Family Social Work*, 7: 253–258.

Gill, O. and Jackson, B. (1983) *Adoption and Race: Black, Asian and mixed race children in white families*, London: Batsford Academic and Educational in association with British Agencies for Adoption and Fostering.

Gilligan, R. (1997) 'Beyond permanence? The importance of resilience in child placement practice and planning', *Adoption and Fostering*, 21: 12–20.

—— (2001) *Promoting Resilience: a resource guide on working with children in the care system*, London: British Agencies for Adoption and Fostering.

—— (2004) 'Promoting resilience in child and family social work: issues for social work practice, education and policy', *Social Work Education*, 23, 1: 93–104.

Glaser, B.G. and Strauss, A.L. (1967) *The Discovery of Grounded Theory: strategies for qualitative research*, Chicago, IL: Aldine Publishing.

Goddard, J. (2000) 'The education of looked after children – a research review', *Child and Family Social Work*, 5: 79–86.

Goldschmied, E. and Jackson, S. (2004) *People Under Three: young children in day care*, (2nd edn), London: Routledge.

Goldstein, J., Freud, A. and Solnit, A. (1973) *Beyond the Best Interests of the Child*, New York: Free Press.

Goody, E.N. (1982) *Parenthood and Social Reproduction: fostering and occupational roles in West Africa*, Cambridge: Cambridge University Press.

Goody, E.N. and Groothues, C.M. (1979) 'Stress in marriage: West African couples in London', in V. Saifullah Khan (ed.), *Minority Families in Britain*, London: Macmillan.

Gordon, D., Parker, R. and Loughran, F. (2000) *Disabled Children in Britain: a re-analysis of the OPCS Disability Survey*, London: HMSO.

Gottesman, M. (ed.) (1991) *Residential Childcare: an international reader*, London: Whiting & Birch.

—— (1994) *Recent Changes and New Trends in Extrafamilial Childcare: An international perspective*, London: Whiting & Birch.

Gray, B. and Jackson, R. (eds) (2002) *Advocacy and Learning Disability*, London: Jessica Kingsley.

Greene, M. (1999) *Over To Us: a report of an advocacy project working with young disabled people living in residential institutions*, Manchester: GMCDP Publications.

Greig, A. and Taylor, J. (1999) *Doing Research with Children*, London: Sage.

Griffiths, C. (2000) *Breaking Their Fall: meeting the literacy needs of looked after children*, London: National Literacy Association/The Who Cares? Trust.

Hagan, J. (1997). Defiance and despair: subcultural and structural linkages between delinquency and despair in the life course', *Social Forces*, 76, 1: 119–134.

Hallden, G. (1991) 'The child as project and the child as being: parents' ideas as frames of reference', *Children and Society*, 5, 4: 334–346.

Hallett, C. and Prout, A. (eds) (2003) *Hearing the Voices of Children: social policy for a new century*, London: Routledge Falmer.

Halsey, A., Heath, A. and Ridge, J. (1980) *Origins and Destinations: family, class, and education in modern Britain*, Oxford: Clarendon Press.

Hammond, C. (2002) *Learning To Be Healthy*, Wider Benefits of Learning Monograph No. 3, London: Institute of Education.

Harbin, F. and Murphy, M. (2000) *Substance Misuse and Childcare*, Lyme Regis: Russell House.

Harder, M. and Pringle, K. (1997) *Protecting Children in Europe: towards a new millennium*, Aalborg: Aalborg University Press.

Harker, R. (2002) *Including Children in Social Research*, Highlight No. 193, London: National Children's Bureau.

Harker, R., Dobel-Ober, D., Berridge, D. and Sinclair, R. (2004) *Taking Care of Education: an evaluation of the education of looked after children*, London: National Children's Bureau.

Haywood, C. and Mac an Ghaill, M. (2003) *Men and Masculinities*, Buckingham: Open University Press.

Health Development Agency (2001) *Teenage Pregnancy: an update on key characteristics of effective interventions*, London: Health Development Agency.

Heath, A., Colton, M. and Aldgate, J. (1989) 'The educational progress of children in and out of care', *British Journal of Social Work*, 19: 447–460.

—— (1994) 'Failure to escape: a longitudinal study of foster children's educational attainment', *British Journal of Social Work*, 24: 241–259.

Heptinstall, E. (2000) 'Gaining access to looked after children for research purposes: lessons learned', *British Journal of Social Work*, 30: 867–872.

Herbert, M.D. and Mould, J.W. (1992) 'The advocacy role in public child welfare', *Child Welfare*, 71, 2: 114–130.

Hetherington, R., Cooper, A., Smith, P. and Wilford, G. (1997) *Protecting Children: messages from Europe*, Lyme Regis: Russell House.

Heywood, J. (1964) *Children in Care: the development of the service for the deprived child* (revised edn), London: Routledge & Kegan Paul.

Higham, P. (2001) 'Changing practice and an emerging social pedagogue paradigm in England: the role of the personal adviser', *Social Work in Europe*, 8, 1: 21–29.

Hill, M. and Tisdall, K. (1997) *Children and Society*, London: Longman.

Hobcraft, J. (1998) *Intergenerational and Life-course Transmission of Social Exclusion: influences of childhood poverty, family disruption and contact with the police*, London: Centre for Analysis of Social Exclusion.

Holman, R. (1973) *Trading in Children: a study of private fostering*, London: Routledge & Kegan Paul.

—— (1980) *Inequality in Child Care*, London: Child Poverty Action Group.

—— (1998) *Child Care Revisited, The Children's Departments 1948–1971: how the child care specialists of the past hold lessons for the future*, London: Institute of Childcare and Social Education UK.

—— (2002) *The Unknown Fostering: a study of private fostering*, Lyme Regis: Russell House.

Home Office, Department of Health, Department of Education and Science, Welsh Office (1991) *Working Together Under the Children Act 1989*, London: HMSO.

Houghton Report (1972) *Report of the Departmental Committee on the Adoption of Children*, cmnd 5107, London: HMSO.

House of Commons Health Committee (1998) *Children Looked After by Local Authorities. Second report. Vol. 1: Report and proceedings of the Committee*, London: HMSO.

Humphreys, C., Berridge, D., Butler, I. and Ruccick, R. (2003) 'Making research count: the development of "knowledge based practice"', *Research Policy and Planning*, 21, 1: 41–49.

Humphreys, M. (1994) *Empty Cradles*, London: Transworld.

Inglis, R. (1989) *The Children's War: evacuation, 1939–1945*, London: Collins.

Ivaldi, G. (1998) *Children Adopted from Care: an examination of agency adoptions in England*, London: British Association for Adoption and Fostering.

Jackson, B. (1984) *Fatherhood*, London: Unwin Hyman.

Jackson, S. (1983) *The Education of Children in Care*, unpublished report to the Social Science Research Council.

—— (1987) *The Education of Children in Care*, Bristol, UK: University of Bristol School of Applied Social Studies.

—— (1989) 'The state as parent: assessing outcomes in child care', in J. Hudson and B. Galaway (eds), *The State as Parent: international research perspectives on interventions with young persons* (NATO ASI Series, 53), Boston and Dordrecht: Kluwer Academic.

—— (1998) 'Looking after children: a new approach or just an exercise in form filling? A response to Knight and Caveney', *British Journal of Social Work*, 28, 1: 45–56.

—— (2000) 'Promoting the educational achievement of looked after children', in T. Cox (ed.), *Combating Educational Disadvantage: meeting the needs of vulnerable children*, London: Falmer Press.

—— (2001) *Nobody Ever Told Us School Mattered. Raising the educational attainments of children in care*, London: British Association for Adoption and Fostering.

—— (2002) 'Promoting stability and continuity in care away from home', in D. McNeish, T. Newman and H. Roberts (eds), *What Works for Children*, Buckingham: Open University Press.

Jackson, S. and Kilroe, S. (1995) *Looking After Children Training Resources Pack*, London: HMSO.

Jackson, S. and Kilroe, S. (eds) (1996) *Looking After Children: good parenting, good outcomes*, London: HMSO.

Jackson, S. and Martin, P. Y. (1998) 'Surviving the care system: education and resilience', *Journal of Adolescence*, 21: 569–583.

Jackson, S. and Roberts, S. (2000) *A Feasibility Study on the Needs of Care Leavers in Higher Education: report to the Gulbenkian Foundation*, Swansea: University of Swansea, School of Social Sciences and International Development.

Jackson, S. and Sachdev, D. (2001) *Better Education, Better Futures: research, practice and the views of young people in public care*, Ilford: Barnardo's.

Jackson, S. and Thomas, N. (1999) *On the Move Again*, Ilford: Barnardo's.

—— (2001) *What Works in Creating Stability for Looked After Children?* Ilford: Barnardo's.

Jackson, S., Ajayi, S. and Quigley, M. (2003) *By Degrees: the first year. From care to university*, London: National Children's Bureau/The Frank Buttle Trust.

—— (2005) *Going to University from Care*, London: Institute of Education.

Jackson, S., Williams, J.G., Love, A., Cheung, W.Y and Hutchings, H. (2000) *The Health Needs and Health Care of School Age Children Looked After by Local Authorities*, Final Report to the Wales Office of Research and Development, Cardiff: The National Assembly for Wales.

Jackson, S., Feinstein, L., Levacic, R., Owen, C., Simon, A. and Brassett-Grundy, A. (2002) *The Costs and Benefits of Educating Children in Care*, CLS Cohort Studies Working Paper No.4, Internet Publication. Available online at <ftp://cls.ioe.ac.uk/pub/Cohort/Acrobat/Cswp4.pdf> (accessed 2 February 2005).

James, A., Jenks, C. and Prout, A. (1998) *Theorizing Childhood*, Cambridge: Polity Press.

Kane, R. and Wellings, K. (1999) *Summary Bulletin: reducing the rate of teenage conceptions. An international review of the evidence: data from Europe*, London: Health Education Authority.

Kemmis, J. (2000) 'Advocacy groups welcome support for children', *Community Care*, 17 February.

Kiernan, K.E. (1995) *Transition to Parenthood: young mothers, young fathers – associated factors and later life experiences*, London: London School of Economics.

Kipling, R. (1999) *The Man who Would be King, and Other Stories*, Oxford: Oxford University Press.

Knight, A., Chase, E. and Aggleton, P. (forthcoming) "Someone of Your Own to Love": experiences of being looked after as influences on teenage pregnancy', *Children and Society*.

Knight, T. and Caveney, S. (1998) 'Assessment and action records: will they promote good parenting?', *British Journal of Social Work*, 28, 1: 29–44.

Lally, J.R. (2005) 'The human rights of infants and toddlers: a comparison of childcare philosophies in Europe, Australia, New Zealand and the United States', *Zero to Three*, 25, 3: 43–46.

Lalond, S. (1995) 'Teenage dads', *New Generation*, 9.

Lambert, L., Essen, J. and Head, J. (1977) 'Variations in behaviour ratings of children who have been in care', *Journal of Child Psychology and Psychiatry*, 18: 335–346.

Laming, H. (2003) *The Victoria Climbié Inquiry*, Cm 5730, London: HMSO.

Lewis, A. and Lindsay, G. (eds) (2000) *Researching Children's Perspectives*, Buckingham: Open University Press.

Lee-Foster, A. and Moorhead, D. (1996) *Do the Rights Thing! An advocacy learning pack*, London: Sense.

Lindley, B. and Richards, M. (2002) *Protocol on Advice and Advocacy for Parents (Child Protection)*, Cambridge: Centre for Family Research, University of Cambridge.

Lindsay, M. (1997) 'Balancing power: advocacy in a Scottish health board', *Research, Policy and Planning*, 15, 2: 31–33.

Local Government Data Unit – Wales (2004) *Social Services Statistics Wales 2002–2003*, Cardiff: Local Government Data Unit. Available online at <http://www.wales.gov.uk/keypubstatisticsforwales/content/publication/health/2004/sdr35-2004/sdr35-2004.htm>.

Lorenz, W. (1994) *Social Work in a Changing Europe*, London: Routledge.

Mainey, A. (2003) *Better Than You Think: staff morale, qualifications and retention in residential child care*, London: National Children's Bureau.

Marchant, R. (1998) 'Letting it take time: rights work with disabled children and young people', in L. Ward (ed.), *Innovations in Advocacy and Empowerment for People with Intellectual Disabilities*, Chorley: Lisieux Hall Publications.

Martin, P.Y. and Jackson, S. (2002) 'Educational success for children in public care: advice from a group of high achievers', *Child and Family Social Work*, 7, 2: 121–130.

Maxime, J. (1986) 'Some psychological models of black self concept', in S. Ahmed, J. Cheetham and J. Small (eds), *Social Work With Black Children and Their Families*, London: Batsford.

McDonald, T.P., Allen, R.I., Westerfelt, A. and Piliavin, I. (1996) *Assessing the Long-term effects of foster care: a research synthesis*, Washington, DC: Child Welfare League of America.

Melton, G. (1987) 'Children, politics and morality: the ethics of child advocacy', *Journal of Clinical Psychology*, 16, 4: 357–367.

Merriam, S.B. (2002) 'Assessing and evaluating qualitative research', in S.B. Merriam (ed.), *Qualitative Research in Practice: examples for discussion and analysis*, San Francisco, CA: Jossey-Bass.

Millham, S., Bullock, R., Hosie, K. and Little, M. (1986) *Lost in Care*, Aldershot: Gower.

Mittler, P. (2000) *Working Towards Inclusive Education: social contexts*, London: David Fulton.

Mittler, P., Jackson, S. with Sebba, J. (2002) 'Social exclusion and education', *Building Knowledge for Integrated Care*, 10, 3: 5–15.

Monckton Report (1945) *Report on the Circumstances Which Led to the Boarding Out of Dennis and Terence O'Neill on Bank Farm, Minsterley and the Steps Taken to Supervise Their Welfare*, Cmnd 636, London: HMSO.

Morgan, P. (1998) *Adoption and the Care of Children*, London: IEA Health and Welfare Unit.

Morris, J. (1998) *Don't Leave Us Out. Involving disabled children and young people with communication impairments*, York: Joseph Rowntree Foundation.

—— (2000) *Having Someone Who Cares? Barriers to change in the public care system*, London: National Children's Bureau.

Moss, P. and Penn, H. (1996) *Transforming Nursery Education*, London: Paul Chapman.

Mount, J., Lister, A. and Bennun, I. (2004) 'Identifying the mental health needs of looked after young people', *Clinical Child Psychology and Psychiatry*, 9: 363–382.

Mumford, G.H.F. and Selwood, T.J. (1976) *A Guide to the Children Act 1975*, London: Shaw & Sons.

Musick, J. (1993) *Young, Poor and Pregnant: the psychology of teenage motherhood*, New Haven, CT: Yale University Press.

National Care Standards Commission (2003) *Children's Views on Complaints Procedures and Advocacy. Report of the Children's Rights Director*, Newcastle: National Care Standards Commission.

National Children's Homes (NCH) (2000) *Factfile 2001. Facts and figures about children in the UK*, London: NCH.

National Foster Care Association (NFCA) (1997) *Foster Care in Crisis*, London: NFCA.

National Statistics Bulletin (2003) *Statistics of Education: Care Leavers, 2002–2003*, London: Department for Education and Skills.

—— (2005) *Statistics of Education: children looked after in England (including adoptions and care leavers) 2003–2004*, London: Department for Education and Skills.

Newby, H. (2004) Memorial Lecture for Colin Bell, University of Bradford, 30 March.

Newell, P. (1993) *The UN Convention and Children's Rights in the UK* (2nd edn), London: National Children's Bureau/Calouste Gulbenkian Foundation.

Newman, M., Papadopoulos, I. and Sigworth, J. (1998) 'Barriers to evidence-based practice', *Clinical Effectiveness in Nursing*, 2: 11–20.

NHS Centre for Reviews and Dissemination (1999) 'Getting evidence into practice', *Effective Health Care Bulletin*, 5: 1–16.

Noon, A. (2000) *Having a Say: the participation of children and young people at child protection meetings and the role of advocacy*, London: The Children's Society.

Notermans, C. (2004) 'Fosterage and the politics of marriage and kinship in East Cameroon', in F. Bowie (ed.), *Cross-cultural Approaches to Adoption*, London: Routledge.

OFSTED (2002) *Raising Achievement of Children in Public Care. A Report from the Office of Her Majesty's Chief Inspector of Schools*. Available online at <http://www.ofsted.gov.uk/public/docs01/publiccare.pdf>.

Oliver, C. (2003a) 'The care of the illegitimate child: the Coram experience 1900–1945', in J. Brannen and P. Moss (eds), *Rethinking Children's Care*, Buckingham: Open University Press.

—— (2003b) *Advocacy for Children and Young People: a review of literature*, London: Department of Health.

Packman, J. (1975) *The Child's Generation: child care policy from Curtis to Houghton*, Oxford and London: Blackwell and Robertson.

Packman, J., Randall, J. and Jacques, N. (1986) *Who Needs Care?*, Oxford: Blackwell.

Page, H. (1989) 'Childrearing versus childbearing: coresidence of mother and child in sub-Saharan Africa', in R.J. Lesthaeghe (ed.), *Reproduction and Social Organization in Sub-Saharan Africa*, Berkeley: University of California Press.

Parker, R.A. (1980) *Caring for Separated Children*, London: Macmillan.

—— (1990) *Away from Home: a history of child care*, Ilford: Barnardo's.

Parker, R.A., Ward, H., Jackson, S., Aldgate, J. and Wedge, P. (1991) *Looking After Children: assessing outcomes in child care*, London: HMSO.

Parton, N. (1991) *Governing the Family: child care, child protection and the state*, Basingstoke: Macmillan.

—— (ed.) (1997) *Child Protection and Family Support*, London: Routledge.

Patel, S. (1995) 'Advocacy through the eyes of a young person', in J. Dalrymple and J. Hough, *Having a Voice: an exploration of children's rights and advocacy*, Birmingham: Venture Press.

Peart, E., Owen, C. and Barreau, S. (2005) 'Semi-formal care work: the case of private fostering', *Care Work in the Twenty-first Century*, London, Routledge.

Petrie, P. (2001) 'The potential of pedagogy/education for work in the children's sector in the UK', *Social Work in Europe*, 8, 3: 23–26.

Petrie, P., Cameron, C. and Boddy, J. (2002) 'All round friends', *Community Care*, 12 December: 34–35.

Petrie, P., Boddy, J., Cameron, C., Simon, A. and Wigfall, V. (forthcoming, 2006) *Working with Children in Europe*, Buckingham: Open University Press.

Pike, N. (2002) 'The neglected dimension: advocacy and the families of children with learning difficulties', in B. Gray and R. Jackson (eds), *Advocacy and Learning Disability*, London: Jessica Kingsley.

Pinchbeck, I. and Hewitt, M. (1973) *Children in English Society*, London: Routledge & Kegan Paul.

Piper, C. (1998) 'Child advocacy', in Y.J. Craig (ed.), *Advocacy, Counselling and Mediation in Casework*, London: Jessica Kingsley.

Pithouse, A., Lowe, K. and Hill-Tout, J. (2004) 'Foster carers who care for children with challenging behaviour: a total population study', *Adoption and Fostering*, 28, 3: 20–30.

Pollock, S. (2001) 'Young first time fathers – influences on commitment', *Young People's Health Network Newsletter*, 15, 8.

Power, S., Edwards, T., Whitty, G. and Wigfall, V. (2003) *Education and the Middle Class*, Buckingham: Open University Press.

Prevatt Goldstein, B. (2000) 'Ethnicity and placement, beginning the debate', *Adoption and Fostering*, 24: 2–4.

Priestley, M., Rabiee, P. and Harris, J. (2003) 'Young disabled people and the "new arrangements" for leaving care in England and Wales', *Children and Youth Services Review*, 2, 11: 863–890.

Pringle, K. (1998) *Children and Social Welfare in Europe*, Buckingham: Open University Press.

Pritchard, C. (2004) *The Child Abusers: Research and Controversy*, Maidenhead: Open University Press.

Prout, A. (2002) 'Research children as social actors: an introduction to the Children 5–16 programme', *Children and Society*, 16, 2: 67–76.

Quinton, D. and Rutter, M. (1988) *Parenting Breakdown: the making and breaking of intergenerational links*, Aldershot: Gower.

Quinton, D., Pollock, S. and Golding, J. (2002) *The Transition to Fatherhood in Young Men – Influences on Commitment*, Bristol: ESRC. Available online at <http: www.regard. ac.uk> (accessed 2 February 2005).

Qvortrup, J. (1994) 'Childhood matters: an introduction', in J. Qvortrup, M. Bardy, G. Sgritta and H. Wintersberger (eds), *Childhood Matters: social theory practice and politics*, Aldershot: Avebury.

Rabiee, P., Priestley, M. and Knowles, J. (2001) *Whatever Next? Young disabled people leaving care*, Leeds: First Key.

Randall, G. (1988) *No Way Home*, London: Centrepoint.

Rashid, S.P. (2000) 'The strength of black families: appropriate placements for all', *Adoption and Fostering*, 24: 15–22.

Reder, P. and Duncan, S. (2003) 'How much should children's views count?', in P. Reder, S. Duncan and C. Lucey (eds), *Studies in the Assessment of Parenting*, Hove and New York: Brunner-Routledge.

Reder, P., Duncan, S. and Gray, M. (1993) *Beyond Blame: child abuse tragedies revisited*, London: Routledge.

Rees, J. (2001) 'Making residential care educational care', in S. Jackson (ed.), *Nobody Ever Told us School Mattered*, London: British Agencies for Adoption and Fostering.

Richardson, J. (2002) *The Mental Health of Looked-after Children*, London: The Mental Health Foundation.

Richardson, J. and Joughin, C. (2000) *Mental Health Needs of Looked After Children*, London: Gaskell.

Rickford, F. (2004) 'Touchy subject', *Zero to Nineteen*, December.

Rinaldi, C. (2005) *In Dialogue with Reggio Emilia*, London: Routledge.

Ross, C.E. and Mirowsky, J. (1999) 'Refining the association between education and health: the effects of quantity, credential and selectivity', *Demography*, 36, 4: 445–460.

Rowe, J. and Lambert, L. (1973) *Children Who Wait*, London: Association of British Adoption Agencies.

Russell, P. (1989) *Self-advocacy and Parents: the impact of self-advocacy on the parents of young people with disabilities*, London: Further Education Unit.

—— (1998) *Having a Say: disabled children and effective partnership in decision-making*, London: Council for Disabled Children.

Saleeby, D. (1996) 'The strengths perspective in social work practice', *Social Work Education*, 41, 3: 296–305.

Sanders, R. (2003) 'Medical research ethics committees and social work research: a hurdle too far?', *Social Work Education*, 22, 1: 113–114.

Sanders, R., Jackson, S. and Thomas, N. (1996) 'The balance of prevention, investigation and treatment in the management of child protection services', *Child Abuse and Neglect*, 20, 10: 899–906.

Sargant, N., Field, J., Francis, H., Schuller, T. and Tuckett, A. (1997) *The Learning Divide: A study of participation in adult learning in the United Kingdom*, Leicester: National Institute for Adult and Continuing Education.

Saunders, L. and Broad, B. (1997) *The Health Needs of Young People Leaving Care*, Leicester: Centre for Social Action, De Montfort University.

Schuller, T., Brassett-Grundy, A., Green, A., Hammond, C. and Preston, J. (2002) *Learning, Continuity and Change in Adult Life*, Wider Benefits of Learning Research Report No. 3, London: WBL Centre, Institute of Education.

Schuller, T., Bynner, J., Green A., Blackwell, L., Hammond, C., Preston, J. and Gough, M. (2001) *Modelling and Measuring the Wider Benefits of Learning*, Wider Benefits of Learning Monograph No.1, London: Institute of Education.

Scott, J. and Larcher, J. (2002) 'Advocacy with people with communication difficulties', in B. Gray and R. Jackson (eds), *Advocacy and Learning Disability*, London: Jessica Kingsley.

Scottish Executive (2003) *Children's Social Work Statistics 2002–03*, Edinburgh: Scottish Executive.

Scutt, N. and Hoyland, C. (1995) 'My special person', *Community Care*, 23 February.

Seale, C. (2002) 'Quality issues in qualitative inquiry', *Qualitative Social Work*, 1: 97–110.

Seebohm Report (1968) *Report of the Committee on Local Authority and Allied Personal Social Services*, Cmnd 3703, London: HMSO.

Seglow, J., Kellmer Pringle, M. and Wedge, P. (1972) *Growing Up Adopted*, Windsor: National Foundation for Educational Research.

Seligman, M.E.P. (1998) 'Building human strength: psychology's forgotten mission', *APA Monitor*, 29, 1.

—— (2002) *Authentic Happiness*, New York: Free Press.

Seligman, M.E.P. and Csikszentmihalyi, M. (2000) 'Positive psychology: an introduction', *American Psychologist*, 55: 5–14.

Sheldon, B. (2001) 'The validity of evidence-based practice in social work: a reply to Stephen Webb', *British Journal of Social Work*, 31: 801–809.

Sheldon, B. and Chilvers, R. (1995) *Evidence-based Social Care: a study of the prospects and problems*, Dartington, Devon: Dartington Social Research Unit.

Short Report (1984) *Children in Care: Second Report from the Social Services Committee*, HC360, London: House of Commons.

Simons, K. (1995) *I'm Not Complaining, But . . .: complaints procedures in social services departments*, York: Joseph Rowntree Foundation.

Sinclair, I. and Gibbs, I. (1996) *Quality of Care in Children's Homes*, York: University of York.

—— (1998) *Children's Homes: a study in diversity*, Chichester: Wiley.

Sinclair, R. (2004) 'Participation in practice: making it meaningful, effective and sustainable', *Children and Society*, 18: 106–118.

Skuse, T. and Evans, R. (2001) 'Directing social work attention to education: the role of the Looking After Children materials', in S. Jackson (ed.), *Nobody Ever Told Us School Mattered: raising the educational attainments of children in care*, London: British Agencies for Adoption and Fostering.

Skuse, T. and Ward, H. (1999) *Current research findings about the health of looked after children. Paper for Quality Protects Seminar: improving health outcomes for looked after children*, 6 December, Totnes: Dartington Social Research Unit and Loughborough University.

Social Care Institute for Excellence (SCIE) (2004) 'Improving the use of research in social care practice', *Knowledge Review*, 7, London: SCIE.

Social Exclusion Unit (1998a) *Rough Sleeping: report by the Social Exclusion Unit*, London: Stationery Office.

—— (1998b) *Truancy and School Exclusion*, London: Stationery Office.

—— (1999) *Teenage Pregnancy: Report by the Social Exclusion Unit*, London: Stationery Office.

—— (2003) *A Better Education for Children in Care*, London: Office of the Deputy Prime Minister.

Social Policy Research Unit (2002) *Estimating the Cost of Being 'Not in Education, Employment or Training' at Age 16–18*, London: DfES.

Social Services Inspectorate (SSI) (1994) *Signposts: findings from a national inspection of private fostering*, London: SSI.

—— (1998) *Somebody Else's Children: the inspection of planning and decision making for children looked after and the safety of children looked after*, London: SSI.

Solesbury, W. (2002) 'The ascendancy of evidence', *Planning, Policy and Practice*, 3, 1: 90–96.

Song, M. (2003) *Choosing Ethnic Identity*, Oxford: Polity Press.

South Glamorgan Advocacy Unit (1994) *South Glamorgan Advocacy Scheme for Children and Young People Who Are Looked After. First Year Report, August 1993–September 1994*, Cardiff: The Welsh Office.

Speak, S., Cameron, S. and Gilroy, R. (1997) *Young Single Fathers: participation in fatherhood – barriers and bridges*, London: Family Policy Studies Centre.

Statham, J., Candappa, M., Simon, A. and Owen, C. (2002) *Trends in Care: exploring reasons for the increase in children looked after by local authorities*, London: Institute of Education, University of London.

Stein, M. (1986) *Living out of Care*, Ilford: Barnardo's.

—— (1997) *What Works in Leaving Care?*, Ilford: Barnardo's.

—— (2002) 'Leaving care', In D. McNeish, T. Newman and H. Roberts (eds), *What Works for Children*, Buckingham: Open University Press.

Stein, M. and Carey, K. (1986) *Leaving Care*, Oxford: Blackwell.

Stein, M. and Rees, G. (2002) 'Young people leaving care and young people who go missing', in J. Bradshaw (ed.), *The Wellbeing of Children in the UK*, York: University of York/Save the Children.

Stein, M. and Wade, J. (2000) *Helping Care Leavers: problems and strategic responses*, London: Department of Health.

Stephens, J. (2002) *The Mental Health Needs of Homeless Young People. Bright futures: working with vulnerable young people*, London: The Mental Health Foundation.

Stroud, J. and Pritchard, C. (2001) 'Child homicide, psychiatric disorder and dangerousness: a review and an empirical approach', *British Journal of Social Work*, 31: 249–269.

Stuart, M. and Baines, C. (2004) *Progress on Safeguards for Children Living Away From Home: a review of action since the People Like Us Report*, York: Joseph Rowntree Foundation.

Swann, C., Bowe, K., McCormick, G. and Kosmin, M. (2003) *Teenage Pregnancy and Parenthood: a review of reviews*, London: Health and Development Agency.

Sweeting, H. and West, P. (1995) 'Family life and health in adolescence: a role for culture in the health inequalities debate', *Social Science and Medicine*, 40, 2: 163–175.

Taylor, M. (2000) 'Children must be seen and heard', *Community Care*, 24 February.

Thomas, N. (2000) *Children, Family and the State: decision-making and child participation*, London: Macmillan.

Thomas, N. and O'Kane, C. (1998a) 'The ethics of participatory research with children', *Children and Society*, 12: 336–348.

—— (1998b) 'When children's wishes and feelings clash with their "best interests"', *International Journal of Children's Rights*, 6, 2: 137–154.

Timms, J. (2001) 'Best interests and best practice: improving outcomes for children', *Representing Children*, 14, 3: 145–159.

Triseliotis, J., Borland, M. and Hill, M. (1995) *Teenagers and the Social Work Service*, London: HMSO.

—— (2000) *Delivering Foster Care*, London: British Agencies for Adoption and Fostering.

United Nations Children's Fund (UNICEF) (2001) *A League Table of Teenage Births in Rich Nations*, Innocenti Report Card No. 3, Florence, Italy: UNICEF.

Utting, Sir W. (1991) *Children in the Public Care: a review of residential child care*, London: HMSO.

—— (1997) *People Like Us: the report of the review of the safeguards for children living away from home*, London: Department of Health and Welsh Office.

Vernon, J. (2000) *Audit and Assessment of Leaving Care Services in London*, London: National Children's Bureau, for Department of Health and Rough Sleepers Unit.

Vernon, J. and Fruin, D. (1986) *In Care: a study of social work decision-making*, London: National Children's Bureau.

Voice for the Child in Care (1998) *Sometimes You've Got to Shout to be Heard: stories from young people in care about getting heard, and using advocates*, London: VCC.

Wade, J., Biehal, N., Clayden, J. and Stein, M. (1998) *Going Missing: young people absent from care*, Chichester: Wiley.

Wagner, G. (1982) *Children of the Empire*, London: Weidenfeld & Nicolson.

Walker, T. (2002) *Caring for the Education of Looked After Children*, Manchester: National Teaching and Advisory Service.

Ward, H. (ed.) (1995) *Looking After Children: research into practice*, London: HMSO.

Ward, H. and Skuse, T. (1999) *Looking After Children: transforming data into management information. Report for first year of data collection*, Totnes, Devon: Dartington Social Research Unit.

—— (2001) *Looking After Children: using data as management information. Report from the first year of data collection*, unpublished.

Ward, L. (ed.) (1998) *Innovations in Advocacy and Empowerment for People with Intellectual Disabilities*, Chorley: Lisieux Hall Publications.

Warren, D. and McAndrew, G. (1997) *Foster Care in Crisis: a call to professionalise the forgotten service*, London: National Foster Care Association.

Waterhouse, Sir R. (2000) *Lost in Care: report of the tribunal of inquiry into the abuse of children in care in the former county council areas of Gwynedd and Clwyd since 1974*, London: The Stationery Office.

Waterhouse, S. (1997) *The Organisation of Fostering Services: a study of the arrangements for the delivery of fostering in England*, London: National Foster Care Association (NFCA).

Webb, S. A. (2001) 'Some considerations on the validity of evidence-based practice in social work', *British Journal of Social Work*, 31: 57–78.

Weick, A. and Saleeby, D. (1995) 'Supporting family strengths: orienting policy and practice toward the 21st century', *Families in Society*, 76, 3.

Wellings, K., Nanchahal, K., Macdowall, W., McManus, S., Erens, B., Mercer, C.H., Johnson, A.M., Copas, A.J., Korovessis, C., Fenton, K.A. and Field, J. (2001) 'Sexual behaviour in Britain: early heterosexual experience', *Lancet*, 358: 1843–1850.

Westcott, H.L. and Jones, D.P.H. (2003) 'Are children reliable witnesses to their experiences?', in P. Reder, S. Duncan and C. Lucey (eds), *Studies in the Assessment of Parenting*, Hove and New York: Brunner-Routledge.

Whittaker, D., Archer, L. and Hicks, L. (1998) *Working in Children's Homes: challenges and complexities*, Chichester: Wiley.

Whitty, G., Aggleton, P., Gamarnikov, E. and Tyrer, P. (1998) *Independent Inquiry into Inequalities in Health*, Input Paper 10, Education and Health inequalities, London: Institute of Education.

Who Cares? Trust (WCT) (1999) *Equal Chances Practice Guide: acting on the facts*, London: WCT.

—— (2001) *Right to Read*, London: WCT.

—— (2003a) *Believe in Me: supporting designated teachers supporting literacy*, London: WCT.

—— (2003b) *Education Matters: for everyone working with children in public care*, London: WCT.

—— (2004) *Measuring Progress*, London: WCT.

Who Cares? Trust/Quality Protects (2001) *Who Cares about Education? An action guide for young people*, London: Department of Health.

Who Cares? Trust/The Paul Hamlyn Foundation (2001) *Right to Read: promoting the benefits of reading to children and young people in public care. Project findings and recommendations for good practice*, Christchurch: The National Literacy Association.

Williams, J., Jackson, S., Maddocks, A., Cheung, W-Y., Love, A. and Hutchings, H. (2001) 'Case-control study of the health of those looked after by local authorities', *Archives of Disease in Childhood*, 85, 4: 280–285.

Willow, C. (1996) *Children's Rights and Participation in Residential Care*, London: National Children's Bureau.

Winnicott, D. (1957) *The Child and the Outside World*, London: Tavistock Publications.

Wyler, S. (2000) *The Health Needs of Care Leavers: a draft report to the King's Fund*, London: King's Fund.

Wyllie, J. (1999) *The Last Rung of the Ladder: an examination of the use of advocacy by children and young people in advancing participation rights in practice within the child protection system*, unpublished paper for the Children's Society.

# Subject index

# Name index

Lightning Source UK Ltd.
Milton Keynes UK
10 February 2011

167296UK00002B/68/P